Building a Nation

A history of Botswana from 1800 to 1910

J. Ramsay
B. Morton
T. Mgadla

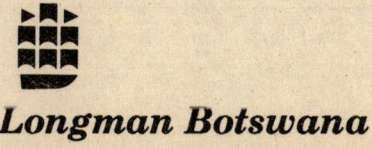

Longman Botswana

Longman Botswana (Pty) Ltd.
P O Box 1083
Gaborone
Offices at:
Plot 14386
New Lobatse Road
Gaborone West Ind. Site

Associated companies, branches and representatives
throughout the world.

Longman Botswana 1996

All rights reserved. No part of this publication may be reproduced, stored in
a retrieval system, or transmitted in any form or by any means, electronic,
mechanical, photocopying, recording or otherwise, without the prior written
permission of the copyright owner.

First published 1996
ISBN 99912 66 68 2

Typeset by: Sygma Publishing
Cover illustraion by Steve Jobson
Cover design: O P Design

Printed and bound by Creda Press

Acknowledgements

The authors of Building a Nation owe a considerable debt to others. A great deal of research in Botswana's nineteenth century history has been undertaken over the last two decades by student as well as staff scholars based at the University of Botswana and elsewhere. Their work, together with the writings of earlier scholars, has been an important factor in the appearance of this volume. We, furthermore, wish to express our collective gratitude to our colleagues at the University for their creative stimulation and comradeship over the years.

Material and moral support has been received from many. We wish to thank the (now former) Director, (Mrs.) T.M. Lekaukau, and staff of the Botswana National Archives for their cooperation over the years. In this respect we wish to give special thanks to veteran archivists Gilbert Mpolokeng and Mmapula Khiwa for their always good natured support. For access to other valuable materials thanks is due also to (Mrs.) K.H. Raseroka and the University of Botswana Library staff, more especially the staff of the library's invaluable Botswana Collection.

We acknowledge with thanks the following photographic sources: Botswana Collection of University of Botswana Library, Kgosi Sechele I Museum, Kevin Shillington, Alec Campbell.

For their comments and assistance in preparing the manuscript we wish to thank Neil Parsons, Lillian Mokgosi and the staff of Longmans Botswana. We also wish to especially acknowledge

Isaac Schapera, the mentor of modern Botswana social science, for his encouragement over the years.

And, for their patience and support during the long months of writing, the two married authors are ever grateful to their wives Rebecca Mgadla and Sekgabo Ramsay.

Contents

Acknowledgements i

Maps, Pictures & Illustrations v

Time Line History of Botswana to 1912 ix

Section I: Peoples of Botswana before the Difaqane

1. The foundations of Botswana's History 1

2. Southern Botswana before 1820 19

3. The north before 1820 31

4. Botswana's traditional culture 41

Section II: The Emergence of new states

5. Time of tumult - the Difaqane 61

6. Trade and the 1852-3 Batswana-Boer War 80

7. State - building in the South - East 101

8. The Batawana conquer Ngamiland 116

9. The Bangwato and their neighbours 132

Section III: The Coming of Colonial Rule

10. British occupation and colonization   145

11. The consolidation of colonial   159

12. The new Tswana culture   178

13. The mid - 1890s: Years of pestilence   199

Section IV: Under the Protectorate

14. The Kgalagadi and Chobe   216

15. Changes in the North   228

16. Realities of 'protection' in the Bechuanaland Protectorate   243

APPENDICES

18th - 19th Century Traditional Rulers   259

Glossary   266

List of Suggested further reading   269

INDEX   272

Maps

Peoples of Botswana by 1800, p. 6.

Difaqane in Botswana, p. 65.

1852- 53 Batswana-Boer War, p. 93.

Botswana in 1875, p. 113.

British Imperial Expansion in Southern Africa by 1902, p. 147.

Pictures & Illustrations

Large traditional structures at Gaditshwene (J. Campbell Travels into the Interior of South Africa, 1822), p. 4.

Nineteenth century Batswana iron workers (S. Jobson), p. 11.

Ovaherero woman c. 1890 in traditional dress (Botswana National Archives), p. 16.

Khoisan besides Tshodilo rock paintings (A. Campbell), p. 35.

A 19th century rainmaker (J. MacKenzie Day Dawn in Dark Places, 1883), p. 47.

Ngaka throwing bones (A.M. Duggin-Cronin The Bechuana, 1929), p. 48.

A Motlhaping girl initiate (A.M. Duggin-Cronin The Bechuana, 1929), p. 52.

v

European traders with Bakalanga in 1890s (R. Churchill <u>Men, Mines and Animales</u>, 1893), p. 59.

Ratumagole, a Makololo veteran at Tsau 1908 (Royal Commonwealth Society), p. 67.

Kgosi Sechele in 1865 (G. Fritsch <u>Drei Jahre in Sud-Afrika</u>, 1868), p. 69.

Seven barrelled Knocks volley gun of type ordered by Sechele (School of Infantry, Warminister), p. 84.

Sechele's cannon (Kgosi Sechele I Museum, Molepolole), p. 85.

Kgosi Mosielele in 1865 (G. Fritsch <u>Drei Jahre in Sud-Afrika</u>, 1868), p. 88.

Batswana raiding Boer farms (S. Jobson), p. 92.

Kgosi Gaseitsiwe in 1865 (G. Fritsch <u>Drei Jahre in Sud-Afrika</u>, 1868), p. 102.

Ostrich Hunting (J. Chapman <u>Travels in South Africa</u>, 1868/1971), p. 103.

Elderley Sechele with Matsheng's widow MmaKgari (A.J. Wookey <u>Dico</u>, 1922), p. 107.

Kgosi Kgamanyane being flogged by Kruger (S. Jobson), p. 109.

Bekuhane Kishi dancers (E. Holub <u>Seven Years in South Africa</u>, 1875, p. 116.

Letsholathebe dining with European trader (W.C. Baldwin African Hunting and Adventure, 1894), p. 122.

Battle of Khutiyabasadi (S. Jobson), p. 123.

Kgosi Sekgoma I (E. Holub Seven Years in South Africa, 1875), p. 133.

Warren at Molepolole 1885 (S. Jobson), p. 155.

Offices of Bechuanaland Border Police (R. Churchill Men, Mines and Animales, 1893), p. 160.

Gaborone Camp in 1890s (MacGregor Museum, Duggin-Cronin Collection), p. 165.

Dikgosi exchange gifts with Queen Victoria (The Graphic, November 30, 1895), p. 174.

Missionary Wookey and Wife (A. Campbell), p. 179.

An early Motswana Evangelist (W.C. Willoughby), p. 182.

Batswana migrants (J. MacKenzie Day Dawn), p. 192.

The Railroad (W.C. Willoughby), p. 203.

Cattle being shot by police (S. Jobson), p. 208.

Shua Khoe at Chobe 1906 (A. Hodgson Trekking the Great Thirst), p. 222.

White settler at Gaborone (Botswana National Archives), p. 229.

Dikgosi Bathoen I and Sebele I speak against Union of South Africa (s. Jobson), p. 249.

Time line for history of Botswana, to 1912

500,000 years ago: Early Stone Age tools in Botswana.

25,000 BCE: Late Stone Age in Botswana. Rocks paintings in the region.

By 200 BCE: Pastoralism in Botswana.

By 200: Bantu speakers in Botswana.

By 350: Iron Age in Botswana. Spread of arable agriculture.

By 700: Emergence of larger semi-permanent settlements, Botswana region integrated into coastal trading networks.

1100: Late iron age in eastern Botswana

13-1500: Evidence of depopulation, possible dry phase.

c. 1450: Bakalanga Kingdom of Butwa emerges.

1690s: Bakalanga Kingdom under Nichasike defeats Portuguese.

By 1800: Bakgalagadi, Bakalanga, Batswana, Bayie, Babirwa, Bapedi, Hambukushu, and Bekuhane settled in Botswana.

1801: Truter-Somerville expedition. First official British contact with Batswana.

1816: LMS missionaries begin work among Batswana.

1821: Execution of Bakwena Kgosi Motswasele II

1822: Robert Moffat visits Kgosi Makaba II of the Bangwaketse, first missionary in Botswana.

1823: The Bakololo of Sebetwane begin their two decade invasion through eastern, central, and northwestern Botswana leading to the temporary breakup of many merafe.

1825: Bangwaketse, Bakwena and Bakgatla bagaMmanaana defeated by Bakololo, Makaba II killed.

1826: Battle of Dithubaruba Bangwaketse defeat Bakololo with help of armed Cape traders. Bakololo subsequently move into northern Botswana.

c.1828: Battle of Matopos. Kgosi Kgari of Bangwato defeated and killed by Bakalanga.

1831: Amandebele move into western Transvaal. Defeat Barolong at Khunwana.

1833: Sechele becomes Kgosi of Bakwena.

c.1834: Sebego defeats Amandebele at Dutlwe, subsequently invades western Kgalagadi.

1834-54: "Great Trek"- Boer's invade South African highveld seizing land from Batswana and other Africans.

1835: Sekgoma I becomes Kgosi of Bangwato.

1836: Barolong Kgosi Moroka rescues Boers at Vegkop

following an Amandebele attack. Temporary Boer-BaTswana alliance formed.

1837: Batswana, Boers, and Griqua drive the Amandebele out of the Transvaal. Amandebele subsequently invade Zimbabwe via Botswana.

1840: Amandebele join Amangoni in conquering the Bakalanga Kingdom.

1841: Beginning of David Livingstone's career among the Batswana.

1842: Last Amandebele raid into south-eastern Botswana.

1843: Sechele builds fort at Tshonwane, prepares to fight Boers.

1844: Bangwato under Kgosi Sekgoma drive Amandebele away from Shoshong.

1847: Livingstone's mission at Kolobeng founded, first church and school in Botswana. Letsholathebe becomes Kgosi of the Batawana.

1848: Bakaa driven out of Shoshong hills by Banwato, flee to Bakwena.

1849: Europeans begin traveling to Ngamiland.

1852: The Batswana-Boer war begins. Bakgatla ba-ga-Mmanaana flee to Botswana to escape Boers. Pan-Batswana alliance led by Sechele resists Boer invasion at Dimawe. Batswana raid the western Transvaal.

1853: Batswana drive Boers back to Rustenburg and Potchstroom. Sechele agrees to a ceasefire after Boers ask for peace. Balete, Batlokwa, Bahurutshe migrate to southeastern Botswana.

1854: Battle of Kwebe, Batawana defeat the Bakololo.

1857: Peace agreement between Sechele and Transvaal President Pretorius. Arrival of Lutheran missionaries in Botswana. Gaseitsiwe defeats Senthufe to become undisputed Kgosi of the Bangwaketse.

1858: Sechele installs Matsheng as Bangwato Kgosi in place of Sekgoma. Nharo-Khoe in Ghanzi defeated by Batawana.

1859: Sechele reinstalls Sekgoma as Kgosi of Bangwato in place of Matsheng.

1863: Amandebele attack on Shoshong defeated by Bangwato. Merafe in Southeastern Botswana spread out from Dithubaruba to found new settlements.

1865: Gaseitsiwe, Montshiwa, and Sechele threaten to go to war if Transvaal Boers seize Lehurutshe. The Boers back down.

1865-66: Bangwato Civil War between Sekgoma and his son Khama. Sechele reinstalls Matsheng.

1867: German explorer Karl Mauch finds gold in the Northeast District.

1869: Paul Kruger flogs Bakgatla ba-ga-Kgafela Kgosi Kgamanyane. Many Ba-ga-Kgafela then move from the western Transvaal to settle at Mochudi.

1871: British annex Batlhaping lands around Kimberly as Griqualand West. Ludorf draws up constitutions for united Bangwaketse, Bakwena, Barolong, and Batlhaping confederation.

1872: Sechele installs Khama as Kgosi of Bangwato in place of Matsheng.

1873: Sekgoma installed once more as Bangwato Kgosi in place of Khama.

1875: Inter-merafe conflicts breakout in throughout southern Botswana. Bakgatla ba-ga-Kgafela defeat Bakwena at Mochudi. Khama outsits Sekgoma in Gammangwato, remains in power till 1923 death.

1876: Bakwena defeat Ba-ga-Kgafela, Balete, and Batlokwa at Molepolole. Breechloading rifles introduced. British occupy the Transvaal. Balozi destroy Bekuhane (Basubiya) state.

1878-79: First Anglo-Batlhaping War. British forces under Warren occupy Batswana lands south of the Molopo.

1881: British withdrawal from the Transvaal and southern Batswana lands. Balete defeat Bangwaketse at Ramotswa. inter-merafe wars in southern Botswana end.

1883: Bakwena, Bangwaketse, and Barolong renew attempt to form a confederation to counter growing British and Boer threats.

1884: British re-occupy Batswana lands south of the Molopo. Battle of Khutiyabasadi, Batswana defeat Amandebele.

1885: The British unilaterally proclaim the Bechuanaland Protectorate to counter Germany's occupation of Namibia.

1886: British land commission awards 92% of Batlhaping and Barolong land south of the Molopo to whites.

1887: Battle of Ngwapa. Bangwato defeat Baseleka with British support.

1888: Rudd Concession become basis of British South Africa Co. claims to Zimbabwe.

1889: Most Batswana Dikgosi object to colonial rule at the Kopong Conference. The British South African Company (BSACo) is awarded a royal charter to administer Botswana and Central Africa in the name of the British Crown. Khama move capital from Shoshong to Palapye.

1890: Overriding local objections, the British grant themselves the right to exercise colonial control over Botswana through the Foreign Jurisdictions Act. Protectorate extended to Ngamiland and Chobe. BSACo Pioneer Column passes through Botswana in route to Zimbabwe.

1891: Order-in-Council gives the High Commissioner wideranging administrative powers. Sekgoma Letsholathebe becomes Kgosi of Batswana.

1892: Tati (Northeast District) joined to the Protectorate. Sechele dies.

1893: Bechuanaland Border Police and Bangwato help the BSACo destroy the Amandebele Kingdom in Zimbabwe. Concessions Commission meets.

1894: Bangwato rule extended into Bukalanga region.

1895: Bathoen I, Khama III, and Sebele I, travel to Britain to oppose the proposed transfer of their territories to BSACo administrative control.

1896: Failure of Jameson Raid ends the immediate threat of the Protectorate's transfers to BSACo control. Rinderpest (bolwane) destroys livestock and wild life. Batswana south of the Molopo annexed to the Cape Colony.

1897: Mafikeng to Bulawayo railway built. Second Anglo-Batlhaping War

1898: Boers settle in Ghanzi.

1899: The major Batswana "reserves" are demarcated and Hut Tax is introduced.

1899-1902: Batswana fight in the South African (Boer) War. Bakgatla conquer territory between Kgatleng and Rustenburg but are forced by the British to give it up. Barolong and others defend Mafikeng.

1902: Khama moves capital from Palapye to Serowe.

1903-05: Thousands of Ovaherero and Nama refugees flee to Botswana to escape German genocides in Namibia.

1906: British depose and detain without trial Kgosi Sekgoma

Letsholathebe of the Batawana.

1908: Bathoen and Sebele petition against incorporation into proposed Union of South Africa. Germans invade southwestern Botswana in failed effort to defeat Nama of Simon Kooper.

1909: Batswana continue to protest against the Union of South Africa. Bathoen and Sebele send Gerrans to London as their representative. Germans occupy Eastern Caprivi causing many local Bekuhane to flee across Chobe into Botswana.

1910: Bathoen I dies. Union of South Africa formed with provisions for future incorporation of Botswana. Sekgoma Letsholathebe loses case in Privy Council.

1911: Sebele I dies.

1912: Native Recruiting Corporation begins systematic recruitment of migrant labour for mines. Batswana delegates attend the inaugural conference of the African National Congress. Sekgoma Letsholathebe settles at Kavimba, dies 1914.

Chapter 1
The Foundations of Botswana's History

History is the story of mankind's past. It can be about events that occurred long ago. The fall of Babylon, which is mentioned in the Bible, is a true historical event that took place about 2,500 years ago. History can also be about recent happenings. The 1994 election of Nelson Mandela as President of South Africa is already described as an important historical event.

Whose Story?

Obviously not everything that occurred yesterday is significant enough to be remembered as history. How do people decide what should be recorded for the future? This is not an easy question. Historians, that is people who specialize in studying history, do not always agree about what is important. Often the way people see the present determines the way they see the past. For example many history books about South Africa begin in 1652, the year white settlers from the Netherlands began to settle at the Cape. White South African authors wrote these books. They were brought up in a society in which white people alone had political power. To them South Africa's history was a story about the actions of white people.

Southern Africa had a history long before the arrival of white people. A thousand years ago this region, including Botswana, had hundreds of stone walled settlements. These places were connected to one another by trade networks stretching between the Atlantic and Indian Oceans. On the borders of the Kgalagadi today people sometimes find seashells, which were brought to Botswana by ancient traders for use as jewellery.

The history of Botswana has not always been taught in schools. From 1885 to 1966 Botswana came under British overrule. During this period the British rulers tried to justify their authority. They told Batswana that they had no past worth remembering. Instead Batswana were taught that they had been saved by the British. The British Queen Victoria, known locally as Mmamosadinyana, was said to have stopped the Boers from taking Botswana. One of their books about Bechuanaland, as they called Botswana, written in 1965, stated:

> **Happy is a nation that has no history. By this standard there can be few nations in Africa happier than the Bechuanaland, for apart from the inter and intra tribal conflicts normal to the African continent before its emergence into modern life and thought, its record is remarkably free of incident of any kind. The Batswana offered an equally friendly reception to missionaries, traders and soldiers alike when they came to offer their various receipts for happiness and since the British drew a line on the map and said "This is Bechuanaland" they have lived quietly and undemandingly for seventy uneventful years.**

In 1970 this nation's first President, Sir Seretse Khama, rejected such ignorance, stating:

> **We were taught, sometimes in a very positive way, to despise ourselves and our ways of life. We were made to believe that we had no past to speak of, no history to boast of. The past, so far as we were concerned, was just a blank and nothing more...**
>
> **It should now be our intention to try to retrieve what we can of our past. We should write our own history books, to prove that we did have a past and that it was a past that was just as worth writing and learning about as any other. We must do this for the**

simple reason that a nation without a past is a lost nation and a people without a past are a people without a soul.

Around the world people living in different nations study their own history to know more about themselves. Batswana must follow Sir Seretse's advice and do the same. Botswana's old British rulers understood that people who did not know their past were like trees without roots that could be pushed aside easily. Imagine if you woke up one morning having completely forgotten where you came from. You would be confused and uncertain of what to do. It is the same for a community or nation. To know where to go you need to know where you have been.

Sources of History

Unfortunately there is much about Botswana's past that we will never know. Here, as elsewhere in the world, many important events and personalities of the past have now been forgotten. Historians are limited in what they can know of long ago. They use three main types of historical evidence; material evidence, oral evidence and written evidence.

Written evidence about Botswana only goes back to the beginning of the nineteenth century. Oral evidence usually takes us no further than the seventeenth century. So in recovering Botswana's early history material evidence is important.

Material Evidence
Objects both large and small can be used as material evidence. A glass bead once traded from the Indian Ocean is a piece of material evidence. So are the remains of old settlements, like

Great Zimbabwe. Pictures such as ancient rock paintings or photographs are also material evidence. Old tools and bones are other examples. One can see much material evidence about Botswana's past in museums. The National Museum and Art Gallery in Gaborone is the biggest in Botswana. There are also local museums in Francistown, Mochudi, Molepolole and Serowe.

Material evidence is often collected by archeologists, people who study mankind's distant past. Since independence archeologists have discovered many new things about the early history of Botswana. For example the remains of cattle, sheep and goats tell us that people in Botswana have been keeping livestock for over 2,000 years. We also know that 1,500 years ago local communities were making iron tools.

This 1820 drawing of a very large house belonging to a wealthy Motswana at Gaditshwene are an example of material evidence. The actual material remains of Gaditshwene (near Zeerust) are now being excavated by archeologists.

Oral evidence
Many events that have never been written down exist in the memories of people as oral evidence. Elders often remember significant events that were part of their own lives. They can thus give us eyewitness accounts of their experiences. The information we receive from eyewitness accounts may be about big events, such as Seretse Khama's return from exile to Botswana. Older people can also teach us important things about the changes in everyday life that have occurred in their lifetimes. Elders who know traditional Batswana conservation practices, for example, can help Botswana protect its environment today.

Oral traditions are another kind of oral evidence. Traditions are stories about past events that have been passed down from generation to generation. People often learn traditions by listening to grandparents, aunts and uncles. A few oral traditions were even written down as early as the nineteenth century. This has helped historians because traditions are usually forgotten or distorted as years pass. Fortunately, there have been efforts to record surviving oral traditions for future generations. In recent years staff and student researchers at the University of Botswana have been especially active in the preservation of oral traditions.

Written Evidence
Written evidence can include official documents, letters, old newspaper articles and books. Written historical evidence is divided between *primary sources* and *secondary sources*. History books are secondary sources. This is because when we read them we get our information about the past second hand, that is from a the book's author(s). Primary written sources provide historical researchers with original information about the past. An old diary kept by a person travelling through

Botswana during the 1860s is an example of a primary source. It will provide a first hand account of its writers observations from the period.

Other Sources of Information

Historians occasionally use other types of evidence, Languages, for instance, can provide historical information. Languages like Setswana, Isizulu and Kiswahili belong to a common Bantu language family. This tells us that the people who speak those languages were once closely related. Setswana has words of foreign origin, such as *tafole* from the Afrikaans word *tafel* (table). This is evidence of past contacts between Batswana and Afrikaners.

Evidence about mankind's past can also be found in the natural environment. For example, the rings of an old tree trunk can indicate past years of drought. The existence of foreign plants and animals in a region shows where it was connected to by trade. Maize, for example, came to southern Africa from South America only three centuries ago.

Using the Evidence

There are advantages and disadvantages in using each of the various sources of historical evidence. Material evidence can tell us many things about the way people lived in the past. A pile of animal bones in old settlements shows whether the inhabitants were primarily hunters or herders. But objects do not talk and cannot tell us everything we need to know. In an old battle field archeologists may dig up weapons of war, such as spears and axes. Such evidence will tell them something about how people once fought there, but not why they were fighting. An object cannot tell us the name of its owner or what language he or she spoke.

Written and oral evidence is always affected by human biases or points of view. During the nineteenth century many missionaries came to Botswana and wrote about their experiences. These writings are a good primary source for local history. Historians who read the missionaries' books must be careful, though. Missionaries often made little attempt to understand local life and culture, which they saw as un Christian. They usually dismissed Tswana medicine, for example, as witchcraft. Many traditional doctors (*dingaka*) though, were able to cure diseases. Missionaries also spoke well of those who accepted their teachings. So they praised Kgosi Khama of the Bangwato and denounced his father Sekgoma, who hated Christianity. Likewise the British who ruled Botswana after 1885 liked those dikgosi who cooperated with them. But they called dikgosi like Linchwe I of the Bakgatla and Sebele I of the Bakwena 'troublesome chiefs' because they stood up for their people's independence. So historians must try to understand the biases that exist in written and oral evidence.

Migration and settlement before 1800

While Botswana's population of approximately 1.3 million is relatively small, it has long been the home of many different peoples. Most of the African peoples living in Botswana today were there by 1800. They spoke different languages, had different beliefs and customs and were organized into different types of societies. Botswana's modern population reflects this long standing variety. This book will describe how, after 1800, all these groups came together to form a nation.

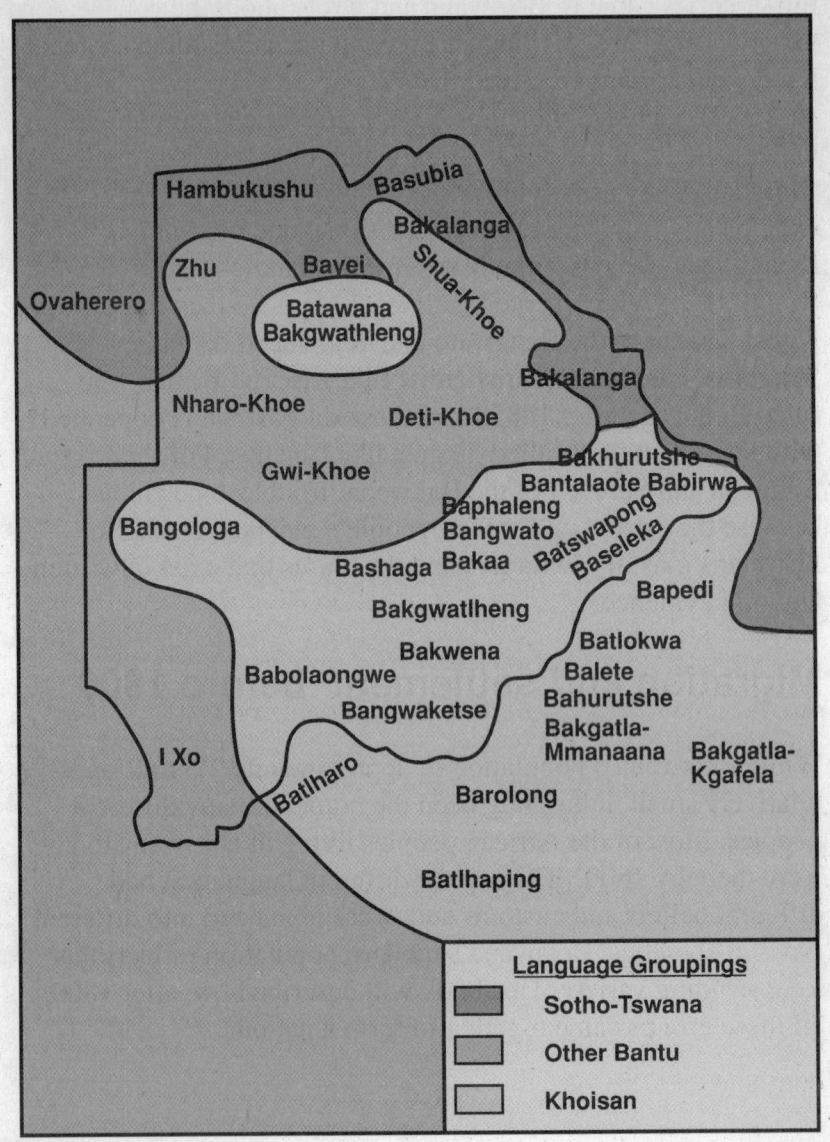

The diversity of Botswana's population is also due to the fact that different communities had to adapt themselves to different environments. Some people have settled in the dry Kgalagadi, others have settled in the Okavango swamps. Such different situations encouraged people to adopt different ways of life. But, despite their differences, the peoples of Botswana have always been similar in many ways.

Early times

People have lived in Botswana since the beginning of mankind. Early Stone Age tools and skeletons that are 500,000 years old have been found in eastern Botswana. Other tools that have been found show that these Stone Age peoples never left the region. They kept using stone tools until some 1,500 years ago and lived by hunting game and gathering wild foods.

Botswana's earliest known inhabitants spoke Khoisan languages. Today their descendants are commonly called Basarwa, Bushmen or San. The Khoisan languages can be divided into three groups, Khoe, Zhu and !Xo. Khoe, Zhu and !Xo languages are very different from each other. Even the languages within a group are very different from others in the same group. Most Basarwa speak one of a dozen or so major Khoe (or Khoi) languages. Other languages like Zhu and !Xo are very different from Khoe. Khoisan peoples acquired Iron Age technology over 1,500 years ago. Most of them abandoned hunting and gathering then and took up other activities such as owning livestock, farming, fishing and mining.

Batswana often think Basarwa live only in remote areas of the country. But long ago they lived all over the country and continue to do so.

The Keeping of Livestock

The remains of domestic animals have been found in Botswana that are 2,200 years old. Pastoralism came to this region then. Livestock keeping was probably introduced by Khoe communities living in northern Botswana. This helps to explain why the Setswana words for cow (*kgomo*), goat (*podi*) and sheep (*nku*) may all be of Khoe origin.

Once pastoralism began people started to live in bigger villages. The oldest known permanent settlements in Botswana are 2,100 years old. They have pottery, cattle dung and rubbish heaps. Similar settlements were also started by fisherman in the Okavango-Chobe area.

Iron tools appeared in Botswana 1,500 years ago. When iron comes to an area the Stone Age ends and the Iron Age begins. Iron making brings many advantages because it makes farming easier. Intensive farming was made possible by the iron axe and hoe. People began trading iron goods and other items. This trade, combined with intensive farming, allowed larger settlements to develop. Between 600 and 1100 AD many Iron Age settlements grew throughout the North east and Central Districts. The people of that time and their culture are called Zhizo by archeologists. Perhaps they were the ancestors of the modern Bakalanga.

It may have been Bantu speakers who brought iron technology to Botswana from central Africa. The word "Bantu", like Khoisan, refers to a group of languages. Bantu languages commonly spoken in Botswana include such Sotho Tswana languages as Setswana, Sekgalagari and Sepedi. Ikalanga, Otjihererero, Seyei, Tjimbukushu and Chikuhane (Sesubia) are not Sotho Tswana but they are also Bantu. Bantu speakers began to settle in Botswana by 200 AD. All of the above Bantu languages were locally represented by 1800.

Early nineteen century Batswana iron workers (bathudi) forging assagais.

The Late Iron Age

By 1100 AD the people of Botswana were living a much more advanced kind of life. They cultivated big fields, traded over long distances and had complex cultures. It was after 1100 that larger Setswana and Ikalanga settlements began. This later part of the Iron Age lasted until 1800.

The Bakalanga and related Vashona, are known for building Late Iron Age stone walled structures called zimbabwes. The largest and most famous of these is the Great Zimbabwe. Between 1250 and 1450, Great Zimbabwe was part of a settlement of some 10,000 inhabitants. After 1450 much of north eastern Botswana and western Zimbabwe came under the rule of the Bakalanga Kingdom of Butwa. This kingdom lasted until 1840 under the rule of the Chibundule (*Tolwa*) and Nichasike (*Rozwi*) dynasties. The wealth of Butwa was partially based on gold mining. Over 200 ancient gold mines are known in the Tati area alone.

Butwa had several large and impressive towns, such as Khami, Naletale and Danangombe (Dlhodlho). All are located in western Zimbabwe. Remains of many smaller stone walled settlements, such as Domboshaba, Old Tati and Majojo, are in Botswana. These Botswana based settlements had hundreds of residents. The patterns of their homes are similar to those of the modern Bakalanga.

One of the most studied of Botswana's Iron Age settlements is Toutswemogala. It first emerged around 700 AD as a Zhizo type village. For centuries it prospered as a trading site, while dozens of smaller Toutswe-type settlements were established in the Central District. Between 1300 and 1500 there seems to have been a population decline in the Toutswe settlements. People may have left due to overgrazing and prolonged drought. Toutswemogala was finally abandoned around 1700. This settlement is important because the ancestors of the modern Batswana and Bakalanga are believed to have lived there.

The known origins of Batswana settlement date back to fifth century Iron Age sites in south eastern Botswana and the western Transvaal. Over time larger stone walled settlements emerged. Aerial photographs have revealed thousands of stone-walled ruins between the Limpopo and Orange rivers. Usually they were built on hilltops so that their inhabitants could defend themselves easily. Large populations of Sotho Tswana speakers lived in the South African highveld before the coming of the Europeans. Batswana settlements increased in size rapidly after 1500. By the seventeenth century many Batswana communities in what is now South Africa lived in villages of 5,000 or more. Settlements in Botswana tended to be smaller. They only became bigger after 1850, when trading expanded.

Sotho-Tswana origins

Archeology suggests that Batswana and Bakgalagadi have been present in Botswana since 400 AD. Oral traditions, though, only talk about what happened more recently. Different Sotho Tswana groups migrated in and out of Botswana long before 1500. There was, though, a period of depopulation between about 1300 and 1500. Perhaps this is why oral traditions differ from the archeological evidence.

In some of their oldest traditions both the Batswana and Bakgalagadi actually claim to have originated in Botswana. Both groups claim to be descended from an early hero named Matsieng. In the beginning of time Matsieng was held as a prisoner in the underworld, below the earth's surface, by a god like figure known as Tintibane. Then a one legged being called Lowe showed Matsieng how to escape from the underworld to Botswana through a cave. Matsieng's supposed cave is located near Mochudi.

The above tradition is almost certainly not true. The story, however, underscores the important point that the Batswana and Bakgalagadi peoples of this country see themselves as belonging to the land. Other oral traditions indicate that the modern Bakgalagadi groups settled in most areas of Botswana before the Batswana.

The Bakgalagadi

The name Bakgalagadi means people of the Kgalagadi. Bakgalagadi is a collective term for a number of related groups who all speak the Sekgalagadi language. Sekgalagadi is related to, but separate from, Setswana. The Bakgalagadi groups in Botswana include the Bakgwatlheng, Baphaleng, Baboloangwe, Bangologa and Bashaga.

According to oral tradition the first four of the above groups were once a single people who later split up. All four claim to have once been a part of the Barolong and to have settled in Botswana by 1500. The Bashaga also claim to have broken off from the Barolong, but at a much later date.

Bakgalagadi, as their name suggests, have long lived in the Kgalagadi desert. During the seventeenth century, though, many Bakgwatlheng and Baboloangwe lived in south eastern Botswana. During the 1600s most of this region came under the political control of the Bakwena. Rather than submit to Bakwena rule many Bakgwatlheng and Baboloangwe then migrated into the Kgalagadi. There they joined other communities of Baboloangwe and Bangologa. At about the same time the Baphaleng broke off from the Bakgwatlheng and established themselves in the Central District.

The Batswana

The Bakwena-ba-ga-Kgabo of Botswana are among the oldest Batswana communities in Botswana. They broke away from the Bakwena-ba-ga-Mogopa of South Africa during the early seventeenth century. But other traditions indicate that Bakwena groups had been in the area much earlier. When the Bakwena came they seized the region around Molepolole from the Bakgwatlheng. From there they began to build up their wealth through trading animal skins.

During the eighteenth century two sections of the Bakwena broke away to form their own merafe. These were the Bangwaketse and Bangwato. The Bangwaketse moved to Seoke, near modern Lobatse, where they remained until the early nineteenth century. Seoke's stone walled remains still survive. After breaking away from the Bakwena, the Bangwato established themselves in the Shoshong hills. Later still the Batawana broke away from the Bangwato and settled in Ngamiland during the last decade of the eighteenth century.

Other Batswana groups that were settled in Botswana before 1800 include the Bakaa and Bakhurutse. The Bakhurutse are a branch of the Bahurutse who eventually settled in north eastern Botswana. It was their Bakalanga neighbours who called them Bakhurutse. The Bakaa are an offshoot of the Barolong. Their name comes from 'ba ka ya'. When they broke away, the Barolong kgosi is reported to have said 'ba ka ya jaaka ba boletse' (they can go). Other, smaller, groups of Barolong had also settled throughout Botswana by 1800.

Other Sotho-Tswana groups

Other Sotho Tswana groups who had settled in Botswana by 1800 included the Babirwa, Bapedi and Batswapong. Babirwa have been living in the region around Bobonong for several centuries. Their name is derived from an ancient ruler named Mmirwa, who apparently paid tribute to the Bakalanga kings of Butwa. The Sebirwa dialect is closely related to the Sepedi or Northern Sotho language.

Batswapong is a collective name for a number of different groups that have lived together around the Tswapong hills for a long time. Most of these groups claim Bapedi origin. By 1800 other groups of Bapedi had also settled throughout the Central

District. The Bakalanga-ba-ka-Nswazwi trace their origins to one of these groups. During the eighteenth century they moved into the Bukalanga region and then adopted Ikalanga language and culture.

Ovarero women c.1890 in the then traditional dress.

The Batalaote were once Bakalanga who gradually adopted the Setswana language and culture of neighbouring Central District groups. The name Batalaote is derived from an early leader, Dalaunde, who was known as Ntalaote by the Batswana. Traditions say that Dalaunde and then his son, Sankoloba, led the group from Zimbabwe to the Shoshong hills. There they lived near the Bakaa and Bangwato.

Many other Bantu speakers live in the Ngamiland Chobe region. The Bayei, Hambukushu and Bekuhane or Basubia are the biggest of these. All three of these peoples migrated into Botswana from central Africa, but no one knows for sure when they first came. Some may have been here by 1500, while others arrived in more recent times. We know that Hambukushu were living in Ngamiland before 1800, but in recent years others have arrived as refugees from Angola. As far as we know the Bayei, Hambukushu and Bekuhane had not formed any large states before 1800.

Another large Bantu speaking group found in Botswana is the Ovaherero. Most local Ovaherero left Namibia after 1897 to escape German rule there. But some Ovaherero had lived along the Namibian border in earlier times. Today Ovaherero can be found throughout Botswana. The largest communities are at Mahalapye and in Ngamiland.

Questions

1 What did Sir Seretse Khama mean when he said "we were taught, sometimes in a very positive way, to despise ourselves"?
2 a. What are the three main categories of historical evidence
   b. What are their advantages and disadvantages?

3 a. What is meant by pastoralism?
   b. When did it begin in Botswana?
   c. Which people probably first practiced it in Botswana?

4 a. What is meant by Iron Age?
   b. What changes occurred in agriculture during the Iron Age?

5 What is meant by Bantu and Khoisan groups in Botswana?

6 The Bakgalagadi in Botswana claim to have originally belonged to which Batswana group?

7 a. What is the significance of Toutswemogala?
  b. When was it occupied?

8 a. When did the Bakalanga kingdom of Butwa begin and end?
  b. What were the names of its two ruling families or dynasties?

Chapter 2
Southern Botswana before 1820

For centuries southern Botswana has been the home of Batswana, Bakgalagadi and Khoisan (or Basarwa) communities. Before the 1820s all three were linked together closely.

Long ago a pattern emerged in southern Botswana in which many Khoisan were forced to work for Bakgalagadi masters. In turn, many of the Bakgalagadi ended up under the control of Batswana. This system of forced labour is generally referred to as **bolata** and is a form of slavery or serfdom. Although **malata** were rarely sold by their masters, they were not free to move around without permission. A master could transfer his control over malata to others, such as his relatives and children. Malata can thus be said to have been people who were virtually owned by others.

Bolata began hundreds of years ago. As far back as the fifteenth century the Bakgalagadi conquered and ruled Khoisan communities in southern Botswana. Later on during the seventeenth century, Batswana defeated the Bakgalagadi and made them into malata as well. In the course of these wars, a number of people avoided bolata and remained free by fleeing into the remote areas of the Kgalagadi.

By 1820 most of southern Botswana was controlled by the Bangwaketse and Bakwena, who were militarily strong. Both of these merafe had many Bakgalagadi and Khoisan malata. But in areas more to the west, the modern day Kgalagadi district, many Bakgalagadi and Khoisan lived independently.

Khoisan speakers: The Khoe and !Xo

Southern Botswana's oldest inhabitants spoke Khoisan languages. Most of these southern Khoisan speak one of the various Khoe languages and belong to such groups as the Qana-Khoe, Gwi-Khoe, Nama-Khoe and Cara-Khoe. The first two of these groups live today in the Central Kgalagadi. The Cara Khoe are found in the Kweneng and Kgatleng. The Nama Khoe today mostly live in Namibia, but they have long hunted and traveled in western areas of Botswana. During the early twentieth century many fled to Botswana as refugees from Namibia (see Ch. 15).

The other Khoisan speakers of southern Botswana are !Xo, who also live in Namibia and South Africa. Their language is very different from that of the Khoe. Unfortunately very few speakers of !Xo survive today. Boers killed and enslaved most of them two hundred years ago, while others were conquered by the Bakgalagadi and Nama Khoe.

A strange result of the !Xo losing their identity was the way in which whites came and gave them another one. By the 1870s it was common for white entertainment promoters to go to the Cape Province or southern Botswana to look for a member of the 'vanishing race of Bushmen'. Anyone unfortunate enough to meet one of these promoters was then often kidnapped and taken to Europe or America. People there paid money to see these people talk or dance or take their clothes off. Often they were exhibited as being members of the 'oldest race on earth'. Due to such forms of entertainment, all sorts of strange ideas arose about who the Khoisan were. Many people still believe these notions today.

Later chapters will describe the Khoisan in more detail and show how their way of life was destroyed.

Bakgalagadi groups

In the last chapter it was noted that the Bakgalagadi are divided into five major groups. Four of these groups have lived for centuries in southern Botswana: the Bakgwatlheng, Babolaongwe, Bangologa and Bashaga. The fifth group, the Baphaleng, have lived in the north since breaking away from the Bakgwatlheng during the seventeenth or early eighteenth century.

According to many oral traditions the Bangologa and Babolaongwe also once separated from the Bakgwatlheng. Mongologa is said to have been the name of a Morolong royal who fled to Matsheng, the region around Hukuntsi, Lehututu and Tshane, after failing in an attempt to take bogosi from his brother. With a few followers he then established his rule over the Bakgwatlheng in the area, who were thereafter called the Bangologa. The earliest known leader of the Babolaongwe was Mbolawe. After breaking from the Bakgwatlheng, Mbolawe moved his subjects to Mabuasehube. Both of these splits had occurred by the sixteenth century.

The Bashaga have a separate origin from the above three groups. They originally broke away from the Barolong. In the eigteenth century the Bashaga moved into southern Botswana under a kgosi named Modikele.

As the Bakgalagadi moved deeper into the Kgalagadi they came into conflict with its original Khoisan speaking, Basarwa inhabitants. The following account of an early war between the Babolaongwe and the Khoe was recorded by a Mokgalagadi royal named Gaoongwe Seloilwe. It tells how Bakgalagadi began to own Khoisan as malata:

> Long ago the Basarwa were a nation, they were not owned by the Bakgalagadi . . . It came about once that the Basarwa kgosi assembled the Basarwa and said to them, 'Let arrows and quivers be made, the time may come when we will fight with the Bakgalagadi . . . And on the day which the Basarwa kgosi had appointed as the day of battle the Bakgalagadi kgosi chose a man to go and see if the Basarwa were in their village and he did so (and found them dancing). And early in the morning the (Kgalagadi) army set out; and at daybreak it found the Basarwa still dancing and the army fell upon them. And the armies came together, starting at sunrise; and at noon they were still fighting together. Thus Basarwa shot with arrows, but did not injure the Bakgalagadi; and the Bakgalagadi killed many of the Basarwa, killing them with great slaughter. At last there remained only the kgosi of the Basarwa. And as they were pursuing him his arrows got finished and the Bakgalagadi seized him, saying, 'Come on into the shade, that we may cut off your head, a kgosi cannot die in the sun.' He came and stood in the shade and his head was severed. Thereupon the Bakgalagadi kgosi ordered that the Basarwa women and the small Basarwa children should be rounded up and brought home. Beginning here, in the time of Kgosi Seloilwe I, the Bakgalagadi began to own the Basarwa . . .

Many Bakgwatlheng were living at Dithejwane, near Molepolole, under Kgosi Magane in the seventeenth century. At that time the Bakwena under Kgosi Kgabo arrived in the area and eventually defeated the Bakgwatlheng in a series of wars. Some of the Bakgwatlheng became malata, while others fled into the Central District and the Kgalagadi. So Bakgwatlheng spread far and wide in Botswana.

As a result of their defeats the Bakgwatlheng became poorer than they had previously been. Their poverty is reflected in a praise poem of the Bakwena Kgosi Tshosa (1803-7), who claimed that it was a waste of time to fight them:

> I oppose the killing of Bakgalagadi in battle,
> They are but paupers who own nothing of their own;
> A rich man conquers those rich like himself,
> A handsome man eats those as handsome as he is.

One of the greatest Bakgwatlheng heroes is Magane's grandson Mabeleng. Sometime around the year 1770 he and his people were the malata of the Bangwaketse. So Mabeleng decided to break away and lead his people deeper into the Kgalagadi. Kgosi Mongala heard of this breakaway and he pursued the Bakgwatlheng. Mongala was killed in battle. After his death wars continued, until most of the Bakgwatlheng were captured in the time of Mabeleng's son, Seeiso. Then the Bangwaketse kgosi broke them up and divided them as malata among his followers, so that they would not revolt again.

Tribute or sehuba

While some Bakgalagadi were forced to work for Batswana every day as malata, others only had to pay them tribute. **Sehuba** was an important feature of life in Botswana before 1900. It operated in several ways. A master, for instance, could demand that his lelata bring him a certain number of skins every month. Sehuba did not necessarily depend on the existence of bolata. For instance, if one morafe defeated another in battle, it could then send over a group of men every year to collect sehuba from the other. Then, the weak morafe might hand over cattle, skins, grain or other food, ivory or even people, to the more powerful group. A third way that sehuba operated was for all members of a morafe to give gifts every year to the kgosi. All dikgosi gained their wealth in this way.

Even though sehuba operated in several different ways, it always did one thing; it allowed senior groups to take wealth from groups junior in rank.

Because the Bakgalagadi split up into a number of small groups after their defeat by the Bakwena, they did not have any strong chiefs. Bakgalagadi kept living in very small communities, mostly of around several hundred people. Gradually these groups gave themselves names, but they were originally Bakgwatlheng. One of the groups, perhaps the largest Bakgalagadi group in Botswana, is the Bangologa. Before 1700, a Morolong named Mongologa had left his country because as he was one of the chief's younger sons and could not assume power there. This man and his followers took control of the Bakgwatlheng in the Hukuntsi area, distinguishing themselves by engaging in trading skins with Batswana in the south.

The Batswana

Prior to the 1840s the Batswana were not a particularly powerful or numerous force in the Kgalagadi region. They only came to prominence later on. Even today most Batswana do not live within the boundaries of modern day Botswana, but instead many millions live in South Africa. For instance there are the Bahurutshe, Bakwena and other groups in the Transvaal. Large numbers of Barolong and Batlhaping also live in the Cape and the Orange Free State. The Batswana of Botswana are closely related to these groups, especially the Bakwena-ba-ga-Mogopa and the Barolong. Sometime deep in the past, the Batswana were more or less concentrated in one place. Gradually they split up and began to move to other areas.

It is unclear when the Batswana first arrived in the southern

Kgalagadi, but sometime before 1700 AD a group later known as the Bakwena ba-ga-kgabo split off from their old **morafe**, the ba-ga-Mogopa and moved into the Kweneng. Many of the Batswana who live in Botswana today are descended from these original Bakwena.

Splitting

The origin of the name 'Batswana' is not agreed on by everyone. One explanation is that it comes from 'ba a tswana' (those who came out of each other). Another possibility is that it comes from 'ba a tshwana' (they are the same people). Of course, the Europeans who came along could not pronounce these words correctly and so the term Batswana arose. Interestingly, each of the explanations make the same point, Batswana keep splitting up and forming new merafe.

Throughout history, the Batswana merafe have always been prone to split up. This is usually because the kgosi has many sons, who then argue over who should succeed their father as leader. On many occasions, one of the sons has simply left the morafe with his own followers and established a new group.

The Bangwato and Bangwaketse get their names from their earliest dikgosi, Ngwato and Ngwaketse. But they were not independent rulers, they were both Bakwena. Many traditions say that Ngwato and Ngwaketse were the brothers of Malope, who was a Kwena kgosi. He then allowed his brothers to have their own separate **dikgotla**. Over time these dikgotla grew and began to become merafe of their own.

During the mid eighteenth century the Bangwaketse split from the Bakwena peacefully, under Kgosi Mongala. Sometimes they had minor clashes with their old morafe, but the two groups were not enemies. By about 1790 the Bangwaketse had become powerful, under a renowned leader, Makaba II. He won a series of wars against the Batlhaping, Bakgatla and others, taking many cattle. During this time, Makaba moved to the Kanye area and his people were thought to be one of the strongest and largest morafe of all the Batswana.

The Bangwato finally broke away from the Bakwena during the middle of the eighteenth century. Mathiba was their first independent ruler even though he is said to have been reluctant to leave the Bakwena. Traditions say he was forced to leave his morafe. Mathiba had lived happily at Boswelakgosi in the time of his father, Moleta. But after Moleta's death Mathiba's uncle Mokgadi became the Bangwato regent (*motshwaredi*). Mathiba's mother disliked Mokgadi because she thought he wanted to kill her son and become kgosi. So she sent Mathiba to live with Motswasele I, kgosi of the Bakwena.

At this time Motswasele was married to Mokgadi's daughter. He then asked to marry her sister as well, but Mokgadi refused. Motswasele became angry and asked Mathiba why Mokgadi was refusing. Mathiba was afraid of his uncle and did not want to get involved. So he said: "Why do you ask me, am I the kgosi?" Then Motswasele replied: "You are not the kgosi now, but if I make you kgosi what will your attitude be?"

Hearing this, Mathiba knew Motswasele wanted him to get rid of Mokgadi. So one night he and some friends went to Mokgadi's house and strangled him. The next morning some Bangwato were shocked to find their leader's corpse and guessed that Mathiba had killed him. So they went to Motswasele's kgotla to report what they had found. Motswasele told them Mathiba, who he called a mature young man, had been with him all the previous night. He was really saying that he had given Mathiba permission to kill his uncle.

Soon he made him kgosi of the Bangwato section.
One of Mokgadi's sons, Mongwe, wanted to take revenge. But first he and his friends pretended to accept Mathiba as kgosi. He advised the new kgosi to do things without permission from Motswasele, such as ploughing. Motswasele, though, did not care. So Mongwe waited until it was time for Bakwena girls to enter initiation (*bojale*). Then he told all the Bangwato that the Bakwena were stealing their cattle and Bangwato men got angry and went into the bojale camp. As if that was not serious a crime enough, they then stripped two of Motswasele's wives and sent them to their husband naked. This time Motswasele was very angry and he declared war. His warriors went out and defeated the Bangwato at Kgope hill. After being defeated, the Bangwato then went north. Their history will be followed in the next chapter.

The Bakwena

Meanwhile, the Bakwena continued to be a fairly prosperous group, despite losing people. During the eighteenth century they lived mainly in modern day Kgatleng, at Oodi and Mochudi (which is named after the Kwena kgosi of that time). In the following years the Bakwena moved closer to Molepolole, where they are based today. During this time they lost a number of battles, to the Bangwaketse, Bakgatla and Babirwa and were divided by a number of internal conflicts. Eventually, a ruler known as Motswasele II, came to power around 1807 and he managed to unify his people and win some military victories. Despite his generalship, Motswasele made many enemies among his people due to his cruelty and his unwillingness to abide by customary law. He refused to take advice and change his behavior and so ended up being executed in 1821 by his own people.

Batswana life before the Difaqane

Like other peoples of Botswana, the southern merafe had many ways of making a living. Women tended to be heavily involved in agricultural production, mainly growing sorghum and other vegetables. Men were more likely to herd cattle or to hunt. It is doubtful that Batswana owned nearly as many cattle as they do today. Gathering wild food was extremely important to the Batswana during the winter months and during droughts. There was also a good deal of trade carried on. During the drier months traders moved goods by oxen and exchanged them with neighbouring peoples. From the north, Batswana exchanged copper, iron, and beads from the Bakalanga and Batswapong. From the south they obtained goods like dagga and **sebilo**.

It is incorrect to think of these early Batswana living lives of luxury. Only a small portion of any morafe owned many cattle. Batswana were continually on the edge of starvation due to the dry climate and generally had very little food. A favourite greeting at that time was not saying "dumela". Instead they greeted by asking, "What are you eating?" and replying, "Absolutely nothing." All agriculture had to be done with human labour alone using the hoe, since there were no ploughs or any kind of animal power. This meant that much less food could be produced then. And since droughts were always possible it was difficult to produce enough in wet years to compensate for the dry ones. Usually the wealthiest people were men with more than one wife who could thus benefit from having more farming land.

Batswana at this time lived on a largely vegetarian diet, eating a lot of sorghum porridge and beer, vegetables and if they were lucky, they had cattle that provided them with sour milk and cheese (thick/hard madila). Otherwise they were forced to gather food in the veldt or hunt wild animals. Gathering was far easier than hunting, because Batswana only had spears with which to kill animals. Without guns, they often organized **matsholo** and tried to drive game into fenced in areas where they could spear and club animals to death. Meat was generally dried and made into biltong. Hunters also saved the fat and used it to smear on their skin or to make their porridge more tasty.

By 1820 the Bakwena and Bangwaketse may have had as many as 10,000 people each. Each morafe controlled territory in the same area that they do today, as well as other land further to the south. There were very few European travelers who visited the Batswana before the Difaqane and for that reason there are not many written descriptions of the time. Robert Moffat, visited the Bangwaketse in 1822. He wrote:

> **The town in which Makabbe (Makaba II) lives is very large. I am not able to judge the number of inhabitants, but the town itself appears to cover at least eight times more ground than any other town I have yet seen among the Bechuanas.**
>
> **Their premises and houses are rather on a different plan to other tribes which I have seen. The houses are no larger, but built with more taste and comfort. The accuracy with which circles are formed and perpendiculars raised, is quite astonishing. Their outer yards and house floors are very clean and smooth as paper . . . . Their front cattle fold or place where public meetings are held, is a circle of 170 feet diameter . . . . Behind this lies the proper cattle fold, capable of holding many thousand oxen.**

Questions

1. Name four groups in Botswana who can be described as Khoisan.

2. Why are the !Xo such a small group today?

3. Are the Bakgalagadi much different than the Batswana? Explain your answer.

4. How did bolata start?

5. Which Bakgalagadi leader tried to restore his people's independence from the Bangwaketse?

6. What is sehuba?

7. Who are the Batswana in Botswana descended from?

8. Why is it that Batswana kept splitting up?

Chapter 3
The north before 1820

Northern Botswana is quite distinct from the southern parts. This is because ethnic Batswana do not make up the majority of the area's population. The inhabitants of the north include many Bakalanga, Khoisan, Bakgalagadi, Bayei, Hambukushu and Batswapong.

Batswana

Three Tswana groups lived in what is today the Central District, the Bakaa, Bakhurutshe and Bangwato. The first to move there were the Bakhurutshe, who split off from the Bakhurutshe in the Transvaal hundreds of years ago. Originally the bahurutshe lived at Shoshong, but later split into two groups that moved to the Boteti and Mahalapye. The Bakaa, an offshoot of the Barolong, also began living in the Shoshong area long ago. They had many Bakgalagadi malata and took tribute from a Bakalanga group, the Batalaote. They remained dominant in the area until the Bangwato arrived.

The Bangwato moved into the Central District from the Kweneng around 1770, settling at Shoshong. For a decade or so they lived on friendly terms with the Bakaa and paid them tribute. But then they fought and drove them east towards the Limpopo River. However the Bangwato did not become that powerful immediately, since they split not long after their victory. A succession dispute arose around 1795 during the reign of Kgosi Mathiba, who had several sons by several wives. His son, Tawana, by his first wife, was initially designated heir. Tawana's mother, though, was not the **mohumagadi**, who had another son.

Tawana and his faction split from the Bangwato and eventually moved north. They settled in the Kgwebe Hills, an old iron mining center near Lake Ngami just outside the tsetse fly and malaria zone. His morafe became known as the Batawana, although it was known until the 1840s as the Bampuru. The Bangwato at first let Tawana go. But about fifteen years later they attacked him and suffered a major defeat just south of Lake Ngami. Despite their victory the Batawana did not live peacefully afterwards. They too had a succession dispute, fought a short civil war and split into two factions.

The Bangwato, on the other hand, soon became a much stronger morafe following the accession of Kgari I to the bogosi around 1817. Kgari tried to end succession disputes by increasing the power of the kgosi and reducing the power of the royal family. He made the headmen more powerful by granting them large numbers of cattle. These cattle were herded by Khoisan malata, who were captured in fairly large numbers by Bangwato mephato. Headmen, who became known as the batlhanka-ba-ga-kgosi (servants of the chief), had their own property rights restricted when they accepted the kgosi's cattle. If the headmen failed to support the kgosi in disputes, they were liable to lose all their property, not merely the cattle given to them by the chief. Kgari also sought to increase the power and population of the Bangwato through other measures. He forced all people to live in the main village. Then he made many Bakhurutshe, Bakalanga and Bakgalagadi become part of his morafe. Kgari also made many Khoisan become malata.

The effects of his reforms eventually enabled the Bangwato to become a powerful morafe after his death.

Khoisan (Basarwa)

Of the inhabitants of Botswana, the Khoisan are those who have lived there for the longest time. Previous chapters explained that there are three main Khoisan language groups, the !Xo, Zhu and Khoe. While the !Xo in southern Botswana were almost all exterminated in past centuries, there were no such wars of genocide in northern Botswana. Many Khoisan speakers still live there.

Khoe is the most widely spoken Khoisan language. It is very similar to that formerly spoken by the Khoikhoi (sometimes called Hottentots) of South Africa, who have since adopted Afrikaans and are called Coloureds. It is probable that the ancestors of the Khoikhoi once lived in northern Botswana two thousand years ago until they obtained cattle and moved south to the Cape. Some of the Khoe include the Bateti who live on the Boteti River, the Shua Khoe of the Nata area and the Qanikhwe of the Okavango Delta. Zhu is spoken largely in the western side of Ngamiland, especially north of Ghanzi.

Khoisan culture
Khoisan are often thought to be nomads who roam around the Kgalagadi hunting animals. In fact the Khoisan have very specific territorial customs and only a small number of them claim land ownership. Usually, a family owns land, which is passed on from father to son over generations. The landowning family is then joined by people who have married into it or by more distant relatives seeking a place to live. In general about thirty people tended to live on any one piece of land.

In the past Khoisan landowners, both Khoe and Zhu, were called **Xhaihasi**. They controlled large pieces of land but did not use it all the time. Instead, they would move around to different parts of their territories depending on the time of year. Xhaihasi received the largest share of food and were the political leaders of their groups. During the dry winters, the group lived at a central waterhole, which was sometimes shared with neighbouring families. But after the rains came the inhabitants would move away from the central waterhole and live near pools of standing water. Usually they split up into small sub groups and stayed away from the waterhole for as long as possible. Finally they moved back there as winter returned. Khoisan did not leave their own territory very often and, in fact, were likely to be attacked by their neighbours if they trespassed.

Most people think of Khoisan as hunters, but in fact most of their food comes from sources other than meat. It is true that Khoisan men are expert hunters. But in the past they were limited in their ability to kill large animals since they only had bows, arrows and spears. Women gathered the majority of the food from wild plants. There were also many Khoe who owned cattle and lived on the milk these animals produced. Less well recognized is that many Khoisan traded in order to obtain grain, particularly from the Bakalanga. Khoisan have been involved in long distance trade for over 1500 years. They traded goods such as skins, biltong, ostrich eggshell beads and salt from the Kgalagadi to their neighbours for goods such as metal, grain, beads, dagga and tobacco.

Khoisan are commonly recognized as having exceptional talent in painting. Artists used rock canvases to paint highly abstract pictures, in which the eland often figures as a sacred animal. In these pictures, animals and other symbols were used to represent elements of religious experience. Painters often represented the experiences of going into trances, which was done fairly regularly at all night fireside dances. Dancers entered a trance through the constant repetition of movements and the smoking of dagga. In this state they were able to cure the sick and talk with spirits.

Many of the Khoisan in northern Botswana maintained their independence until the middle of the nineteenth century.

Others, though, became the malata of the Batswana long before then. Those groups that kept their independence had their own leaders and traditions. One famous man of Shua Khoe descent is Kgaraxumae, a ruler in the Nata and southern Chobe area who was renowned as a great hunter and a resister of Batswana rule.

Bakalanga

One of the largest groups in northern Botswana are the Bakalanga. They are a branch of the Shona speakers and have been living in their present areas for over 1500 years. At one time the Bakalanga had the largest kingdom in southern Africa.

Around 1450 AD the Bakalanga who lived in the Tati area and further west inside Zimbabwe formed a powerful state known as Butwa. It seems that before that time they had not controlled the gold they produced but were under the rule of another empire. But after 1450 Butwa became a huge kingdom. Traders from Butwa sent gold and other products along the Limpopo River to be sold to Europeans and Asians at the Indian Ocean. The capital of Butwa was Khami, where about 7 000 people lived, a very large population for that time in history.

Until the 1680s the king of Butwa, called the Mambo, came from a family known as the Chibundule (Torwa). But then another group of Bakalanga entered the area, led by the Nichasike (Rozwi) family. This group of people revolted and took over the kingdom, which they ruled until the 1830s. Among descendants of the Nichasikes in Botswana are the Mengwe clan, which were once the most senior Bakalanga group.

Due to the nature of their history, the Bakalanga are really a collection of many different sections of people. Those Bakalanga in Botswana who were associated with the original Butwa kingdom before 1680s are called the Balilima. Meanwhile, the immigrants who came with the Nichasikes and ruled Butwa after 1700 are called the 'Banyayi'. Both of these two groups see themselves as pure Bakalanga or Bakalanga Dumbu.

Because Butwa was a huge and prosperous kingdom, it attracted large numbers of settlers of various origins who adopted Bakalanga culture. Most of these people were Bapedi and Babirwa who had lived south of the Limpopo.

Though the Bakalanga were a powerful and independent group before 1840, they would come to be dominated by the Amandebele and Bangwato later on. During their years of power the Bakalanga had a vast trading network stretching from the Makgadikgadi salt pans, where they got copper and salt, all the way to the Indian Ocean. They even traded in southern Botswana, selling goods among the Bakwena and Bangwaketse.

Other peoples of the Central District

Apart from the Batswana, Khoisan and Bakalanga, there were several other large groups living inside what is today the Central District.

The Batalaote
The Batalaote were originally Bakalanga, but split off from their Banyayi relatives hundreds of years ago. After Dalaunde (called Ntalaote by the Batswana), the son of the Mambo, argued with his older brother, he moved with his followers into the Shoshong area. There they adopted the Setswana language. By the year 1800 the Batalaote were closely connected with the Bangwato, among whom they lived.

The Batswapong
The Batswapong are a diverse group of people living in the Tswapong Hills. Like the Batswana, they are said to have originated in South Africa. Some were originally Bapedi and others Transvaal Ndebele (Bapedi and Transvaal Ndebele are Sotho-Tswana speakers living in the Transvaal). All of the Batswapong live in a scattered way, divided up among various small villages throughout the hills they live in. Originally these villages each had its own leader, but early in the nineteenth century a group of Transvaal Ndebele led by a man named Malete conquered the area. For this reason the Batswapong are sometimes called Bamalete (but they have no connection with the people who live in the Ramotswa area). Due to the fact that there is a lot of iron ore in the Tswapong Hills, there have always been a number of skilled iron workers, living there. They traded their iron goods as far south as the Kweneng.

The Baphaleng
A large number of Baphaleng live in the Central District and they are of Bakgalagadi origin. They are the descendants of the Bakgwatlheng who in Chapter 2 fled from the Bakwena and went to live in the Shoshong area. They were independent for some time. Eventually the Bangwato defeated them a little before 1800.

Peoples of Ngamiland

The Bayei
Ngamiland's largest ethnic group are the Bayei, who migrated to Ngamiland from southern Zambia hundreds of years ago. The Bayei were primarily fishermen who travelled around the Okavango Delta in canoes they called makoro.

Since the Bayei lived in scattered communities over a wide area they did not have strong rulers. They did have a kgosi who was supposed to be the head of the entire group, but he never had substantial power. In fact the Bayei appeared to have avoided warfare at all costs, preferring to live peacefully with the Khoe fishermen who also lived in the Okavango Delta.

The Bayei did not live by fishing alone. They also produced a lot of food by planting gardens on the islands and riverbanks of the Okavango delta. Like all the other people of Botswana, they were also expert hunters. The Bayei specialized in trapping hippopotami. Regarding trade, the Bayei sold fish, grain and metal to the Khoisan. They also sent goods to Angola and obtained beads, cloth and other goods in return.

The Hambukushu
Also living in the Okavango area, in the drier areas to the north of the marshes, were the Hambukushu. In the past, far fewer lived in Botswana than today. Like the Bayei, the Hambukushu were split up into a number of small groups. But they had a king with far more power than that of the Bayei chief. By 1800 the Hambukushu were living all along the Okavango River up into Angola. They kept cattle, farmed and traded all sorts of goods and people.

The Bakgalagadi

There were a fair number of Bakgalagadi in Ngamiland, mainly of Bangologa descent. Most of them lived in the Kgwebe area near Lake Ngami. The Batawana made them malata after 1800. In later years, many Bangologa fled Batawana rule and moved north and lived next to the Hambukushu.

Questions

1 a. What are the four Batswana merafe in northern Botswana?
  b. Which two are most closely related?

2. What languages do the Khoisan speak?

3. How do the Khoisan maintain their ownership of land?
4. What is the relationship between the Banyayi and the Balilima?

5. Why were many of northern Botswana's peoples not strong in military terms?

6. Compare the lifestyles of the members of the Bayei, the Khoisan and the Butwa.

Chapter 4
Botswana's traditional cultures

What is Culture?

Culture can be defined as a manner of life of any particular group of people. The way in which human beings in any society live is their culture and each society on this planet has its own culture. All societies, for instance, have their own language, their own way of addressing elders, their own way of running affairs, their own system of medicine and their own way of dealing with outsiders. Because each society has its own culture, we are able to distinguish one society from another.

Before Europeans came to this country Batswana had their own way of life and a traditional culture of their own. This culture made the Batswana different from other groups in the region, such as the Amandebele, the Amaxhosa and the Khoikhoi of South Africa.

Traditional leadership

Bakgalagadi and Batswana had leaders called dikgosi or chiefs. Dikgosi are going to be important in this book, because it was they who dealt with the Europeans. Also, the dikgosi as leaders of their people, were decisive in shaping political events. Most of the dikgosi tried to rule by consensus. In other words people would discuss ideas at length and then make a decision when almost everybody agreed. Important matters were usually discussed in private by the kgosi and his councillors first and then were taken to the people at a public assembly for further discussion. This public assembly was known as the kgotla, which was located next to the kgosi's residence. In the old days a meeting was held every morning at the kgotla around a fire. All important decisions went through the councillors and the kgotla.

It was at the main kgotla that the kgosi tried cases, held public meetings, met all visitors to his land and held important ceremonies. He might also hold special meetings, such as *phuthego*, in which all men in the village were summoned or *pitso*, in which all male subjects from across the land were called to the kgotla. These kinds of meeting were only rarely called. Often they settled serious disputes that arose between a kgosi and his people. Sometimes new laws were introduced in this way.

The kgosi, though, did not control everybody's affairs on his own. His subjects were divided up into different wards (*makgotla*), which were led by the headmen and the royal family members (*dikgosana*). These wards were given land that was often far from the central village and the headmen ran the affairs of those areas for the kgosi. Usually most matters were dealt with by the headmen in their makgotla, but if a severe dispute or issue arose then it might be brought to the attention of the kgosi.

Due to his position, the kgosi was treated in a special manner. He was referred to by his subjects according to the totem (*sereto*) of his morafe. Among the Bangwato, the kgosi was called Phuti, while the Bangwaketse and Bakwena referred to their kgosi as Kwena. The dikgosi were also praised by their subjects in a special way and praise songs were composed that glorified their deeds. Dikgosi also wore different clothes from the common people and only they were allowed to wear leopard skins when not in battle. Dikgosi were installed into office in elaborate ceremonies, with all their subjects present.

Social organization of the Batswana

Batswana were an unusual group in Africa in the sense that the kgosi tried to make all the people live in a central village (*motse*). Many of the subjects would not live there for much of the year, but they were expected to maintain a home in the main village. These villages were often located in a hilly area suitable for defense, and also had good water supplies.

The three residence system
Most Batswana families tried to maintain three places of residence. They had a home in the motse, as well as lands for ploughing (*masimo*) and a cattle post (*moraka*) to keep their stock. Usually these places were some distance apart and families would be split up for much of the year. The women would spend much of the time from November to May at the masimo, where they cultivated and harvested crops. If the family had cattle, then the men would spend a lot of time at the moraka. Since cattle had to be herded all year round there would always be a need for people to look after them. The head of the family and the grandparents, meanwhile, might live in the motse for much of the year.

The mafisa system
Among the Batswana, it was very common for families to try to work closely with other families. Batswana were poor people and they needed a large number of friends in order to be able to survive during difficult periods.

How were such contacts made? One method was for poor families without cattle to obtain loans from wealthier families. If a wealthy man gave a poorer man a loan of cattle this was known as mafisa. The number of cattle loaned out varied a great deal. Sometimes only a couple of cattle were given away, which the borrower could use for milk or for ploughing. At other times, rich men could give away as many as thirty animals, which would then be herded full time by the borrower and his sons. In return for herding the mafisa cattle, the borrower would be given one female animal a year.

When a person took mafisa from another, he lost some of his personal independence to the man he borrowed cattle from. The owner could come to the borrower's moraka and look at the cattle at any time. He could take them away if he wanted to. Borrowers could also find that they were asked to do other favours for the owner of the cattle. He could be asked to help harvest the owner's crop or perhaps support him in a court case. Sometimes families ended up working closely with each other for many generations.

Marriage and family life
Long ago marriages did not occur simply because the couple involved were in love. In almost every case, marriage was arranged in order to bring two families closer together. When a man was seen as old enough to marry, his parents and relatives would look for a suitable partner for him. In some cases, they had already thought about this matter for a long time. Most families tried to look for marriage partners from wealthier families. When a family decided on an appropriate bride, it would approach her parents and conduct negotiations. Neither of the potential married couple played any part in the talking. If the negotiations succeeded then the man could visit the woman. She would give him a gourd of water if she accepted

him as her husband.

Once the marriage was arranged, it had to be finalized with the payment of bridewealth (*bogadi*). The family of the man would pay a certain number of cattle, goats or sheep, to the woman's family. If the woman was from a wealthy or royal family then perhaps over ten cattle would be paid. Women from poor families with little influence accepted bogadi of two head of cattle or even goats. This payment did not symbolize that the woman was being bought. What it meant was that the families were being drawn closer together and that they took the marriage seriously. If the couple were to divorce, and there were no children involved, then the bogadi would have to be repaid to the man's family. For that reason, both families would put pressure on the married couple to stay together rather than divorce. Bogadi also showed that the bride was moving from one family to another. She was obliged to leave her own parents' home and move to the husband's courtyard. If her husband paid bogadi, then all her children came under the jurisdiction of her husband's family and kgotla, not her own.

The vast majority of men married only one woman. But perhaps ten percent or so married more than one woman, a practice known as polygamy. Usually only richer men who owned many cattle married a second woman. The reasons for having a second wife varied, but in general it brought a man extra status. When a man married for the second time, his first wife usually retained senior status in the family. Her children would inherit most of the property as well as any position her husband held.

Daughters of wealthy or royal families tended to marry people of similar status. In fact, among the wealthier Batswana, it was extremely common for people to marry their cousins, which was known as serara. Richer people preferred serara because they knew that they would not be paying bogadi to people from outside their own family. All the inheritance would remain in the family too. Many people liked serara because the families involved knew each other very well and thus there was a good chance of a successful union.

Once a wife moved to her husband's residence she was given her own independent household. This consisted of a house, ploughing land and any cattle that she might own and other property. All these things were owned by her and her children and were completely separate from the property belonging to that of the other wives.

Religion

All societies have their own way of worshipping a superior being or God. Before the arrival of Christianity the Batswana worshipped the spirits of their dead ancestors *(badimo)*. The badimo were thought to pay close attention to the lives of their living descendants. Batswana therefore tried hard to please them.

Batswana had always believed in the existence of one God *(Modimo)* who had created the earth. They did not, though, have a very good idea of what Modimo was and they did not have any ceremonies that worshipped this God. But they recognized that Modimo was the most powerful force on the earth.

The kgosi was at the centre of religious activities. He was known to be directly descended from the first ancestor of the morafe. So he was involved in many religious ceremonies.

Also, in times of drought or danger, he would communicate with the badimo and ask them to improve the situation.

An important annual ceremony was rainmaking. No person was allowed to plough before it was complete. Every year when ploughing time approached, the kgosi and his favourite ngaka would appeal to the ancestors for rain. They would kill a black cow specially selected for the occasion. Then they would take its blood and mix it with herbs. Finally they would spread the mixture across the countryside with the branch of a mosetlha tree. Rain was then supposed to fall soon. If it did not it meant that the badimo were unhappy about something and other measures had to be taken to appease them.

A 19th century rainmaker

Ordinary people also communicated with the badimo to make sure that they were not offended. On important occasions they would set aside food and drink for their badimo to enjoy. Every year the kgosi also gave part of the first crops to the ancestors. Only after that could people prepare food from the harvest. There were also ceremonies where cattle (either all white or all black) were sacrificed to the badimo. Then the blood of these animals would be mixed with special herbs by various **dingaka** and eventually poured onto a fire that was kept in a holy location.

Bongaka and boloi—traditional medicine and sorcery

Batswana, like most other peoples in the pre-industrial period, believed that unfortunate events were not caused by chance. Instead, they often felt that misfortune was caused by sorcery (*boloi*). They believed, for instance, that if a person got sick or died, then that person's enemies had caused the problem through the use of boloi. This system of beliefs was different from that of the Europeans, who believe in such concepts as fate, chance and random occurrences.

Ngaka throwing bones

People who had the power to use witchcraft were called baloi. They used herbs and other ingredients to hurt other people. Baloi were said to possess special powers. They were thought to be able to enter houses at night and then to turn their enemies into animals (which they rode around on). At other times, baloi might try to poison their enemies or aim lightning at them. The use of boloi was not allowed in any morafe. People who were suspected of using it were put on trial. If found guilty they were liable to be put to death.

The traditional doctors, *(dingaka)* were different from the baloi in that they used their powers in a positive manner. Each ngaka tended to have a specialty and attracted a separate range of customers. Some were skilled at curing the sick, treating them with herbs they grew or collected in the bush. Other dingaka were skilled at 'throwing the bones'. They would throw a set of bones on the ground and then interpret them. In doing so they tried to help solve a person's problems. In this way, for instance, a ngaka could help a sick man identify who was using boloi against him and then come up with a cure. Another group of dingaka were skilled at the protection and curing of cattle and livestock.

The range of activities in which baloi and dingaka took part was very large. In all the large villages there were a number of them, who lived by charging fees for their services. Usually they charged a goat, but if they cured a serious illness they would ask for a cow. If you wanted a moloi to harm your enemy, then the price was much higher than that. Successful dingaka tended to be among the most prosperous citizens of any morafe, even though they were not from the royal family.

Education

In all societies, education is used to train young people to think and act like their older counterparts. Long ago the Batswana had a very rigid system of education, although there were no classrooms then. Traditionally, Batswana received formal training during initiation ceremonies and informal training from parents, relatives and elders. Unless a man had received this education, he was not allowed to take part in public affairs. Uneducated women, likewise, could not marry and start families. Just as important was the fact that uneducated people were regarded as children, no matter how old they were. To be taken seriously, then, a person had to be educated.

Batswana education tended to promote very conservative ideals. By that we mean that children were encouraged to keep things the way they were. Adults were expected to act in the same manner as their elders and ancestors, the badimo, had done. If not the badimo would be upset and they would cause things to go wrong in the morafe. People were also taught to respect the kgosi's authority and not to disturb the political order.

Informal training

All Batswana children received informal training from a young age. Children were taught practical skills by their parents. Mothers taught their daughters various household duties such as fetching water, wood and cooking. Girls were taught how to build houses, how to keep them clean and how to decorate them. At the lands they learned to grow and harvest crops and to prepare them for eating. In some families, basket making or pottery was also taught.

Boys meanwhile learned from their fathers and older boys. Hunting, tending cattle, clearing fields, carpentry, tanning and sewing were among the skills they acquired. Seven year olds were sent to look after goats and calves and by the age of ten they usually looked after cattle. Herding cattle was a job with much responsibility. Boys were situated far from home at a cattlepost and worked by themselves for much of the day. Herd boys were always on the lookout for good grazing land and, during the driest part of the year, they had to dig for water in the beds of streams. Boys were disciplined to do a good job. If a boy did not put much effort into herding cattle or was found sitting far away from the animals, he could be beaten by any adult who walked by. Boys who let cattle go astray could expect to be severely punished.

Elders usually tried to educate the children by telling them stories and riddles. This exercise often took place in the evenings around a fire. These stories were often about animals, which were acting in ways similar to adults. They always had a lesson to them and would warn children never to be foolish. Riddles challenged youngsters to use their intellect. One of these, for instance, asked: "What sinks and then emerges?" The answer—a needle.

Formal education
Batswana's formal education, known as initiation, was a far more serious affair than the telling of stories around fires. During this exercise children were transformed into adults through intensive instruction, corporal punishment, denial of comfort and seclusion. Initiation ceremonies for boys were known as bogwera, while those for girls were called bojale. These ceremonies occurred every five to ten years and all people except malata were expected to participate. Most of the participants were aged between thirteen and eighteen.

Bogwera was a harsh exercise. All the boys would be sent off into the bush during the winter, where they could not be visited except by the people in charge of the ceremony. Then they went through a three stage course. First of all, the boys (*magwane*) were circumcized, which was an extremely painful and dangerous operation. Once they had recovered from their wounds, which took several days, the magwane then went through physical training. At this time they were moulded together into a fighting regiment (*mophato*). They were taught military tactics and also to handle weapons. Like soldiers everywhere, they had to complete long marches and other tests of their endurance and courage. Hunting was thought to be an excellent form of learning for soldiers and every day the magwane had to hunt for food. After bogwera was over, the magwane would be expected to fight and conduct other duties together for the rest of their lives.

Motlhaping girl initiate.

During the final part of bogwera the magwane were taught the laws governing Tswana society. They learned law, custom and the historical traditions of their morafe, as well as the duties of the kgosi, headmen and ordinary citizens. In addition, the young men were taught the responsibilities of being a husband and the head of a family.

Undergoing bogwera was a painful process. Not only was circumcision painful, but military training was arduous. Constant beatings made the magwane learn their lessons and all magwane returned home with scared backs. They were denied normal amounts of food and sleep. In the mornings they would be awakened by having cold water thrown on them. Due to this training, it was not uncommon for magwane to die. In fact, the organizers of the ceremony always ensured one person died, as a sacrifice to the badimo.

Once the process had finished the magwane were presented to the kgosi, who gave the new mophato a name. Maletamotse, for instance, is the name of a mophato in several merafe. Mephato were always led by the senior royal family member in the regiment, often a son or nephew of the kgosi. He and his men could be called upon at any time by the kgosi to defend the morafe or to perform public tasks such as hunting dangerous animals, rounding up stray cattle or destroying locusts.

Girls' initiation ceremonies were usually held at the same time as the boys' and were known as bojale. This ceremony took place far from the village in a private location. Initiation for girls was not designed to be as rigorous for them as it was for boys. For example, there was no equivalent of circumcision and girls were not expected to go hunting or to learn military tactics.

Girls undergoing initiation were smeared all over in white clay and given clothes made out of reeds. In addition they carried around large sticks with which they could beat anyone who came near them.

The girls were not well fed at this time and they did quite a lot of walking. But the main aspect of their education was not physical. They were taught how to be good wives and mothers. Like the boys, they learned the laws and customs of the morafe and what duties they were expected to perform as adult citizens. When, after some six weeks, the initiation was finished, they were also presented to the kgosi and the mophato given a name. From then on, for the rest of their lives, the mophato could be called on to perform public duties such as building huts for the kgosi, preparing a feast or any other such thing.

Once boys and girls had been initiated they were full citizens. As such they were allowed to marry and to go to court as an adult. Batswana felt that initiation taught youngsters all the things they needed to know in order to be useful to society.

Women in traditional society

Traditionally women in Botswana occupied an inferior position to men. This can be seen in that men were in control of making public decisions, while women were expected to perform most of the work done in the morafe.

Only men were allowed to take part in political affairs. Women were not supposed to be public officials such as the kgosi or an advisor to the kgosi, nor were they allowed to go to kgotla, where all political and legal matters were decided, unless they were giving evidence in a court case. Women were expected to rely upon their fathers, brothers or husbands if they wanted any legal matter to be taken up.

Socially, women were expected to perform far more than half of all work done in the morafe. Women and their daughters were expected to perform all house work, such as cooking, cleaning, fetching water and firewood and caring for children. Men rarely did these things. In addition, women performed almost all the agricultural work, while men looked after cattle and hunted. It was agriculture that provided families with the majority of their food, not cattle or game meat.

An indication of a woman's position can be seen through laws relating to cattle ownership. The majority of cattle were owned by men. When a man died, his cattle were then divided up into shares with the majority going to his oldest son. His younger sons got smaller shares, while his daughters could usually expect one or two beasts at most. It was men who controlled almost all of the inheritance (*boswa*). Nor did a woman gain any share of bogadi that came into her family. When a woman was married, the bogadi that was paid went to her father and his brothers only. Through such laws as these, women were traditionally denied the means to obtain cattle. Women thus remained dependent upon men, who controlled the family wealth.

Other cultures in Botswana

This chapter has so far looked at Batswana culture only. This is because other groups have already been discussed or will be in later chapters. But also because the culture of all the groups in Botswana were to a large extent similar.

A big difference between Batswana and the other merafe is that the Batswana lived in much larger groups. Peoples like the Bayei and Batswapong were scattered, they tended not to have a strong kgosi. Instead, they had many local rulers whose power extended over a small area and who were quite weak. Because their numbers were small, these groups did not divide themselves up into makgotla like the Batswana.

These merafe were similar to the Batswana in many ways. They practiced bogadi, traditional medicine and educated their children through initiation and circumcision. All believed also in sorcery, rainmaking and worshipping ancestors.

Mwali cult and Hambukushu rainmaking

Bakalanga and Batswapong had a different religion from the Batswana. The Mwali cult was practiced in eastern Botswana as well as in neighbouring parts of Zimbabwe and the Transvaal, by a wide variety of people. This religion had originated with the Butwa empire many centuries ago and then spread into other areas. Bakalanga and others believed in a powerful being named Mwali, the son of God, with whom they communicated in times of need. Such help was needed because the Bakalanga believed that bad luck, drought or illness were brought by angry badimo. To appease the badimo, Bakalanga had to talk to Mwali through priests and priestesses who lived in remote and sacred places, such as caves.

To communicate with Mwali, Bakalanga had to visit the priest, bringing big pots of traditional beer and a lot of food. The priest would then offer the food to Mwali, who would drink the beer and leave only foam inside the pots. Once the sacrifice was given, the priest would ask Mwali for aid or guidance. In the evening that the sacrifice had been given, dingaka would have another ceremony in which they would dance barefoot through a fire in a public ceremony. If they succeeded, it showed that Mwali had heard the people and would get rid of the evil spirits that had been bringing misfortune.

Another group of people with a separate religious tradition were the Hambukushu, who lived in the northern part of Ngamiland. The rulers of the Hambukushu claimed to control all the waters that flowed down the Okavango River and were thought to be the area's best rainmakers. Other leaders from Zambia, Namibia and even Botswana would send him cattle every year so that he would make rain come and keep the rivers flowing. Part of the Hambukushu rulers power came from the fact that for many months of the year he lived by himself in the bush, apart from his people. He would only emerge from his seclusion once rains had fallen.

Khoisan culture

Khoisan differed depending on where they lived. Many owned cattle and livestock, while others relied more on hunting and foraging. A lot of Khoisan had dikgosi, while some smaller groups did not have any formal leader. Most of the Basarwa conducted initiation ceremonies for boys and believed in a similar system of religious beliefs as the Batswana.

One way in which Khoisan are quite distinct from Batswana is in the way they put pressure on each of their friends and relatives to share their food and belongings. For instance, among the Zhu a custom known as hxaro exists, in which people exchange belongings. So Zhu can borrow things from relatives or friends when they need them. In return they know that at some point in the future they will be asked to give a gift back to the person that they borrowed from. This custom allows Zhu to be confident that in times of drought or poverty they will be able to turn to someone for help. Some engage in hxaro with several dozen people at a time for that reason.

Another feature of Khoisan life quite different from that of the Batswana is their system of medicine. Besides having their own traditional doctors to heal them, when a person who got sick a trance dance might be held. During these ceremonies, people gather around a fire and begin singing. A group of dancers begin moving around in a circle. After moving around and pounding their feet for some time, usually one or more of the dancers would enter a trance and attempt to cure the sick person. These dancers are not dingaka, they are just ordinary people. It is believed that all people keep a healing substance called *n/um* in their stomachs and that dancing can bring this substance up into their heads. Once the *n/um* has arrived in the head, the dancer will rub sweat all over the sick person and make a series of strange moaning sounds. It is believed that the evil spirit that caused the disease will then go away.

The challenge to Tswana culture

During the course of the nineteenth century, Europeans began to interact with the peoples of Botswana. Before Botswana became a Protectorate, there were two groups of Europeans with whom the Batswana dealt regularly. These were the missionaries and the traders. Both groups had a great deal to do with changing Tswana culture.

What is a missionary? These are people who try to spread their religion in other countries. In the case of Botswana, the missionaries were British and German. They came to Botswana to spread Christianity. The most prominent group was the London Missionary Society (LMS). Missionaries were important in the nineteenth century because they tried to change the way in which Batswana thought about life. They wanted to get rid of many traditional customs. So they told Batswana that if they practised these things they were sinning against God and would spend their afterlives in a place called Hell. They wanted to replace Tswana customs with practices based upon the laws of their God, found in the Bible.

Another group who made a lasting impact on the Tswana way of life were traders. These were businessmen who came to Botswana to exchange products which they had brought with them for things the Batswana had. Traders did not care how the Batswana thought or acted, but came to Botswana in order to make money. Some of them, perhaps, wanted to hunt or have some adventure in what was for them a strange and distant land. Most traders came to Botswana from the Cape Colony and the Transvaal, which was where they returned to sell the goods that they acquired.

European traders with Bakalanga in 1890s.

Traders changed the way in which Batswana behaved for one main reason. They brought items that the Batswana had never seen before and wished to obtain. These included guns, clothes, new kinds of food, wagons and horses. Because the traders did not want sorghum and cattle, Batswana were forced to change their lifestyle in order to produce things the traders wanted.

In some ways the traders and missionaries were closely tied together. For instance, many missionaries such as David Livingstone and Robert Moffat, also traded with the Batswana. In cases where missionaries went to Tswana merafe and did not trade, traders were quick to follow them because the kgosi was likely to favour the presence of whites. Meanwhile, the Batswana dikgosi often invited missionaries to live among their people so trade would increase and ties with the Cape Colony would be strengthened. Missionaries and traders will appear in many later chapters. They played an important role in nineteenth century Botswana.

Questions

1 Why was the kgosi so important in Tswana society?

2 What is mafisa and what makes it crucial to some poorer people?

3 Describe the type of marriage you would have wanted if you had lived in nineteenth century Botswana.

4 For what reason did Batswana and the Bakalanga worry so much about the badimo?

5 How could Batswana try to harm their enemies without the use of physical force?

6 Describe the main elements of bogwera.

7 How were women discriminated against traditionally?

8 Compare Tswana and Sarwa healing techniques.

Chapter 5
Time of tumult-The Difaqane

No period in Botswana's history has been more destructive than the Difaqane, also known as Mfecane. During the 1820s and 1830s two groups of foreign invaders, the Bakololo and Amandebele, attacked merafe throughout the country, seizing people and livestock. Some communities were completely ruined, while others were weakened and scattered. To make matters worse famine and internal conflicts also occurred, as local groups turned on one another to survive.

What happened in Botswana also occurred elsewhere in Africa. The Sesotho term Difaqane and Isixhosa term Mfecane are used by historians as labels for the great upsurge in violence that occurred throughout much of Eastern and Central as well as Southern Africa during the early decades of the nineteenth century. Both words are commonly translated as expressions for the crushing sound made by grinding stones. Difaqane and Mfecane thus refer to a 'time of crushing'.

In the past Batswana had other names for the period. Local oral traditions speak of a 'time of tumult'. Some elders, when referring to the Bakololo as well as Amandebele, speak of Matebele invasions. Another indigenous term is the 'time of the black ants' (*ditshoswane tse dintshonyana*).

The last term comes from an incident involving the Bakwena. In the years just before the invasions, the Bakwena were governed by Kgosi Motswasele II, who is remembered as a powerful but abusive ruler. His misrule led some of his subjects to plot his execution. Before he was beheaded Motswasele is said to have warned that: 'If I am killed my father's ants will come to avenge me'. He is further said to have prophesied that the countryside would first be overrun by 'black ants' and later by 'white ants' (*ditshoswane tse ditshweunyana*). Batswana remembered the slain kgosi's prophecy. Later most identified the black ants as being the Bakololo and Amandebele and the white ants as the Boers who followed them.

What caused the time of tumult?

Historians do not agree about the origins of the Difaqane. A number of explanations have been offered. It is likely that several factors contributed to its outbreak. Until recently experts assumed that the Difaqane began among the Northern Nguni of Natal, the people we know today as the Amazulu. But recent studies have focused attention on events elsewhere in southern Africa, which also contributed to the time of tumult.

Prior to the Difaqane the Northern Nguni lived in small clans, which were sometimes loosely united into larger confederations. After 1810 these clans fought one another for control over all of Natal in an increasingly bloody series of wars. It is uncertain why these wars broke out. The growth of the region's human and cattle population may have led to greater competition for land, especially good grazing land. The outbreak of a period of prolonged drought, around 1800-10, may also have increased competition for food and cattle. This drought was made more severe by a growing dependency on maize, which had been introduced from the Americas. Maize is less drought resistant than African grains such as sorghum. Another probable factor for the Difaqane in Natal was competition over trade routes to the Portuguese ports in

Mozambique. Among the products that the Portuguese sought were ivory and slaves. Ivory trading could have encouraged war through the formation of large armed hunting parties, which competed over remaining elephant herds. As hunters began to acquire guns in exchange for their ivory, the region became more insecure.

The spread of slave trading has always been connected with increased violence. In the past people were generally enslaved by being captured in wars. Some suggest that the Difaqane may have been begun by slavers. The outbreak of the Difaqane coincided with the export of thousands of slaves from Delagoa Bay (now called Maputo) in southern Mozambique. Perhaps Northern Nguni communities combined into stronger states with larger armies in order to defend themselves from slave traders. This would be an example of defensive state building.

Still another factor that contributed to the Difaqane was the military talents and ambitions of rulers like Dingiswayo, Sobhuza, Zwide and Shaka. The greatest of these was the Amazulu leader Shaka who, between 1818 and 1828, conquered most of Natal. Rather than live under Shaka some groups fled from Natal, usually with little property or food. To survive these same refugees often fought against other groups whom they encountered. In this way they carried the death and destruction of Shaka's wars to other parts of Africa. The Amandebele were one such group.

Slave Trading along the Orange River

Events outside of Natal also contributed to the Difaqane. Like the Portuguese in Mozambique, the Boers in the British ruled Cape Colony were eager to acquire slaves. In 1790 there were 25,000 slaves living in the Cape Colony. They had been imported from other parts of Africa and Asia. These slaves, along with another 20,000 indigenous Khoe, worked without pay for the 22,000 Boers.

In 1809 the British banned the further import of overseas slaves into the Cape Colony. Some Boers then began to buy women and children from across the Orange river, which then formed the Cape Colony's northern border. These women and children were often captured in raids carried out by Griqua and Korannas, both Coloured groups of mixed European and Khoe descent who had acquired guns and horses. Most of the captives were either Basotho or southern Batswana, such as the Batlhaping, though many Khoisan speakers were also captured. There are written eyewitness accounts of this trade. For example a missionary writing in 1829 noted:

> Amongst the Griquas and Bergenaars (a breakaway Griqua group), who are in considerable connection with the Cape, slaves obtained by barter or by capture from Bootchuanas (Batswana) and Bushmen (Khoisan), are a common article of saleable property.

In 1834 a newspaper, *The Grahamstown Journal*, reported:

> Among the Basotho, cattle have now become scarce, and commandos do not now as usual go out in search of them so much as of children, whom they carry off in great number and dispose of them to farmers, who readily give a horse or inferior gun for each.

As happened in Natal, Basotho and southern Batswana began to engage in defensive state building to defend themselves against slavers. The most successful of these states was Moshoeshoe's Kingdom of Lesotho. Some merafe also began to acquire guns, which greatly increased their ability to defend themselves. Other communities fled north to escape the effects of the slavers. The Bakololo belong to this latter category.

Communities in Botswana were not directly affected by slavers from either the Cape Colony or Mozambique. Neither were

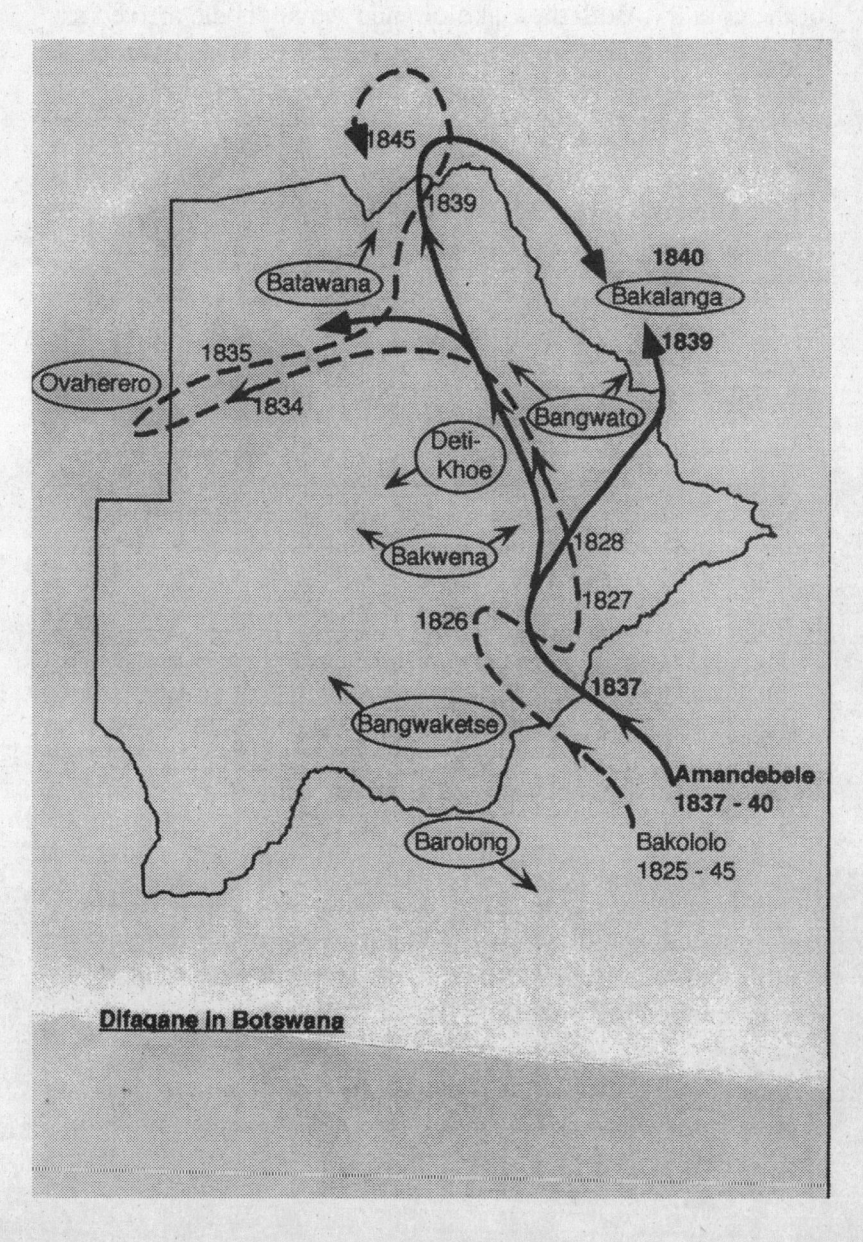

Difagane in Botswana

they involved in Natal's warfare. Yet the refugees from these conflicts to the south and east ultimately affected every corner of the country. Both the Bakololo and Amandebele arrived as powerful, semi nomadic military groups. Each was led by a talented warrior, who built up his following through the assimilation of defeated peoples.

The Bakololo of Sebetwane

During the Difaqane the Bakololo emerged as fierce raiders under the leadership of Sebetwane. Between 1823 and 1840 they attacked merafe throughout eastern and northern Botswana. Sebetwane began his career as the kgosi of a small southern Botswana morafe, the Bafokeng-ba-ga-Patsa. Later he called his followers the Bakololo, in honour of his senior wife whose extended family was called Kolo. In 1822 the Ba-ga-Patsa lost their cattle. Sebetwane is said to have then told his people:

> My masters, you see that the world is collapsing. We shall be eaten up one by one. Our fathers taught us peace means prosperity, but today there is no peace, no prosperity! Let us march!

Sebetwane then joined up with another southern Botswana group, the Bataung, in 1823. Together the two merafe raided the Bahurutshe, Barolong, Batlokwa and Bangwaketse. The Bahurutshe were defeated in a battle near Zeerust, while the Barolong and Batlokwa fled for safety. The latter group moved north to join the Bangwato. Only the Bangwaketse, under the strong leadership of Makaba II, were able to repulse the attackers.
In 1824 the Bakololo raided merafe further to the east. Among their victims were the Bakgatla-ba-ga-Kgafela, then living in the Transvaal under the regent (*motshwarelela kgosi*) Motlotle.

Following his defeat he fled westwards, towards Botswana, where he was later killed.

Ratumagole, a Mokololo veteran posing in old war dress at Tsau in 1908. Except for the headress, his outfit is the same as those worn by Bakwena, Bangwato and Bangwaketse warriors during the Difaqane.

The Bakololo again invaded Botswana in 1825. Sebetwane left the Transvaal because the arrival there of the more powerful Amandebele. The Bakololo initially moved into Kweneng, where the Bakwena had been divided since Motswasele II's assassination. One of the kgosi's assassins, Moruakgomo, led one section of the morafe. Another faction, which included Motswasele's young heir, Sechele, had moved to Gammangwato. There the Bangwato Kgosi Kgari treated Sechele like a son. According to some accounts, Kgari encouraged Sebetwane to attack Moruakgomo on Sechele's behalf. At any rate Sebetwane drove Moruakgomo out of his stronghold at Dithubaruba.

Early in 1826 Moruakgomo's Bakwena joined forces with the Bangwaketse and their allies the Bahurutshe and Bakgatla-ba-ga Mmanaana. Makaba II led this combined force in a great battle against Sebetwane at Losabanyana. According to some accounts Makaba's son, Sebego, betrayed Makaba by staying out of the battle. Makaba was slain. For the Bakololo it was a costly victory. Sebetwane was seriously wounded in the chest. He recovered but a quarter century later the same wound reopened causing his death.

After Makaba's death the Bangwaketse, like the Bakwena, were divided. In August 1826 the largest faction, led by Sebego, launched a surprise dawn attack on the Bakololo at Dithubaruba. It was completely successful and the Bakololo were forced to flee eastward. During the attack Batswana observed the importance of firearms in battle. Two white traders assisted Sebego with their muskets. This incident encouraged others to trade for guns.

The Bakololo move north

The Bakololo recuperated at Mochudi during the 1826-27 planting season. Sebetwane then decided to advance into the Central District. There he took cattle and captives from nearly every community living south of the Motloutse river. After suffering a Bakololo raid the Bangwato tried to rebuild their herds by invading the Bakalanga Banyayi (Rozwi) Kingdom north of the Motloutse. They reached as far as the Matopos, where they were ambushed by the Banyayi. Kgari and about half of his men were killed. During this battle Batswana once more witnessed the power of guns: the Banyayi had acquired muskets from the Portuguese.

In 1829 the surviving Bangwato were once more attacked. The Bakololo took more captives, including the exiled Sechele and Kgari's son Sekgoma. Both were eventually released. During their captivity the two princes learned to appreciate Sebetwane's leadership qualities.

Sechele in 1865.

Faced with continued local resistance, in 1830 Sebetwane decided to move further north into the Boteti region. There, after losing many cattle in the arid central Kgalagadi, he was able to replenish his herds by stealing from Deti Khoe (Bateti), who were then known for their long horned cattle. In 1834 Sebetwane moved his forces into Ngamiland. The Batawana fled into the Okavango and Chobe swamps, where they joined the Bayei and Bekuhane, commonly known as the Basubiya, in holding out against the invaders. Sebetwane then pushed westwards towards the Atlantic, hoping to find white men who could sell him guns. But, in Namibia, he was turned back by Ovaherero and Naro-Khoe archers who made effective use of poisoned arrows.

After this defeat Sebetwane returned to Ngamiland. This time he encountered and defeated the Batawana. Most of the Batawana were then temporarily reduced to the status of Bakololo servants. Moving up the river he also defeated the Bekuhane before crossing over the Zambezi, in 1840, to conquer western Zambia. In the aftermath of this conquest Sebetwane was finally able to settle down and build up his own kingdom. The Bakololo, who by then included many other

Batswana who had been captured during Sebetwane's long march, formed the ruling class of this new state. As a result the major language spoken in western Zambia today, Silozi, is similar to Setswana.

Except for the Bekuhane (Basubia) and Batawana, the peoples of Botswana were free of the Bakololo after 1840. The Bakololo invasion is important because of the tumult it caused. For two decades one community after another was attacked and robbed, weakening once strong merafe such as the Bangwaketse, Bangwato and Bakgatla. As a result the region was left more vulnerable to the second wave of Difaqane invaders, the Amandebele. Yet, during their migration the Bakololo had not always been victorious. Local resistance had been a factor that caused Sebetwane to keep moving northwards until he reached Zambia.

The Amandebele of Mzilikazi

Throughout the 1830s Botswana also suffered aggression by the Amandebele of Mzilikazi. The Amandebele originated in Natal. Mzilikazi began as the leader of a small Northern Nguni group known as the Khumalo. For a period he submitted himself to the authority of Shaka of the Amazulu. But Mzilikazi was too ambitious to accept this subordination. To build up his own power he captured cattle from the Basotho, which he then refused to surrender to his Amazulu overlord. In 1821 Shaka sent an army to punish Mzilikazi. Mzilikazi, along with most of his Khumalo followers, escaped across the Drakensburg mountains into the eastern Transvaal.

At the time Batswana living in the Transvaal referred to all Nguni as Matebele. This name is said to be derived from Motebele who was defeated by his younger brother Motebeyane in an ancient struggle over Bahurutshe chieftainship. Motebele had been supported by some Northern Nguni, who were therefore called Matebele. While staying in the Transvaal Mzilikazi's people adopted the name, modifying it to Amandebele.

Once in the Transvaal Mzilikazi began to build up his power by attacking local Basotho and Batswana. At first no merafe could withstand his age regiments (*amabutho*) which were well trained and disciplined. Like other Northern Nguni the Amandebele had adopted the long shield and short stabbing spear *(assegai)* as their principal weapons. They often attacked their enemies using the buffalo horns formation, which had been favoured by Shaka.

Usually the Amandebele fought to completely destroy their opponents. They then captured their women, children and cattle after battle. The women and girls became Amandebele wives and were charged with growing food. The boys herded Mzilikazi's cattle before being trained as members of the amabutho. As a result of this policy many Batswana became Amandebele. By 1835 over 80% of the Amandebele were said to have been of Batswana origin.

Among the groups that Mzilakazi's amabutho fought with were the Bakwena-ba-ga-Magopa. The Ba-ga-Mogopa were the mother morafe of Botswana's Bakwena, Bangwaketse and Bangwato. Although independent, during the early nineteenth century members of these merafe sometimes still identified themselves as Ba-ga-Magopa. The Ba-ga-Mogopa were renowned fighters, though their kgosi, More, had grown old and weak. After a series of fierce battles, the Ba-ga-Mogopa eventually surrendered to the Amandebele in 1827. More, along with his sons, was executed. His fate may have convinced his Botswana relatives never to surrender to Mzilikazi.

Some merafe did submit. Among these were the Bakgatla-ba-ga-Kgafela, who were forced to pay tribute to Mzilikazi and herd his cattle. In 1831 the Ba-ga-Kgafela ruler, Pilane, tried to break out of this subservience by joining the Griqua against the Amandebele. This alliance was defeated. In revenge about a thousand Ba-ga-Kgafela were killed and their cattle, along with many women and children captured. Pilane fled into the northern Transvaal, where he found refuge with the powerful Bapedi-Balaka ruler, Mapela.

In 1832 the Amandebele moved into the Lehurutshe region adjacent to south eastern Botswana. Having swallowed over two dozen merafe, Mzilikazi was being addressed by many Batswana as the *Tautona*. He now demanded tribute from all the merafe. Among those who refused were the Barolong-boo-Ratshidi. Led by their prince Montshiwa, they executed the Tautona's tribute collectors.

In response Mzilikazi sent his regiments to crush the Boo-Ratshidi, who retreated southwards. Eventually they joined their cousins the Barolong-boo-Seleka, other Batswana and Griqua in an anti Amandebele coalition based at Thaba Nchu. The principal leader of this grouping was the Boo-Seleka kgosi, Moroka.

Sebego's Bangwaketse also killed the Tautona's tribute collectors and were attacked. The Bangwaketse were outnumbered and they retreated into the Kgalagadi, drawing the enemy after them. The Amandebele were not used to the arid environment and grew weak. Sebego sent spies to guide the invaders away from water sources. Finally, at Dutlwe, the Bangwaketse attacked and destroyed the Amandebele regiment.

The Batswana-Boer-Griqua Alliance

In 1836 the Batswana and Griqua at Thaba Nchu were joined in their struggle by a new group, the Boers. Small groups of Boers had begun to pass by Thaba Nchu on their way to hunt for ivory in the Transvaal. At the time the Batswana did not know that these newcomers were the beginning of a major migration, known as the "Great" Trek (see Chapter 6). Initially the Boers ignored Batswana warnings about the danger of trespassing into Mzilikazi's territory.

Two parties of Boers were nearly wiped out by the Amandebele in September 1836. A month later a third party, under Hendrik Potgieter, was left stranded with little ammunition or food, after barely surviving an Amandebele attack. Hearing of their predicament Moroka decided to rescue the Boers, who were escorted back to Thaba Nchu.

A new Batswana-Boer-Griqua alliance was formed in December. Its leaders, Moroka, Potgieter and the others, decided to attack the Amandebele at Mosega, near modern Zeerust. The joint Batswana-Boer-Griqua force struck at dawn on 17 January 1837. The Amandebele assegais were no match for the attacker's guns. A resident American missionary, reported:

> Sometime before sunrise we were aroused by a startling cry, A commando! a commando! In half a minute after this alarming cry a brisk fire commenced on a kraal of people a few hundred yards from our house. The fire of one followed that of another in quick succession and at the thrilling report of every gun the thought would rush on our minds, there falls one and another and another of the poor heathen of whose salvation we had once had some hope. In a few minutes we were in the midst of the slaughter...The Boers attacked and destroyed thirteen, some say fifteen, kraals. Few of the men belonging to them escaped and many of the women were either shot down or killed with assegais.

Although Mzilikazi, along with most of his warriors, had been further north when the attack occurred, the Mosega massacre was a heavy blow. Some 1,000 Amandebele had fallen. The attackers suffered only two casualties, both Batswana.

In the aftermath of the massacre, Mzilikazi's position in the western Transvaal became increasingly desperate. On all sides groups joined the southern Batswana Boer Griqua alliance in challenging the Amandebele. To the north refugees like Pilane reinforced the position of Mapela's Bapedi. From the south east the Amazulu, now under Shaka's brother Dingane, defeated a large Amandebele force in August 1837. To the west Sechele's Bakwena, Sekgoma's Bangwato and Sebego's Bangwaketse engaged in hit and run attacks.

On 4 November 1837 a force of Barolong and Boers burned Mzilikazi's capital, e Gabeni and other Amandebele settlements along the Madikwe river. Once again Mzilikazi himself escaped the attackers. He had gone north to fight Mapela. Some other Amandebele had already been sent to scout out an alternative route through Botswana. In the face of the new Barolong Boer offensive, Mzilikazi decided to move the rest of his people. On 12 November 1837, the Batswana and Boers watched together as thousands of Amandebele crossed into Botswana at Sikwane.

The Amandebele in Botswana

For the Batswana of Botswana the struggle against the Amandebele now entered a new and more dangerous phase. Sechele and Sekgoma suddenly found themselves in the path of Mzilikazi's advance. With the entire Amandebele population pouring across Kweneng's eastern frontier, Sechele pulled back from Kopong to the relative safety of his Lephephe hideaway. Bakwena scouts kept a careful eye on the invaders' movements. They reported that the Amandebele had divided into two columns. Mzilikazi and most of his warriors were moving quickly to the northwest, while a second column under a general named Gundwane went north east. Sechele saw his opportunity and attacked the second column, capturing many cattle.

Further north Sekgoma was also bold. He raided the Bakaa cattleposts around Shoshong after hearing that they had been entrusted with Amandebele mafisa or loan cattle. Mzilikazi then sent a force against Sekgoma, which recaptured the cattle and took many Bangwato captives. According to some accounts, Sekgoma then surprised the enemy by launching a counter attack at Paje, where he recaptured most of his losses before retreating to the Makgadikgadi pans. It was there that Sekgoma's eventual heir, Khama III, was born. After the Amandebele had left the region Sekgoma returned to the Shoshong hills. There he began rebuilding Bangwato power by establishing his authority over the Baphaleng, Batalaote and Batswapong.

The fall of the Bakalanga Kingdom

While moving through Botswana, Mzilikazi's ultimate destination had been western Zimbabwe, the core area of the Bakalanga Banyayi (Rozwi) Kingdom. For decades the Kingdom had been weakened by internal tensions. Its King *(Mambo)*, other members of the royal Nichasike dynasty, the chief tribute collector *(Tumbale)* and the high priest of , the state god *(Mwali)* all quarelled. Local chiefs *(boshe)* used these arguments as an opportunity to take more power for themselves. Many of these boshe, including most of those in Botswana, belonged to the Balilima rather than Banyayi branch of the Bakalanga.

From 1832 the Bakalanga Kingdom was further disrupted by Ngoni (Northern Nguni) invaders who, like the Amandebele, had fled Shaka's wars. One of these groups, led by a woman named Nyamazuma killed the Mambo Chilisamhulu just before the arrival of the Amandebele in 1840. Mzilikazi subsequently married Nyamazuma, resulting in her soldiers joining his army. Thereafter surviving members of the Nichasike dynasty fled to the east, leaving most of their subjects to the Amandebele.

After 1840 Mzilikazi consolidated his authority over the Bakalanga of north eastern Botswana and western Zimbabwe by diplomacy as well as force. He respected the Mwali priests and distributed loan cattle to boshe who accepted his rule. In return, however, the boshe had to pay tribute and send young men to be brought up as Amandebele warriors. Amandebele society was now divided into three classes: the Northern Nguni upper class *(Khumalo)*; the middle class of predominately Batswana origin *(Zansi)*; and the lower class comprised of Bakalanga and their Vashona cousins *(Holi)*.

The fall of the Bakalanga kingdom marks the end of the Difaqane in Botswana. Some communities in northern Botswana, though, continued to live with the threat of Amandebele raids up until the 1880s.

Consequences of the Difaqane

The Difaqane had many adverse consequences for Botswana. Communities lost lives and property to the invaders. For example, it is estimated that between 1820 and 1840 the

Bakwena in Botswana were reduced to one quarter of their previous population. While many were killed, many others were taken as captives, often never to return. Thus a large proportion of the Sindebele speakers of Zimbabwe today are descended from Batswana.

Other people were simply scattered across the countryside. This fact partly explains why people of many backgrounds live side by side today. As we saw in previous chapters, it has long been common for people to break away from their own group to join another. The Difaqane simply increased this trend.

Not all of the adverse consequences of the era were a direct result of foreign aggression. As in the case of other parts of Africa affected by the Difaqane, many victimized communities in Botswana turned into victimizers themselves. Examples of this include the Bangwaketse attacking Bakgalagadi communities and the Bangwato attacking their Central District neighbours. While some merafe were able to recover from the effects of the Difaqane, others were less fortunate. The Bakalanga Banyayi Kingdom was gone forever.

Although the Difaqane reduced the size of many communities, it also provided a foundation for subsequent state building. During the period many merafe came together for their common defence. In some cases these alliances turned into long term relationships. Two examples are the Bakhurutshe and Bakalanga-ba-ka-Nswazwi, both of whom became allies of the Bangwato against the Amandebele.

Another important development of the Difaqane was a growing appreciation by Batswana of the power of guns. By the end of the period rulers like Sechele and Sekgoma were trying to trade for guns with Griqua and Europeans. This, in turn, had important consequences when the Batswana were forced to confront Motswasele's white ants, the Boers.

Summary

Between 1820 and 1840 communities in Botswana were destroyed by Bakololo and Amandebele invaders. Many merafe were reduced in size while the Bakalanga Kingdom was completely destroyed. The period, however, was also marked by the emergence of strong local leaders, such as Sebego, Sechele and Sekgoma, who began building up strong states of their own.

Questions

1 a. What does the term Difaqane mean?
  b. What other names have Batswana had for the Difaqane?

2 a. Name four possible reasons for the outbreak of the Difaqane in Natal.
  b. Which seem most plausible to you?
3   How might the trade in slaves and ivory to Mozambique and the Cape have contributed to the Difaqane?

4   What might have caused Sebetwane to choose to initially invade Kweneng rather than Gangwaketse in 1825?

5 a. Name six merafe who fought the Bakololo?
  b. How might the history of the Bakololo invasions been different if these merafe had been united in 1823?

6   What were the major results of the Bakololo invasion for

Botswana and Zambia?
8. Why might the execution of More and his sons have encouraged Sechele, Sebego and Sekgoma not to give in to the Amandebele?

Chapter 6
Trade and the 1852-53 Batswana Boer War

Chapter 5 focused on the impact of the Difaqane, when Botswana was invaded by the black ants of Motswasele II's prophecy, that is the Bakololo and the Amandebele. In this chapter we will learn about Motswasele's 'white ants', that is Europeans or white settlers, who he said would follow the earlier invaders.

Before the 1885 imposition of colonial rule three types of Europeans had a major impact on Botswana: Boers, traders and missionaries. This chapter will look at the first two categories, while the role of the missionaries is discussed later. Not all the Europeans who arrived, though, fell into just one of these three groupings. A lot of missionaries and Boers engaged in trade. There were also a few Boer missionaries.

In many ways the whites proved to be more troublesome to the Batswana than the earlier invaders. They brought new ideas and technologies, which made them both useful and dangerous. From the beginning the response of Batswana to the coming of the Europeans was shaped by their determination to remain free of foreign rule. In this respect it was the military power of the whites that was most impressive. Fascination with European consumer goods, knowledge and religious ideas were of secondary importance. This was because during the Difaqane, Batswana had already learned two important lessons: firstly that the Europeans posed a far greater threat to them than either the Bakololo or Amandebele; and secondly that to defend themselves against future invaders they needed to acquire guns.

The arrival of the white ants coincided with a boom in Botswana's external trade. Game products, mainly ivory, ostrich feathers and karosses or skins, were sold in return for guns and other goods imported from Asia, the Americas and Europe. By selling game products and acquiring guns, the Batswana were able to defend their independence in the Batswana Boer War of 1852-53.

External Trade

People in Botswana have had trade links with the outside world for a long time. By the eighteenth century trade existed with the Boers at the Cape and the Portuguese stations of coastal Angola and Mozambique. Until the nineteenth century Botswana products reached these European markets through African middlemen. Thus for many years trade with the Cape was conducted through Khoe and Batlhaping intermediaries. Trade with Mozambique was likewise dependent on Vashona middlemen, while much of the Angolan trade passed through the hands of the Ovimbundu.

This early, indirect trade with the Europeans was part of an extensive regional trading system in which African communities exchanged goods with one another. Through this system iron tools made by local Bakalanga, Bakgatla and Barolong craftsmen reached the shores of Namibia and the Cape. Copper, livestock and game products were also traded across long distances.

During the Difaqane much of Botswana's external trade passed into the hands of the Griqua, a Khoe group of mixed descent whose culture had been influenced by European ways. Like the European traders who followed them, the Griqua used ox wagons, horses and guns. These three things allowed them to defend themselves while carry goods across long distances. This gave the Griqua an advantage over other Africans in the region, who had no firearms and mostly transported goods by foot.

Missionaries and trade

During the Difaqane a few Europeans had also begun to appear in Botswana, often accompanied by Griqua. Thereafter their numbers grew. In 1838 David Hume established the first European trading company to operate in Botswana. Hume's base was at a mission station at Kudumane, but in 1847 he posted an agent named Evans to live among the Bakwena at Kolobeng. Evans thus followed Botswana's first resident missionary, David Livingstone, who had just established himself there.

The connection between Hume's stores and mission stations shows that early European traders often preferred to work in places where missionaries were present. Livingstone, himself, acknowledged that:

> Wherever a missionary lives, traders are sure to come; they are mutually dependent and each aids the other.

This mutual dependence of missionaries and traders is partially reflected in accounts of local changes in dress. A German who toured eastern Botswana in the 1860s, noted that in the larger villages "the blacks viewed dressing up (in European clothes) on Sunday as an essential part of their religion". Another early visitor observed that for prominent Molepolole women Sunday dress required imported hats like those worn by the missionaries' wives.

Missionaries encouraged Batswana to adopt European dress. The cloth to make the clothes was bought from traders. Missionary wives and female missionaries played an especially important role by teaching Batswana European methods of tailoring. But the adoption of European clothing was not entirely encouraged by religion. Many non Christians quickly came to prefer the new style of dress for comfort and as a mark of social status.

In addition to tailoring, the missionaries taught Batswana other skills and practices that encouraged them to buy imported goods. Livingstone, for example introduced the plough, which gradually replaced locally produced hoes.

Under missionary influence Kolobeng and later Molepolole and Shoshong, grew into important trading centres. When traders conducted business in other parts of the country, the mission stations often served as places where their goods could be stored safely. Some missionaries were also valued as mediators in commercial disputes between Batswana and traders. A few missionaries even became traders themselves.

For two groups to trade with one another they must each have something that the other wants. This is called supply and demand. In the mid nineteenth century the Batswana were able to supply ivory to the traders who sold it for high prices in South Africa. Batswana had little need for ivory but to the Europeans it was a valuable commodity. In return for ivory Batswana commonly demanded guns. By possessing guns Batswana could both defend themselves and hunt more efficiently. Thus, by the 1850s, a system of exchange had emerged throughout Botswana in which a small elephant tusk was valued at one new gun with ammunition. Although the same tusk could often be resold in the Cape Colony for three times the value of a gun, the Batswana were not cheated. The traders had high costs and were taking large risks by travelling long distances to buy ivory. It is clear then that the Batswana suppliers received a reasonable price for their ivory.

Batswana-Boer relations before 1852

The major motive behind the Batswana demand for guns during the nineteenth century was the fear of Boer aggression. Between 1835 and 1850 some 12,000 Boers left the coastal regions of the British ruled Cape Colony to settle inland. Eventually most settled in the Orange Free State and the Transvaal. Today, the descendants of these Boer settlers call this mass migration the Great Trek.

The Great Trek
This Great Trek was not great for the Africans of the Orange Free State and the Transvaal. For them the arrival of the Boers meant losing their land and independence. It also resulted in slavery. Many Africans were forced to work for the Boers without pay, while others were bought and sold as property. For these Africans the Great Trek was a time of subjugation.
Communities in Botswana also suffered because

A seven barrelled volley gun, Sechelle ordered such a gun through Livingstone and Moffat.

of the Great Trek, though they did not suffer the same fate as their relatives in South Africa. This is because they united successfully to defend their independence in the Batswana Boer War of 1852-53. At the time the Transvaal Boers hoped to make Botswana part of their newly proclaimed South African Republic (SAR). Although the Boers began the hostilities by invading south eastern Botswana, it was they who soon found themselves on the defensive.

Sechele arms his people

The Bakwena Kgosi Sechele I was the principal hero of the Batswana Boer War. In the aftermath of the Difaqane he had emerged as the most powerful Batswana kgosi by trading ivory and other game products for guns. As he obtained more guns he was able to arm ever larger hunting parties. These parties in turn killed even more animals allowing him to obtain still more guns. Because he learned arithmetic, as well as how to read and

Sechele's cannon, now at Mafikeng Museum.

write, Sechele became skillful in his negotiations with the European traders.

Sechele's activities, though, made the Boers nervous. The white settlers knew that their possession of guns gave them power over black people and so they were afraid of any armed Africans. In 1844 the Boers demanded that Sechele give up his guns and submit to their authority. Instead Sechele fortified his village. As a trader noted:

> A short time previous to my arrival, a rumour having reached Sichely that he was likely to be attacked by emigrant Boers, he suddenly resolved to secure his city with a wall of stones, which he at once commenced erecting. It was now completed, entirely surrounding the town, with loopholes at intervals all along through which to play upon the advancing enemy with the muskets which he had resolved to purchase from hunters and traders like myself.

Throughout the 1840s relations between Bakwena and Boers remained tense but peaceful. When in 1846 the Boers confiscated the wagons of one trader for carrying arms to Sechele, the missionary Livingstone calmed Boer fears about Bakwena military strength. Tensions thereafter increased as the Boers began to suspect that Livingstone, himself, was involved in the arms trade. The Boers were correct. Livingstone's own correspondence confirms that he, along with his father in law Robert Moffat, assisted Sechele's efforts in acquiring firearms and moulds for making bullets. In a letter to his parents Livingstone justified this assistance, noting:

> Resistance to such tyrants and murderers (ie. the Boers) is I think obedience to God...The only means which with divine blessing we have preserved our independence as a people are those very guns which you think the people would be better off without. The tribe would never have enjoyed the gospel but for firearms.

Boer concerns about Livingstone and Sechele were heightened

in 1849. The missionary, along with some of his trader friends, including a black American named George Fleming, were the first outsiders to be shown the route to the ivory wealth of Ngamiland. This discovery, which had been organized by Sechele and the Batawana Kgosi Letsholathebe I, increased the level of ivory and gun trading. More guns came quickly into Botswana from the Cape Colony.

The treaty of 'peace and friendship'

Initially the Boers tried to stop the trade by arresting a number of travellers going to Botswana. Other traders still came anyway. So, in December 1850, the Boers demanded that Sechele sign a treaty of 'peace and friendship'. Sechele refused as this treaty would have made the Bakwena and their allies liable to supply the Boers with unpaid labour. In April 1851 the Transvaal's President Andries Pretorius, concluded that Sechele's people would have to be forcibly disarmed. But, noting that it would no longer be an easy operation, he called for caution and consultations with the British.

During August and September 1851 Sechele and the other dikgosi living west of the Madikwe received new demands from the Boers. Again the white settlers demanded unpaid labour. The Bakwena and Bangwaketse continued to resist these demands. But many communities living to their immediate east, such as the Bahurutshe, Bakgatla-ba-ga-Mmanaana, Balete and Batlokwa, submitted in the face of a Boer commando or military expedition.

The war begins

Boer confidence increased after January 1852, when they and the British signed the Sand River Convention. Through this agreement the British accepted the independence of the SAR.

The British also agreed to join the Boers in suppressing the sale of arms and ammunition to all black Africans. Pretorius, in return, agreed to allow British traders free movement in the Transvaal. He also promised to stop his people from enslaving blacks, but this promise was not kept.

Mosielele in 1865.

Pretorius now felt strong enough to invade Botswana. He assembled an invading army made up of some 430 Boer horsemen and over 600 Africans. Because Pretorius was ill, Pieter Scholtz commanded the force. At the time the Transvaal's male Boer population numbered some 5,000. So Scholtz's commando was a big force, which showed that the Boers were determined to win.

Why were Africans in the Boer army? Most had been forced to join. Some rulers, like Kgosi Mangope of the Bakhurutshe boo-Manyana, had been captured as hostages to assure their people's cooperation. Others, like Dikgosi Mosielele and Montshiwa, escaped to join Sechele's resistance rather than submit. Only one kgosi, Moilwa of the Bahurutshe at Dinokana, volunteered to help the Boers. He was thereafter known to blacks and whites alike as 'the dog of the Boers.'

On 17 August 1852, Scholtz's force advanced on Mosielele who, seeing that he was outgunned, retreated with most of his people to Sechele's fortified settlement at Dimawe (near Kolobeng). In the days that followed the Boers destroyed the LMS mission station at Mosielele's abandoned settlement, victimizing those who had failed to escape. Up to 90 Batswana were killed, and many more women and children were captured and made slaves.

The Battle of Dimawe

The Boers arrived at Dimawe on Saturday, 28 August, 1852. In addition to the Bakwena, they found the Bangwaketse, Ba-ga-Mmanaana and Bakaa all ready to fight them under Sechele's leadership. Upon his arrival Scholtz demanded that Sechele surrender Mosielele and 'enter into an arrangement' with the SAR. Sechele replied:

> Wait till Monday. I shall not deliver up Mosielele: he is my child. If I am to deliver him up, I shall have to rip open my belly; but I challenge you on Monday to show which is the strongest man. I am, like yourself, provided with arms and ammunition and have more fighting people than you. I should not have allowed you thus to come in and would have assuredly fired on you; but I have looked into the book (the Bible), upon which I reserved my fire. I am myself provided with cannon. Keep yourself quiet tomorrow and do not quarrel for water till Monday; then we shall see who is the strongest man. You are already in my pot; I shall only have to put the lid on it on Monday.

The negotiations

A two day truce was thus arranged to allow time for negotiation. The Boers were given free passage to the waters of the Kolobeng river, during which time the Batswana made a show of displaying their guns. On the following day a number of Boers attended the Batswana Sunday prayer services led by a Motswana preacher named Mebalwe.

Meanwhile the two leaders exchanged messages. Perhaps hoping that bravado might deter the Boers, Sechele asked Scholtz for some tea and sugar. In return he offered the general gunpowder if he 'had not brought enough with him for a long fight.' Scholtz replied that since men of war did not need sugar he would 'give Sechele chillies instead'. The Bakwena messengers then volunteered to show the Boers where to avoid poisonous grass (*mogau*) for, after the fighting ended, their oxen would surely belong to Sechele. More seriously the two leaders agreed to face to face negotiations at dawn on Monday.

The Monday meeting failed to resolve anything. Sechele called upon Scholtz to justify his demand for Mosielele. Instead, the Scholtz underscored the real issues at stake by calling on the Bakwena and their allies to disarm, to supply the Boers with unpaid labour and to otherwise obey Pretorius. Sechele replied that he would remain a kgosi through the grace of God and his people, not the Boers.

The Boers advance
The battle commenced as soon as the meeting broke up in disagreement. The invaders stormed Dimawe's hillside entrenchments. In their initial advance the Boers marched behind their African troops, using them as human shields. This complicated the task of the defenders, who refrained from shooting their helpless brothers.

After over six hours of battle the Boers burned Dimawe village and overran the Bangwaketse and Ba-ga-Mmanaana positions. But by sunset the core of the Batswana defenders under Sechele's personal command still held their positions on the top of Boswelakgosi hill. Unable to move them and with night approaching, Scholtz called off the attack.

The Batswana regroup

Under the cover of darkness Sechele then retreated, regrouping his forces at Dithubaruba, a natural fortress. On the following morning the Boers are alleged to have massacred the Batswana wounded who had been left behind. For three days thereafter Scholtz divided his forces in pursuit of the now scattered enemy. It was during this period that his men broke into Livingstone's unoccupied Kolobeng mission where they reported:

> **We found several half finished guns and a gunmaker's shop with an abundance of tools. We here found more guns and tools than Bibles, so that the place had more the appearance of a gunmaker's shop than a mission station and more a smuggling shop than a school place.**

In another action Kgosi Senthufe, regrouped the Bangwaketse at Kanye's Kgwakgwe hill and successfully repulsed the pursuing enemy. After this defeat Scholtz's men refused to attack Sechele's Dithubaruba stronghold.

The Boers withdraw

On Friday, 3rd September, Scholtz decided to withdraw from Botswana, taking with him 143 captive women and children and a large number of cattle. Additional property, belonging to the Bakwena and English traders, was also seized and later auctioned. The Boers had failed, however, in their primary mission of subjugating the local population. As they withdrew the Batswana harassed them with hit and run attacks.

For the Boers the invasion had been a failure. According to most sources 36 Boers died as a result of the invasion. The Batswana losses were higher, at 89 dead, but they had succeeded in preserving their independence.

The Batswana strike back

Nine days after he began his withdrawal, Scholtz reported to Pretorius:

> I must regretfully inform you that I have been obliged to disband the commando, owing partly to the weakness of horse and oxen and partly to opposition among the men...moreover I greatly fear, since I cannot keep the commando intact to accomplish anything, that the Marico district will be unsafe...things have not worked out to my liking.

Scholtz's concern proved to be well founded for in the months following Dimawe, Batswana launched retaliatory raids into the Transvaal's Marico District. By November 1852 an English trader noted that:

Batswana raiding Boers farms.

All the Boers are still in laager, they have been in laager a long time. They dare not venture on their farms for fear of Sechilli. Their cattle are dying fast being too many together and disease is amongst them.

A newspaper, the *South African Commercial Advertiser*,

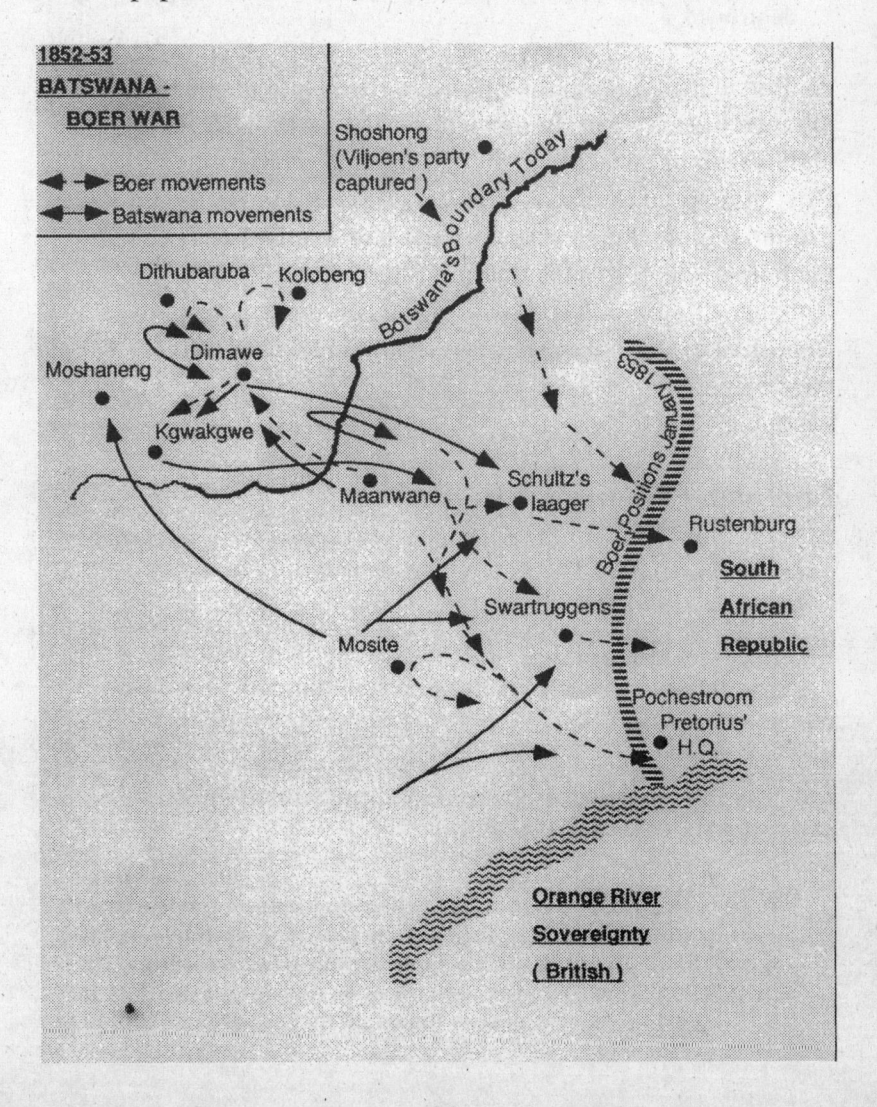

1852-53 BATSWANA - BOER WAR

- Boer movements
- Batswana movements

Shoshong (Viljoen's party captured)

Botswana's Boundary Today

Dithubaruba
Kolobeng
Dimawe
Moshaneng
Kgwakgwe
Maanwane
Schultz's laager
Mosite
Swartruggens
Rustenburg

Boer Positions January 1853

South African Republic

Pochestroom
Pretorius' H.Q.

Orange River Sovereignty (British)

reported that the Batswana natives had united in a strong body against the farmers in the Mariqua district:

> **Great destruction, of course, marked the progress of the conquering natives. Every homestead has been burned and standing corn, ripe for the sickle, together with vineyards and gardens, which then were in full bloom, have been entirely destroyed.**

As Batswana went on the offensive the original anti Boer alliance of Bakwena, Bangwaketse, Ba-ga-Mmanaana, Bakaa and Barolong, was broadened to include other groups. When a Boer attempted to rape one of the wives of the Batlokwa Kgosi Matlapeng, the kgosi shot the villain and led his people to Sechele's. Other groups that migrated into south eastern Botswana to join the resistance included the Balete, Bahurutshe, Batlhako, Barakgologadi and some Griqua. Today the descendants of the above groups can be found throughout south eastern Botswana.

Confusion among the Boers

In an attempt to regain the initiative Pretorius took personal command of the SAR's forces. He then set out to strike a blow against Sechele's ally Montshiwa, by attacking the Barolong at Mosite. According to the Barolong, as soon as the firing started, the already sick Pretorius was wounded. After he left the field the Boers became confused and they retreated without victory. The belief that Pretorius had been killed (he did die a few months later) is reflected in the praise poem of Mokoko Marumo, the man who shot him:

> **The hero of the white horse is nowhere to be seen, the leader of the white troops has bitten the dust, he has been snatched by the eagle of Marumo, he is initiated into colour blind mysteries. His lady is in tears, but her eyes look away, as she curses the tiger of the Makgetla breed, she curses the eagle that is born of Marumo,**

> says that monster has eaten up our husbands and thus condemned them to dismal widowhood.

After their Mosite setback, the Boer position in the western Transvaal became desperate. With their hit and run tactics the Batswana continued to weaken the Boers. Many Boers wished to take no further part in the fighting. Frustrated by increasing Boer disunity in December 1852 the wounded Pretorius warned his people that:

> If this segmentation persists we small number will be surrounded by dozens of enemies, be defeated and vanish. Even if we are united our task is difficult, but with this disunity it has become impossible.

By January 1853 the Boers had been forced to completely evacuate the Marico District. A new defensive line was established from Potchefstroom north to Rustenberg. At the same time the Batlhaping and Bangwato joined the Batswana alliance.

Viljoen makes peace

Also in January some peaceloving Boers succeeded in negotiating an end to the war. These Boers were led by Jan Viljoen. At the time of the Battle of Dimawe Viljoen, together with some other Boers, had been hunting and trading in Gammangwato. Messengers from Sechele arrived asking the Bangwato to intercept and kill any Boers who passed through their territory. But the Bangwato Kgosi Sekgoma I decided to let Viljoen's party leave in peace. He reportedly told Viljoen:

> Jannie, I love you and it is because of this that I let you go...I know you will come back to shoot me.

As it turned out Sekgoma was wrong. Upon his return to the Transvaal Viljoen spoke out in opposition to Scholtz's desire to launch a second attack on Sechele. He accused Scholtz of being 'the sole cause of the losses of the Boers and the enmity of all the tribes.' Viljoen then had the support of many others who, like himself, traded in Botswana's game products.

Viljoen met with Pretorius and obtained the President's blessing to take up Sechele's offer of peace talks. Sechele demanded the release of his son Kgari, who had been captured and enslaved. As a result Pretorius personally purchased Kgari and turned him over to Viljoen.

Viljoen then set out to meet with Sechele's representatives in order to deliver Kgari. Scholtz, who wished to sabotage the negotiations, detained Viljoen. In anger Viljoen told Scholtz that 'the thunder would fetch him'. That same afternoon as a large meeting gathered to listen to Schotlz call for continued war, lightening struck his laager's gunpowder, injuring a dozen people. Scholtz, himself, was afterwards found sitting on a large case of gunpowder. According to an eyewitness 'the lightning penetrated between the box and his body burning his legs and sides.' Happy to be alive, he exclaimed that the Lord in heaven had spoken in favour of Viljoen's peace initiative!

The Cape Town Mission

Kgari's release resulted in the January 1853 peace agreement between the Bakwena led Batswana alliance and the Boers. Only in May 1853, when three Bakwena were murdered in the Transvaal, did the ceasefire breakdown. When the Bakwena killed two Boers in retaliation, peace resumed.

However, relations between the Bakwena and Boers remained tense until 1857. During this time Sechele pressed for the return of the other captives, many of whom escaped or were released. Eventually a lasting peace emerged in which both sides recognized Botswana's current eastern boundary as their common border.

With the Boer threat diminished Sechele turned his attention to the British. Between December 1852 and June 1853 he travelled to Bloemfontein and Cape Town. He hoped to convince the British to set aside the Sand River Convention's ban on the sale of weapons to Africans. He was unable to end the ban. But he succeeded in making friends with whites, many of whom helped him in later years.

From the beginning Sechele had the backing of his traders and missionaries. Two traders, Frederick Green and Sam Edwards, accompanied him. At Bloemfontien Sechele enjoyed an advantage in that Frederick Green was the brother of Henry Green, the British Resident Commissioner. British military officers held a dinner for the kgosi, which raised 119 British Pounds, 'a handsome sum of money to enable him to pursue his journey to England'. After raising more money in Colesburg, Sechele proceeded to Port Elizabeth where he boarded a steamship for Cape Town.

At Cape Town Sechele was prevented from going to Britain by the British Governor General, Lord Cathcart. So Sechele sent a letter stating his views to the British Parliament and returned home. Although Sechele's letter had the support of many missionaries and human rights activists, it was ignored by the Government. Sechele was disappointed. He began denying traders access to the Kgalagadi unless they traded for guns with him. At the same time Sechele and his advisors became angry with the British, saying that the Boers were simply their "Bushmen":

> We have been told that the English are a wise nation. Ashu! What is wisdom? We have been told the English are a strong nation. They have driven their white Bushmen into our country to kill us. Is this strength? Have the English no cattle and slaves of their own that they send their white Bushmen to take our cattle and our children to sell? We are told that the English love all men. They give or sell ammunition, horses and guns to the Boers, who have red teeth, destroy us, and if we ask to buy powder, we get none. No, no, no! Black man must have no ammunition: they must serve the white man. Is this love? The English are not friends of the black man.

In the end the Sand River Convention's ban on the trade in guns was unenforceable. Traders ignored the law and sold guns to Africans.

Batswana-Boer relations improve

Sechele's success in resisting the Boers greatly increased his following. Whereas in 1849 he had 3,620 subjects, including 1,236 allied BaKaa, by 1857 the population in and around Dithubaruba was said to be about 20,000. Other estimates confirm an enormous growth in the mid nineteenth century population of Gammangwato and Gangwaketse, as well as Kweneng. Many blacks had left the Transvaal to live under independent Batswana rule.

In 1857 Batswana Boer relations improved. The SAR took up Sechele's request for new missionaries by arranging for the Hermansburg Mission (German Evangelical Lutheran) to work in Botswana. With the new missionaries came a flowering of economic and social ties.

By 1860 the postal routes to Botswana, as well as most wagon commerce, passed through the SAR. During the same year Sechele travelled to the SAR as a guest of Marthinus Pretorius, the son of Andries, who by then was the Republic's President.

Following this visit some Bakwena began to work for pay in the Transvaal. At the same time small numbers of Boer artisans began to migrate and settle in Botswana. By 1880 some Boer children were even attending Molepolole's Setswana medium school. While a few Boers became part of Setswana society, Batswana adopted aspects of Boer culture. Many, including Sechele's heir, Sebele, spoke Afrikaans, at a time when English was almost unknown.

Summary

In the aftermath of the Difaqane local dikgosi, most especially Sechele, took advantage of the growth in the ivory trade with the Cape Colony to provide their merafe with guns. This allowed them to preserve their independence in the 1852-53 Batswana Boer War. If the Boers had not been defeated then Botswana would have become part of the Transvaal. It is unlikely that Batswana today would enjoy the freedom of living in their own country if Sechele had not been victorious.

Questions

1. Give three examples of how missionaries assisted the activities of early European traders in Botswana.

2. a. What was the Great Trek?
   b. How did it affect the lives of black Africans living in South Africa?

3. a. How did Sechele acquire his guns?
   b. What role did Livingstone play in the arming of Batswana?

4. a. Name four provisions of the 1852 Sand River Convention.
   b. How did it encourage the Transvaal Boers to attack Sechele?

5. a. Which Batswana groups fought in the Battle of Dimawe?
   b. Who won the battle?
   c. Why?

6. a. Where was the Batswana Boer War mostly fought between September 1852 and January 1853?
   b. How did the Batswana gain the advantage?

7. a. What role did Jan Viljoen play in the Batswana Boer War.
   b. Why do you think Pretorius wanted peace?

8. a. Why did some Bakwena blame the British for Boers attacks?
   b. How did Batswana Boer relations change after 1857?

Chapter 7
State building in the South East

The decades that followed the Difaqane saw the emergence of two strong states in south eastern Botswana; Kweneng and Gangwaketse. Between 1840 and 1875 the Bakwena and Bangwaketse rulers expanded their domains in two ways. Firstly they controlled the trade in local game products. Secondly they provided refuge to Transvaal Batswana seeking to escape Boer rule. As we saw in chapter 6 both merafe used guns they bought from traders to defend their independence in the 1852-53 Batswana Boer War. Following this conflict the Bakwena and Bangwaketse prospered as powerful regional partners.

Later, in the 1870s, the regional balance of power was altered when three groups who had come from the Transvaal revolted against the Bakwena and Bangwaketse. These were the Bakgatla-ba-ga-Kgafela, Batlokwa and Balete. Together they began fighting to assert their independence on the eastern borders of Kweneng and Gangwaketse. A costly series of wars between the merafe began. These wars came to a sudden halt in 1881 because whites were threatening to take over the region. So the Batswana stopped fighting and began to once more cooperate in the face of this new threat.

Gaseitsiwe's state

After the death of Makaba II in 1825 the Bangwaketse were divided for thirty years. Sebego ruled from 1825 to 1844 as his nephew Gaseitsiwe's regent. Earlier Gaseitsiwe's father (Sebego's brother) Tshosa had been killed after he tried to overthrow his father Makaba. Sebego's brilliant military leadership during the Difaqane had assured the survival of his morafe, but his ambition to have bogosi for himself caused division. In order to protect Gaseitsiwe's claim a number of Bangwaketse broke away under Segotshane. Sebego's death led to a deeper division when his son Senthufe made himself kgosi over his father's faction.

Gaseitsiwe in 1865.

The Bangwaketse under both Senthufe and Segotshane fought together in the 1852-53 Batswana Boer War. When peace was restored both factions settled side by side in Kanye. In the same year Gaseitsiwe succeeded Segotshane as leader of one faction, but Senthufe still refused to recognize him as kgosi. Despite attempts at mediation by Montshiwa and Sechele, open fighting broke out in 1857. Senthufe was defeated and fled to Sechele. In 1859 he was allowed to return to Kanye after formally submitting to Gaseitsiwe. Thereafter, until his death in 1889, Gaseitsiwe was able to rule in peace.

Under Gaseitsiwe, Gangwaketse prospered and Kanye's population grew from about 6,000 to 20,000. Unlike the

Bangwato and Bakwena, the Bangwaketse had not become heavily involved in the 1840-50s boom in ivory trading. During the 1860s, however, they took advantage of a new growth in demand for ostrich feathers. (Europeans then valued ostrich feathers as fashionable decorations for ladies' hats.)

Most Bangwaketse's ostrich feathers were, in fact, acquired as tribute from their Bakgalagadi subjects. The feathers came from Khakea, Kokong and the Matsheng region (which includes such villages as Lehututu.) During the 1860s the Bangwaketse and Bakwena dominated Matsheng's trade. The Bangwaketse made big profits selling the feathers to white traders in Kanye. But, in the 1880s, the trade collapsed when Batlharo and Barolong refugees fled from the British in the northern Cape and settled in Matsheng. By then overhunting and large scale ostrich farming in the Cape had greatly reduced feather sales.

Under Gaseitsiwe the population of Gangwaketse was

expanded by the arrival of refugees from the Transvaal. Most refugees came in small groups who were placed into Bangwaketse wards, but a number of larger groups also arrived. During the 1860s and 1870s the Bangwaketse shared their territory with the powerful Barolong boo Ratshidi. Between 1853 and 1877 Montshiwa ruled from Moshaneng. Although Montshiwa cooperated with Gaseitsiwe, many Bangwaketse were relieved when he left. They were afraid of having two bulls in one kraal.

Another large immigrant group was the Bakgatla-ba-ga-Mmanaana. These Bakgatla moved to Moshupa in 1863. At the time the area was claimed by both the Bangwaketse and Bakwena. When the Bakwena gave up their claim to the area, in 1880, the Ba-ga-Mmanaana kgosi Pilane accepted Gaseitsiwe as paramount. He wanted to remain independent though and maintained his own authority as an allied ruler. In practice this meant that the Ba-ga-Mmanaana continued to enjoy virtual independence. For this reason Pilane and Gaseitsiwe's successors would quarrel in later years.

Kweneng after the Batswana-Boer war

The two decades that followed the 1853 truce with the Boers was also a time of relative peace and prosperity for Kweneng. By 1874 its population had risen to some 65,000, many of whom were recent refugees from the Transvaal.

During the decade that followed the war most of Kweneng's population lived closely together in the Dithejwane hills surrounding Sechele's fortress at Dithubaruba. In 1864 Sechele moved his capital to Molepolole hill. At the same time a number of the merafe who had joined the Bakwena during the war founded new settlements in south eastern Botswana.

The Ba-ga-Mmanaana moved to Moshupa and the Balete and Bahurutshe boo Mokhibidu went to Mmankgodi. Later, in 1875, the Balete relocated at Ramotswa. The Bahurutshe boo Manyana founded Manyana, next to the old battlesite at Dimawe and the Batlokwa eventually settled at Moshaweng (now called Tlokweng). Smaller settlements were also founded by combinations of Bakwena and other groups in such places as Kopong, Kumakwane, Lentswe-le-Tau and Lephephe.

Before the British occupation of Botswana in 1885, Molepolole rivalled the Bangwato capital Shoshong as the region's leading commercial centre. Although there were virtually no elephants in Kweneng, ivory remained a major trade commodity. Every year Sechele organized hunting parties to shoot elephants in the Chobe region. Outsiders also sold their ivory in Molepolole which, by the 1870s, was a base for six trading companies.

Like the Bangwaketse, leading Bakwena also profited by selling ostrich feathers. Most of these feathers were brought to Molepolole as tribute from subjugated Bakgalagadi and Khoe malata in the central and western Kgalagadi. Many karosses or wild animals skins were also acquired and traded in this way. Some Bakwena became skilled kaross sewers and their products were exported as far away as Europe and North America.

Sechele's diplomacy

Between 1853 and 1875 Sechele remained the most important political leader in Botswana. By using diplomacy as well as the power of his guns, he was able to manipulate the affairs of neighbouring merafe. Between 1857 and 1859 he cooperated with the Barolong Kgosi Montshiwa in supporting the consolidation of Gaseitsiwe's rule over the Bangwaketse. Subsequently he and Gaseitsiwe assured the peaceful succession of his son in law, Pilane, to the Bakgatla-ba-ga-Mmanaana throne. Sechele, Gaseitsiwe and Montshiwa again worked together to secure their eastern borders from the potential of renewed Transvaal Boer aggression. In the west they divided control over the Kgalagadi ostrich feather and skins trade.

Sechele's diplomatic skills were also applied within the Kweneng. He interfered little in the affairs of the refugee groups who migrated into his country. Among the Bakwena, Sechele strengthened the political and economic influence of commoners in order to prevent his royal relatives from having too much power.

Even the status of the Bakgalagadi improved. When his own daughter Gagoangwe blinded a Mokgalagadi servant girl in one eye, Sechele had her brought before his kgotla. There he quoted the biblical passage, "an eye for an eye, a tooth for a tooth". Then he shocked his people by having Gagoangwe also blinded in one eye. On another occasion when he, himself, accidentally killed a servant, Sechele insisted on being tried for murder. In these ways the life and limb of all people in Kweneng came to be respected.

Sechele and the Bangwato

Sechele wanted very much to have a cooperative person ruling over the Bangwato. As one missionary noted at the time:

> It is the life long endeavour of Sechele to obtain such influence in the town of the Bamangwato as would enable him to secure some

of its treasures of ivory and ostrich feathers and furs which are brought from its extensive hunting grounds, extending northward to the Zambese.

Unfortunately for Sechele, the Bangwato rulers proved to be independent minded. Between 1857 and 1872 Sechele intervened four times to overthrow the rulers of Gammangwato. In the process he established peaceful relations with the Amandebele. Sechele's efforts began in 1857. With the aid of the missionary, Robert Moffat, Sechele secured the release of his brother in law, Matsheng, who had been captured by Mzilikazi in 1842. As the senior ranking son of Kgari, Matsheng was the heir to the Bangwato throne. Sechele and senior Bangwato installed Matsheng in place of his half brother Sekgoma as the rightful kgosi at Shoshong. Sekgoma then came to live under Sechele, which resulted in the conversion of his eldest son, Khama to Christianity. Sechele also travelled to Bulawayo, where he convinced Mzilikazi to allow missionaries to work in his country.

Matsheng quickly became unpopular in Shoshong by behaving like an Amandebele, rather than a Motswana, ruler. As a result in 1859 Sechele restored Sekgoma to the throne, while exiling

Elderly Sechele with Matsheng's widow Mmakgari.

Matsheng to Kweneng. Sechele once more intervened to reinstall Matsheng in 1866, taking back Sekgoma. Matsheng's second reign was more popular with the Bangwato, but he foolishly interfered with trade going to the Amandebele. To keep the trade route to the north open Sechele decided to depose Matsheng once more, this time installing Khama as kgosi in 1872. Matsheng died shortly thereafter.

After further conflict with Sekgoma, Khama consolidated his rule over Gammangwato in 1875. But, for some time Khama remained in Sechele's shadow. Besides playing host to the exiled Sekgoma, Sechele married Matsheng's widow in 1883. He thus become the guardian of the late Matsheng's son Kgari.

The coming of the Bakgatla-ba-ga-Kgafela

In 1870 several thousand Bakgatla-ba-ga-Kgafela refugees migrated into eastern Kweneng under their kgosi, Kgamanyane. Like earlier migrants, the Ba-ga-Kgafela had found Boer rule in the Transvaal intolerable. They had lived in the Pilanesburg region of the Transvaal for generations before they fell under Boer rule in the 1840s. Thereafter the Ba-ga-Kgafela Kgosi Kgamanyane was forced to send men to work without pay on Boer farms. He also had to send men to fight in Boer wars against other, still independent, Africans.

Over time these Boer demands on the Ba-ga-Kgafela became too much. In April 1870 Kgamanyane refused to provide the major Boer landowner in the Pilanesburg, Paul Kruger, with additional labourers. In response, Kruger had Kgamanyane tied to a wagon wheel and sjamboked in front of his people. So in November 1870 many Ba-ga-Kgafela left the Pilanesburg when

Sechele agreed that Kgamanyane could settle at Mochudi, which was then part of eastern Kweneng.
Until Kgamanyane's death in 1875 the Ba-ga-Kgafela and Bakwena lived in peace at Mochudi. But Kgamanyane's successor, Linchwe I, was willing to fight to restore his morafe's independence and prosperity. Linchwe made alliances with two other local groups, the Batlokwa and Balete. He then allowed his men to start stealing Bakwena cattle in order to provoke a fight. He succeeded. After Ba-ga-Kgafela were caught with cattle stolen from Sechele's cattlepost on the Ngotwane, the Bakwena demanded war. Sechele tried to have the matter settled peacefully, calling on the Ba-ga-Kgafela to send him a token tribute of a wagon load of sorghum. Linchwe refused.

Inter merafe wars

In August 1875 the Bakwena, accompanied by their Bakaa and Ba-ga-Mmanaana allies, attacked Mochudi under the command of Sechele's son Sebele. The resulting battle was a great victory for the Ba-ga-Kgafela, who had established a strong defensive position in the centre of Mochudi on Phutadikobo Hill. Like the Bakwena, the Ba-ga-Kgafela were well armed. Many of them had worked at the Kimberley diamond fields and bought guns there. Ba-ga-Kgafela spies had also robbed the Bakwena of what they had planned as a surprise attack. Sebele is said to have acted in a cowardly manner during the battle, while the Ba-ga-Mmanaana may not have been eager to fight with fellow Bakgatla. In the end the Bakwena retreated after losing up to 120 men, while the Ba-ga-Kgafela lost about a dozen defenders.

The Ba-ga-Kgafela victory was the beginning of a long struggle that brought much misery to southern Botswana. In November 1875 a second major battle was fought at Thamaga between the Ba-ga-Mmanaana on one side and the Ba-ga-Kgafela and Balete on the other. The Ba-ga-Mmanaana were victorious. Among the Ba-ga-Kgafela who were killed was Maganelo, another son of Kgamanyane's who had been challenging Linchwe's right to become kgosi.

A third major battle was fought in the outskirts of Molepolole in July 1876. The Ba-ga-Kgafela, Batlokwa and Balete had launched a massive raid on Bakwena cattle posts west of Molepolole. While trying to return home with the cattle they were ambushed by Sechele's men, who were armed with a new shipment of rifles. These new guns were breechloaders which fired much more rapidly than the old style muskets. The raiders were defeated. Sechele ordered a ceasefire after about a hundred of his enemy were killed. Linchwe was personally rescued by the Batlokwa prince Gaborone after being wounded.

Following the battle of Molepolole the war turned into a stalemate with the Bakwena and Bangwaketse on one side, the Ba-ga-Kgafela, Batlokwa and Balete on the other, and groups like the Ba-ga-Mmanaana and Bahurutshe sometimes in the middle. Periods of truce were broken by cattle raids and small skirmishes. Only one other major battle took place. This was in 1881, when the Bangwaketse and the Ba-ga-Mmanaana launched a disastrous attack on the Balete at Ramotswa. Although the level of fighting remained modest it was accompanied by enormous suffering. Hunger increased as people feared to watch over their fields. Raiding parties killed and mutilated women and children as well as men. Bakgalagadi herders were especially at risk on isolated cattleposts. In September 1876 a Molepolole missionary wrote that Sechele

> has suffered very heavy losses of cattle, the people are unable to go hunting, the harvest was a failure and worse of all, many lives have been sacrificed and the most revolting murders have been practised.

During the war the Ba-ga-Kgafela, Balete and Batlokwa, had the advantage that they could send their cattle to their relatives living in the Transvaal. Meanwhile the Bakwena cattle remained vulnerable. In 1876 the Transvaal Boer state was on the brink of collapse and no longer able to control its borders. After 1877, when the Transvaal was occupied by the British, the border was closed.

The British withdrawal from the Transvaal in 1881 led to a brief upsurge in fighting, which failed to give any of the merafe a decisive advantage. The following year peace was finally and permanently restored in the region. Some Bakwena say peace between the Bakwena and Ba-ga-Kgafela began when one of

Sechele's junior sons, Sebogiso, decided on his own to return to Molepolole from the Transvaal via Mochudi. Once in the village he went direct to Linchwe's kgotla. After questioning Sebogiso, Linchwe decided to send him back to Sechele with a message that a Ba-ga-Kgafela delegation would follow him to pray for the Bakwena dead. Sechele welcomed and reciprocated the gesture. Thereafter, the Bangwaketse agreed to a truce with the Balete. Soon the Bakwena, as a token of goodwill, allowed the Balete and Batlokwa to graze their cattle in Kweneng.

Another factor that brought the combatants together was renewed fears of white domination. Between 1878 and 1881 the Batlhaping and Barolong had suffered under British occupation. The temporary withdrawal of the British in 1881 was accompanied by new aggression by white mercenary groups which had the backing of the Transvaal Boers. In the face of these threats Linchwe, Gaseitsiwe and Sechele each welcomed Montshiwa's call for a new Batswana alliance.

Consequences of the wars

The restoration of peace left the Balete and Ba-ga-Kgafela practically independent, though Gaseitsiwe and Sechele continued to claim their territories. The Batlokwa once more fell under Bakwena rule.

In addition to the loss of life there was much loss of wealth. The inter merafe wars resulted in a large decline in southern Botswana's cattle herds. Because they had lost much of their best grazing areas to the Ba-ga-Kgafela and Balete, the Bakwena and Bangwaketse had to move many of their cattle into the Kgalagadi. These places were drier and supported smaller herds. As a result of increased herding the Kgalagadi's

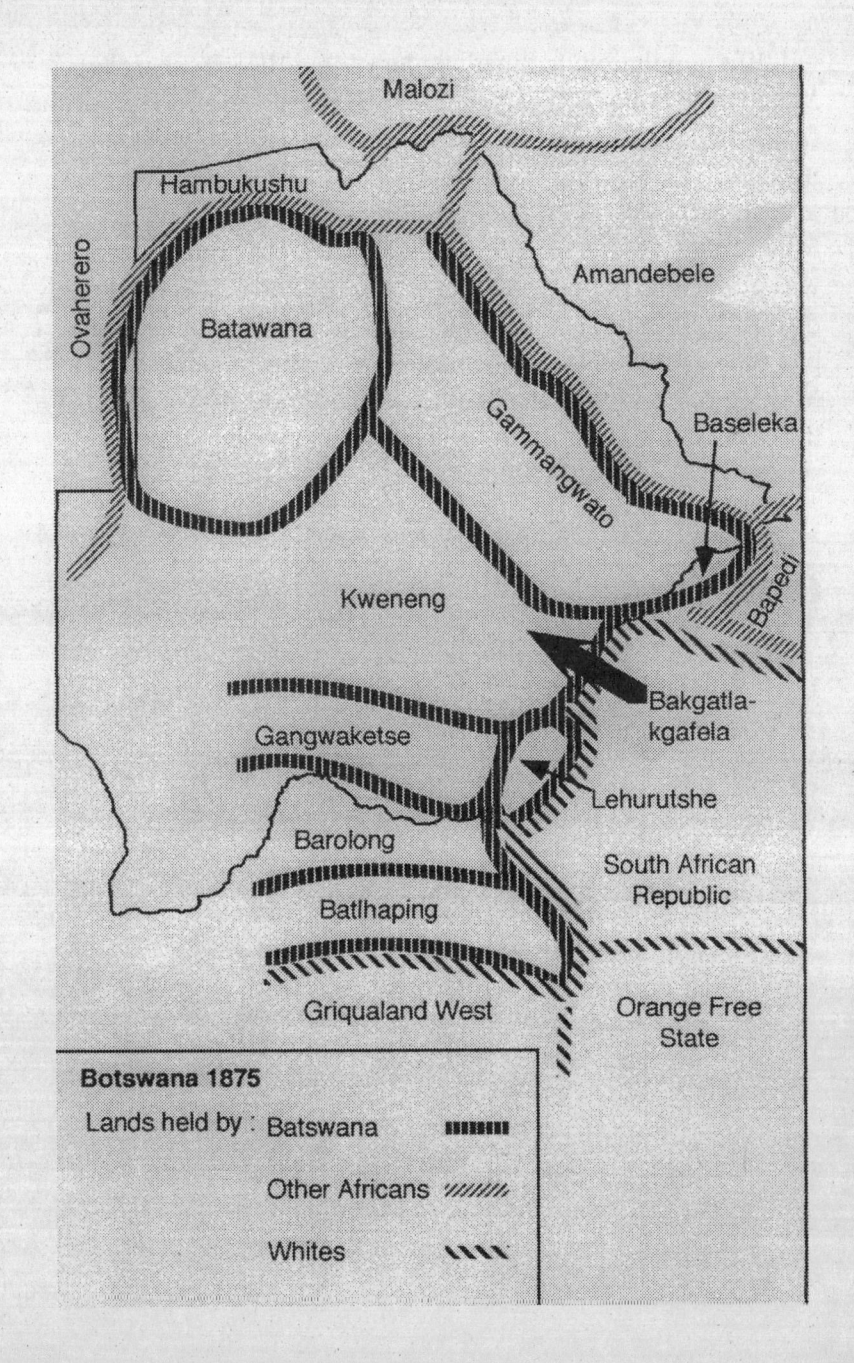

Malozi
Hambukushu
Ovaherero
Batawana
Amandebele
Gammangwato
Baseleka
Bapedi
Kweneng
Bakgatla-kgafela
Gangwaketse
Lehurutshe
Barolong
South African Republic
Batlhaping
Griqualand West
Orange Free State

Botswana 1875

Lands held by: Batswana
Other Africans
Whites

wildlife population declined, undermining the kaross trade. Meanwhile many Bakgalagadi in the region were forced for the first time to herd cattle for their Bakwena and Bangwaketse masters.

Much of the Bakwena and Bangwaketse's previous prosperity was gone. Making matters worse was the end of the ivory and ostrich feather booms due to the decline in wildlife. The war had also disrupted the wagon trade through Kanye and Molepolole. Much of the central African trade now passed through Gammangwato to the Transvaal, thus avoiding southern Botswana altogether.

Questions

1   What difficulty did Gaseitsiwe face in becoming the kgosi of the Bangwaketse?

2   What factors contributed to the growth of the Bangwaketse state under Gaseitsiwe?

3 a. What do you believe was Sechele's motive in intervening in Bangwato politics between 1857 and 1872.
  b. What was Sechele's role in Khama's rise to power?

4   Why did most of the Bakgatla Ba-ga-Kgafela leave the Transvaal in 1870?

5 a. Why did the Bakwena attack Mochudi in August 1875?
  b. What factors might have contributed to the failure of the attack?

6 a. Which groups fought at Molepolole in July 1876?
  b. Why might Sechele have wished to end the war despite his victory in the battle?

7. Why were the Bakgatla better able to protect their cattle than the Bakwena during their war?

8. What effect did the inter merafe wars have on people in the Kgalagadi?

Chapter 8
The Batawana conquer Ngamiland

Following the period of the Difaqane in Ngamiland, there were no strong merafe in the area. The various peoples of the area were scattered around in small groups, each under its own leader. During the fifty years between 1840 and 1890, it was the Batawana who emerged as the rulers of the region. Under the leadership of Mogalakwe, Letsholathebe and Moremi II, they expanded their territory by conquering all the peoples of the area.

It was because of their control of the ivory trade that the Batawana became the strongest power in their region. Batawana leaders encouraged trade with outsiders, just as Sechele had done in the South. Then they obtained weapons with their ivory, which enabled them to become a strong military force.

Bekuhane Kishi-dancers.

Ngamiland's environment and peoples

Ngamiland is a part of Botswana that appears to be very different from the rest of the country. Its environment is distinct in that the Okavango river flows into the region and forms a large delta. It is the only part of Botswana that is not dry. Moreover, the population of Ngamiland has large numbers of people who are not Tswana in origin.

Despite these apparent differences, Ngamiland's circumstances are not very different from the rest of the country's. The abundance of water in the area has not made living there easy. Ngamiland is really a desert of water. Mosquitoes and tsetse fly both live there in great numbers and they spread deadly diseases to humans and their livestock. The soils of the area are not very fertile and producing large amounts of food is impossible. Overall, Ngamiland has a low population density that has supported itself over the centuries largely through hunting and fishing.

Ngamiland's population is diverse and includes such peoples as the Bayei, Hambukushu, various Khoe groups, Bakgalagadi, Ovaherero and Basubia or Bekuhane. During the nineteenth century only about fifteen percent of the Batawana morafe was of Tswana ethnic origin.

These various ethnic groups in Ngamiland were all small societies, scattered over a wide area. There where various local rulers, none of whom had much power. For instance, Sankotse was the paramount kgosi over the majority of the Bayei. Likewise, Kgaraxumae was a well known Khoe leader in eastern Ngamiland, and Lefatshe ruled the Bakgalagadi who lived near Lake Ngami. Meanwhile, the Hambukushu who were in Ngamiland paid tribute to chiefs living in modern day Namibia. None of these peoples or leaders ever attempted to expand their power in the manner that the Batawana did after 1840. Ultimately, this was what led them to lose their independence.

The Batawana during the Difaqane

Like the rest of the country, Ngamiland was disrupted by the Bakololo and Amandebele during the Difaqane. It was the Bakololo who did the most damage. After living on the Makgadikgadi pans for several years, they moved west to Ngamiland sometime around 1834. At first they defeated the Batawana (at the time known as the Bampuru), who had controlled the southern Okavango and Ghanzi. Sebetwane's Bakololo destroyed the Batawana, taking their cattle, killing the regent and making most of them prisoners. Meanwhile, a significant portion of the morafe, who had lived under the kgosi's brother at Ghanzi, fled to Angola, where their descendants live to this day. Most of the members of the Batawana royal family were taken prisoner but Letsholathebe, the infant heir to bogosi, was taken away to the swamps by a group of women. They went to live with Basubia or Bekuhane near the Mababe Flats.

The Bakololo did not stay in Ngamiland long. After defeating the Batawana they marched west of Ghanzi to fight the cattle rich Ovaherero. At this point Sebetwane suffered a major defeat. A Herero Khoe army ambushed him and took all his cattle. Sebetwane then retreated and moved to modern day Zambia, just north of the Chobe river. He soon conquered southern Zambia. With him were the Batawana and many others taken from Botswana, some of whom he even sold to Angolan slave dealers. From Zambia Sebetwane continued to extract tribute from Chobe and the northern Okavango Delta.

A little before 1840 various Batawana began to escape from Bakololo custody. Then a large group escaped and went to the Chobe. The runaways found the young Letsholathebe alive

among the Basubia. Led by a senior kgosana, Mogalakwe, the Batawana then returned to the Toteng area where they grouped themselves with Bakgalagadi and other Difaqane refugees..
At this point the Batawana were scarcely a big force. But during the next fifty years they would defeat the Bakololo and end up controlling all of Ngamiland.

Batawana conquer the region

Around 1840 Mogalakwe, the regent, introduced three practices that would be vital to the spread of Batawana power; kgamelo, ivory trading and bolata. Kgamelo was a system of political control devised by Kgosi Kgari of the Bangwato before the Difaqane. According to this system the kgosi would loan large numbers of cattle out to headmen. In return, the headmen became the servants of the kgosi. If they failed to follow orders, the kgosi could exile the headmen and take their property. Headmen were also allowed to lend out cattle given to them by the kgosi and so a system of political control emerged that was based on cattle. Kgamelo gave the kgosi great power over his headmen, who in turn commanded obedience from those below them. To get the cattle necessary to begin kgamelo, the Batawana took them from the Khoe and Bayei living on the Boteti River and in the southern Okavango.

Ivory trading became important to the Batawana royal family in generating wealth. Mogalakwe began trading it with Angolans in the 1840s for beads and cloth. This trade was to be crucial to the Batawana after 1850. Slavery or bolata, was also reinstituted by Mogalakwe. Conquered peoples such as Bayei and Khoe were expected to work for the Batawana without payment. Male slaves herded cattle, paid tribute in biltong and skins and went on hunting expeditions where they tracked down animals and carried back the meat and ivory. Female malata were taken from their parents and forced to do domestic and agricultural work for their owners.

Mogalakwe handed over power to his young nephew Letsholathebe in 1847. Letsholathebe then used Mogalakwe's reforms to extend Batawana power, conquering large amounts of territory.

First, Letsholathebe expanded the ivory trade greatly. Hoping to get higher prices than trade with the Angolans offered, he invited the missionary David Livingstone to Ngamiland to trade ivory. Livingstone and his Bakwena guides went to Ngamiland in 1849 and opened up the region to traders from the south. Following in the famous missionary's path were large numbers of Coloureds and Europeans from the Cape Colony and Transvaal hoping to earn money from ivory trading.

Before the arrival of Livingstone, ivory had little value. Livingstone wrote:

> **I myself saw eight instances in which the tusks had been left to rot with the other bones where the elephant fell. The Batuana never had a chance of a market before; but in less than two years after our discovery (of Lake Ngami), not a man of them could be found who was not keenly alive to the great value of the article.**

What allowed the Batawana to increase their territory were the trade items brought by these foreigners. Letsholathebe tried to purchase guns and horses at every opportunity. He could easily afford these as he claimed half of all ivory collected in Ngamiland. Even a small number of men could dominate a large area if they owned all the guns and horses and so the ivory trade gave Letsholathebe and his Batawana great military power.

Letsholathebe first expanded into the region north east of the Okavango, the Mababe and Chobe region, which had big elephant herds. The Batawana began killing Bakololo tax collectors in the area and taking tribute from the local population. Of course the Bakololo responded and sent a large army to defeat their former servants. In 1854 this army attacked Toteng but suffered a major defeat. All the Batawana had to do was wait at the top of a hill and kill their spear carrying attackers with their guns. After 1854 the Bakololo presented no more problems to the Batawana as they were too afraid to attack again.

Kgosi Letsholathebe next took Ghanzi, whose Naro-Khoe had stolen huge numbers of Batawana cattle during the Bakololo battle. In 1858 Letsholathebe killed the Naro-Khoe leader Dukuri when he called for a peace conference. Then he turned the population of the Ghanzi area into malata.

Between 1860 and 1880 Letsholathebe gradually established control over the Bayei who lived across the Delta. The Bayei lived in scattered communities and were not unified. For this reason they were unable to combine and defeat Batawana aggressors, who were a much smaller group.

Hunting elephants became the main occupation of the Batawana after 1850 and large parties of hunters went out regularly to shoot them. Usually the Batawana hunters rode on horses, while Khoe and Bayei porters walked, carrying the food and water. Once elephants were found, the Khoe and Bayei stalked them with dogs. This was a dangerous business and the hunters often tried to force the elephants toward swampy areas where they would be slowed down. When the elephants were cornered, the Batawana rode in and killed them with a huge barrage of bullets. Once the animals were killed an even tougher task began the carrying of the tusks and biltong back to Toteng. It was the Khoe and Bayei who performed this exhausting duty and many died of exhaustion due to the heavy loads.

Many thousands of elephants were killed in Ngamiland and later only animals in the remotest regions were left alive. Profits from the trade went largely to the Batawana royals. In addition to buying guns and horses, the wealthy Batawana bought wagons, European clothes and began drinking tea and coffee with sugar. The kgosi's wives, who had looked little different from other Batawana women in 1850, soon distinguished themselves from the masses. By 1880 they dressed in fine clothes and were surrounded by female malata who cooled them with fans and attended to their needs. In the evenings they ate the tastiest meat and other imported delicacies. No longer did they cultivate fields and build houses like the commoners.

Some people think that the European traders cheated the Batswana by giving very low prices for ivory, but this is not true. All the Batswana chiefs knew that ivory was valuable and

Letsholathebe dining with a European trader.

so demanded much in return. One veteran ivory trader wrote:

> Many of the colonial gentlemen who wish to appear well acquainted with the method of procuring ivory but who are as ignorant in reality as one who could not discern the difference between the jaw bone of an elephant and that of a whale, seem to think that a trader has only to find his way to Lake Ngami . . . and, by practising the most gross impositions upon the native possessors of ivory, has an easy task of loading up his wagons and returning home (a rich man).

In reality, not many white ivory traders made big profits. Prices in Cape Town and London went up and down. Only those traders who bought ivory in large quantities and who were good friends of the Batswana chiefs made any significant money.

The lot of the Batawana elite improved through ivory sales, however the same could not be said for the malata. They were treated with great cruelty. Herders whose beasts died or strayed were liable to be killed or tortured. Hunters who failed to provide enough tribute had their children taken and sold. In fact the Batawana were probably the only morafe that sold its malata in large numbers. Letsholathebe sold several hundred youngsters, mainly Bayei and Khoe boys, to Boers from the Zeerust area of the Transvaal.

By the time Letsholathebe died in 1874, the Batawana were the unrivaled masters of Ngamiland. There was no threat to their power.

The rule of Moremi II, 1877-90

Letsholathebe was eventually succeeded by his son Moremi in 1877. Moremi, born to Letsholathebe's second wife, did not change the policies of his father.

His land continued to be the centre of elephant hunting and regiments conquered more land along the western side of the Okavango Delta. During the course of his reign, he shared out this territory to a new group of headmen, who also took kgamelo cattle from him. These headmen were all recent immigrants to Ngamiland from the south. These headmen opened up large new grazing areas, where Batawana cattle increased rapidly. These headmen were known as the basimane ba kgosi (the chief's boys).

The Batawana had won a large number of battles following their victory over the Bakololo in 1854. It was only in 1882 that they were seriously challenged again. In that year the Amandebele sent a large raiding party across the desert to Ngamiland to steal their cattle. This was something that the Amandebele did regularly, as their king relied heavily on his amabutho to move around southern Africa to bring him cattle.

In 1882 the Amandebele forces succeeded in surprising the Batawana and were able to capture many cattle from the Boteti River and Lake Ngami areas. In doing so they burned villages, killed innocents and took large numbers of women and children with them. Two years later they tried to do the same again, but this time they were spotted well in advance.

When the Batawana heard that the Amandebele were on their way, they began removing cattle and their people to the north. Meanwhile a group of gunmen on horseback harassed the Amandebele troops and slowly lured them into a well prepared trap. The horsemen retreated toward a swampy area, east of Nokaneng. At this point the Taoghe river was wide and deep and an island known as Khutiyabasadi provided the site for an ambush.

Battle of Khutiyabasadi.

Together they retreated across the river using canoes and makeshift bridges. The Batawana combined forces with the Bayei, who were very skilled in the wet environment. Because the banks of the island were lined with very high reeds, several Batawana regiments were able to hide behind them. They also dug a huge tunnel into the side of the island where many more men waited. Eventually the Amandebele arrived near the trap, but they were unwilling to cross as they could not swim. The Batawana let a few cattle loose and had several men show themselves to the enemy. This succeeded in getting the Amandebele men to charge and all the warriors ran into the river. They were met by a volley of rifle fire, but more importantly the Amandebele found the water too deep for them as they were unable to swim. Bayei canoers then left the island

and proceeded to drown the Amandebele men. Huge numbers of Amandebele died in this battle and of about 2,500 who left for Ngamiland only a thousand ever returned to Bulawayo.

The victory over the Amandebele was a triumph for Moremi. But the Bayei, who had dominated the battle due to their knowledge of the swamps, ended up worse off. Moremi moved his capital from Toteng to near Nokaneng on the edge of the delta. This allowed Moremi to keep the Bayei under much closer supervision than he had done previously.

Due to the military confidence gained from this battle, Moremi tried further expansion the next year. In 1885 he was asked for military help by Lewanika, who had been deposed in 1884 as kgosi of the Balozi (In 1861 the Bakololo had been destroyed by the Lozi, who then controlled the Southern Zambia area. Batswana call them 'Marotse', 'Barotse'). Moremi took a large force up to southern Zambia. On arrival he found that Lewanika had regained power already, having defeated one of his younger brothers.

But the expedition had not been made in vain. Lewanika gave Moremi access to excellent hunting grounds north of the Chobe river where big game was still plentiful. Moremi also appealed to Lewanika not to execute the leaders of the faction that had originally overthrown him. So Lewanika gave Moremi these people to keep as slaves and they accompanied the Batawana back to Ngamiland where they were distributed among Moremi's relatives. In addition, Moremi decided to return to Ngamiland via the Hambukushu capital, which he wished to conquer. The Mbukushu king at Andara, decided not to fight the Batawana and agreed to be ruled by Moremi. He then sent headmen to control the area. So, by 1885, the Batawana had conquered the entire area of modern Ngamiland.

Social Life

All of the descriptions of nineteenth century Ngamiland are written by European travellers, so it is difficult to describe the lifestyle, feelings and thoughts of the inhabitants of Ngamiland at that time.

Due to the large number of ethnic groups who lived there, Ngamiland was a diverse area. The Bayei, the largest group, were engaged primarily in agricultural production. They grew sorghum and were Botswana's first maize producers. Bayei also exploited the swamps by hunting and fishing. Bakgalagadi were known for hunting and the production of skins and karosses, which they traded over wide areas. Khoe men also focused on hunting, while their wives gathered wild fruits. Meanwhile the Batawana were known for hunting with guns and cattleowning.

These groups had similar lifestyles. Hunting was important to all groups, but the Batawana had a lot more guns to hunt with. Most Khoe in Ngamiland were not full time hunters. Those on the Boteti river kept cattle, while the Qana-khoe in the swamps concentrated on fishing. It was also a common practice for Khoe to leave the desert at harvest time to come and help the farmers. In return for this labour, they received part of the crop. Even Batawana women often went into the bush to gather wild fruits whenever food stocks were low. Moreover, all these groups traded among one another for foodstuffs, meat, tobacco, dagga, metal goods, crafts and jewellery.

Due to their increased power, the Batawana began to impose their culture on members of other groups. Tswana laws replaced the legal systems of other groups, men of conquered merafe were placed into mephato, the formal leaders of the conquered groups were stripped of power and maintained only informal status.

Under such influences, the Bayei and Hambukushu began to change their systems of organization. Both groups were originally matrilineal, in that they traced their descent from their mother's side only. According to the matrilineal system (which is common from Zambia northwards), the relatives of a person's mother take precedence over the relatives of a person's father. Your mother's brothers thus act as your principal guardians. Obviously, the matrilineal system conflicted with the Tswana system where descent is traced through the father. Today the Bayei and Hambukushu no longer trace descent through the mother's side.

As Batawana power increased, it became increasingly desirable to become known as a Motawana. Within Batawana society it was felt important that one's ancestry was pure. All sorts of people made the attempt to become real Batawana. They sought marriages with old families or forged economic links with them. Meanwhile, those who were not seen as Batawana were looked down upon. The Bayei were called Makoba, and all sorts of people came to be known as Masarwa. These were labels that had not been known before the mid nineteenth century.

1885-90: civil war and the approach of colonial rule

Unlike Kweneng, Gammangwato and other southern areas, Ngamiland did not become part of part of the Bechuanaland Protectorate in 1885. This was because in 1885 the British were mainly interested in securing the strip of land where Botswana's railway lies today.

The country which wanted to colonize Ngamiland the most was in fact Germany. Germany had taken over Namibia as a colony in 1884 and during the next few years struggled to take control. In the meantime, a number of German soldiers, traders and missionaries ventured into Ngamiland. By the late 1880s the German government was anxious to expand into Ngamiland.

In the end, however, Ngamiland went to Great Britain. This was due to two concessions that Moremi signed with British traders in the late 1880s. The first of these, the Nicholls Hicks concession was signed in 1889. It gave three white men the right to look for minerals in Ngamiland and to mine if they located any. A second treaty, the Austral Africa concession, gave the same men similar mineral rights in the Ghanzi area.

When Britain and Germany sat down in 1890 to divide Africa between themselves, Britain's claim to Ngamiland was upheld over German claims. The Germans, though, were able to negotiate for the Caprivi Strip, which included a great deal of Batawana and Basubia land.

In 1889 the year before colonial rule came to Ngamiland, a split occurred among the Batawana. One of Moremi's brothers, Sekgoma, took up arms in order to gain the bogosi. Sekgoma was the son of Letsholathebe's seventh wife, a Mongwato woman of royal birth. Sekgoma always claimed that his mother was the mohumagadi. Whatever the truth of the matter, his mother had died when he was born, and another woman had assumed the title of mohumagadi for herself. This woman, the mother of Moremi, was in fact a Mongwaketse pretending to be a pure Motawana.

In 1889, while Moremi was out hunting with his regiment, the 17 year old Sekgoma took over the capital, Kamokaku, with the help of his supporters. Sekgoma, a tough, intelligent and ambitious young man, appealed to those people who wanted to get rid of the fat and alcoholic Moremi. Sekgoma was able to control the capital for some months, before being ejected. He returned some months later with a new force, but was defeated in a bloody encounter.

Sekgoma then retreated to the swamps. The following year, not long after the British government declared its control over Ngamiland, his brother died. Young Sekgoma was soon instituted as his successor.

However, the rift between Sekgoma's men and the supporters of Moremi's family was not to be healed for many years, as will be seen in later chapters.

Questions

1 Why was Mogalakwe important to the growth of Batawana power?

2 a. What product did the Batawana specialize in?
  b. What did they sell it for?

3 What duties did slaves perform for their masters?

4 Describe how the Batawana dikgosi controlled land.

5 How did the Batawana defeat the Amandebele in 1884?

6 What were the results of Moremi's visit to Bulozi in 1885?

7 Did the various merafe in Ngamiland have different lifestyles? Explain your answer.

8 Why did the Germans not become the rulers of Ngamiland?

9 Who was Sekgoma? Why did he revolt against Moremi?

Chapter 9
The Bangwato and their neighbours

The events that took place between 1840 and 1885 what is now the Central District of Botswana were quite similar to those that had taken place in Ngamiland. The Bangwato, a small morafe like the Batawana, were able to conquer a huge amount of land containing a population much larger than their own. In doing so they controlled the ivory and ostrich feather trade. By 1885 the Bangwato were Botswana's largest and most powerful morafe.

Gammangwato before 1840

Early in the nineteenth century a large number of peoples lived in the Gammangwato area, now called the Central District. These included the Bakalanga, Batswapong, Babirwa, Batswana groups like the Bakaa and Bakhurutshe and groups of Bakgalagadi and Khoe. Most of these people lived by a combination of hunting, herding and raising crops, and they all traded among themselves.

Before 1830 none of these groups were in control of a large area. The Bangwato ruled various Bakgalagadi, Khoe and Bakalanga in the Shoshong area. After 1817 the famous kgosi, Kgari I, tried hard to make the Bangwato more powerful. He invented the kgamelo system to make cattle royal property. Those animals were then given to headmen who owed the kgosi total allegiance. This system worked because the Bangwato had big cattle herds. Bolata was also used to exploit conquered peoples. But Kgari's plan never came about in his lifetime, due to his defeat and death at the hands of the Bakalanga Banyayi in 1826.

Following Kgari's death, the Bakololo caused a great deal of chaos by killing many people and stealing cattle. Large numbers of people were forced to migrate to safer places to avoid attacks. The Bakololo left in the early 1830s, but in 1837 the Amandebele arrived and did far more damage than the Bakololo. The Bakaa, Bakalanga and Batswapong were forced to live in caves, while the Bangwato lived in high hills. Grown men were forced to herd their own cattle at this time while carrying spears and shields.

Due to the fact that the Amandebele lived north-east of the Bangwato after 1840, the threat of war was always present. In 1842 the Amadebele sent a raiding party against the Bangwato,

Sekgoma I (standing) in 1873

who fled to the caves and left their cattle behind to be taken. A young Mongwato then made a stirring speech, saying:

> Bangwato, let us die today. Have we not been dying the death of women for years? Today let us die as men. Have we not seen our mother killed before our eyes; our wives, sisters and daughters led away by our enemies? Have we not seen our infants thrown in the air and caught on the point of the Matabele spear? Have we not seen the same spear which had transfixed the old man, thrust at once through the infant and the mother on whose breast it hung? This is worse than death! Therefore let us go and fight with these destroyers of our people and die like men.

Emboldened by this talk, the Bangwato men left the cave, recaptured their cattle and drove off the Amadebele. In 1844 another Amadebele threat was also thwarted. Just prior to the arrival of Mzilikazi's men the Bangwato obtained a huge load of ivory which they exchanged for muskets. Sekgoma had a dozen Amandebele tax collectors killed and his men drove away the others. For the next twenty years, the Bangwato would be free from the threat of the Amandebele.

Trade increases and the Bangwato become more powerful

After 1844 the region's focus changed. Instead of worrying about the Amandebele, hunting elephants became the new occupation. Although white traders had visited the Bangwato in the early 1830s, it was not until 1844 that large scale ivory trading began. Soon, large numbers of traders and hunters from South Africa arrived in Gammangwato. Sekgoma, like Letsholathebe of the Batawana, managed to control this trade.

Due to his desire to control this expanding trade Sekgoma began to conquer his neighbours. In 1848 he defeated the

Malete chiefs who ruled the diverse population of the Tswapong Hills. A year later he conquered the Bakaa, who then fled to the Kweneng.

Next Sekgoma began to look to the Khoisan and Bakgalagadi in the eastern Kgalagadi and Boteti areas, which were fertile hunting grounds. Meanwhile the Bangwato themselves hunted in elephant rich areas around the Limpopo and Motloutse Rivers, which were subjected in the early 1850s. Expansion continued in 1857 as the Bangwato began to collect tribute from the Bakalanga to the north east.

Chapter 7 has already outlined how Kgosi Sechele of the Bakwena began to interfere in the political affairs of the Bangwato because he wanted to obtain part of the riches from the hunting trade of the Bangwato region. Sechele (with Mzilikazi's blessing) installed Matsheng (the son of Kgari) into the Bangwato bogosi in 1857. Both leaders felt they could control the young Mongwato. Matsheng, though, disappointed Sechele by acting more like an Amadebele leader than a Motswana one. Most Bangwato disliked his performance. So in 1859 Sechele sent an army to put Sekgoma back in power. Matsheng then fled to the Kweneng.

On his return to power, Sekgoma proved to be independent of both Sechele and Mzilikazi. He continued to expand, the Bangwato territory. In 1863 he took tribute from the Batalaote, who were then dominated by the Amandebele. Mzilikazi sent his men to attack Shoshong in retaliation. Bangwato regiments, which had a large number of guns, repelled the attack. It was an important victory for the Bangwato, because from then on the Amandebele made no attempt to invade or interfere with Bangwato territory. The two merafe thereafter lived in peace, with a large neutral zone between them.

Sechele, though, continued his desire to interfere in Bangwato affairs. The hunting trade, which had been centered in the Kweneng in the 1850s, had now moved mainly to Shoshong. So in 1864 Sechele started a campaign against Sekgoma and finally succeeded in removing him in 1866. He then installed Matsheng again, who ruled with the support of Christians in Shoshong

Whereas in the 1850s Matsheng had failed to please any of the Bangwato, after 1866 he proved successful at regulating the growing trade of his kingdom. Large numbers of guns were imported. Hunting was carried on across Gammangwato both by Bangwato and their malata. Trade increased dramatically, Shoshong grew and the Bangwato became increasingly prosperous.

Shoshong, a major southern African town

Shoshong, the Bangwato capital, increased dramatically in size as it became the centre for southern Africa's hunting trade. In 1841 Shoshong had a population of about 1,500. By 1870 it was one of the biggest towns in southern Africa. According to one traveller, it was "undoubtedly the most important town in any of the independent native kingdoms in the interior of South Africa". About thirty thousand people lived there, nearly as many as in Cape Town. Where had these people come from? Some were European and Coloured hunters, traders and craftsmen from South Africa. They came to trade for ivory and ostrich feathers and to sell goods to the Europeans who moved through the town in transit. A large part of the new population consisted of various conquered groups forced to live in Shoshong by the Bangwato. But probably more than half the newcomers were refugees from the Transvaal, where Boer rule was becoming tighter. Sekgoma, whose cattle herds were increasing as he became wealthy from ivory, gave these people cattle as mafisa. They were also given fields around Shoshong, which was ringed by kilometres of sorghum and maize. Over time the immigrants came to think of themselves as true Bangwato.

While Shoshong was the biggest town for thousands of kilometres, it was not a pleasant place to live. The town had no sewage or sanitation system of any kind. Disease could spread quickly, especially when it rained. Almost every year large numbers of people died during the rainy season due to various illnesses.

Water was available only from a spring on the side of a nearby hill. Every day the women would have to walk up the hill and wait many hours to get water. Nor was the town that safe at night, hyenas and lions often entered Shoshong and attacked people and animals. A traveler described Shoshong as:

> merely composed of a large collection of huts . . . The whole town is surrounded by a thick hedge of thorns, erected at considerable labour as a bulwark of defense both against surprizes by a hostile tribe and against depredations by wild animals . . . The huts are crowded together as quickly as space will permit, consequently the passages between them, which by extreme courtesy only could be called streets, are tortuous, narrow & inconvenient in the extreme. The whole place is filthy to a degree, not the smallest attention being paid to its sanitary condition, nor any measures being ever taken to remove the refuse. Excrement, bones and filth of every description lie for the most part around each hut . . . . The practice of herding their cattle at night in kraals within the town adds considerably to the prevailing uncleanliness.

It is hardly surprising that many Bangwato preferred to spend their time at the moraka with their cattle or hunting!

However, Shoshong residents lived relatively prosperous lives. They knew how to have a good time, especially once the harvest was finished in May. Young men and women had dances which often went on until the sun came up in the morning. The inhabitants drank sorghum beer (*bojalwa*) in large quantities.

A small number of Bangwato, mainly poor women, became Christians after the arrival of German and British missionaries in 1859. Prior to 1875 however, Shoshong remained a stronghold of traditional Tswana religion. In the face of the missionaries was a determined group who treated the new faith with contempt. Sekgoma had been trained by the finest dingaka in southern Africa and was a skilled practitioner of bongaka. Shoshong had large numbers of dingaka, who brought rain, protected animals and kept people safe from disease and the evil intentions of their enemies.

Khama becomes Bangwato kgosi

In the 1870s, Khama, the eldest son of Sekgoma, became the Bangwato kgosi. Khama is one of Botswana's most famous historical figure. He introduced many new Christian laws to the Bangwato, many of which were copied by other dikgosi across the country.

Khama was born in 1835, when the Bangwato were refugees during the Difaqane. As a young man he engaged in ivory trading and hunting and entered into partnerships with whites from South Africa. In the 1850s he was converted to Christianity by an African preacher and in 1860, was baptized by the Lutheran, Schulenburg.

Khama was deeply devoted to the new values brought by the traders and missionaries. They in turn were highly impressed by him. In addition, Khama appealed to those Bangwato who engaged in trading. He was known as an honest and hard working man of great integrity. Khama was also extremely ambitious as a politician.

So in 1872, he supported Sechele's plan to get rid of Matsheng (who was blocking trade with the Amandebele) and became the kgosi himself. Khama's first year as kgosi was disastrous, because he made a number of Christian reforms and forbade the brewing and drinking of alcohol. Most Bangwato, few of whom were Christians, were quickly dissatisfied by his rule. Sekgoma, Khama's father, easily displaced his son in 1873 and he ruled the Bangwato for the next two years.

Unable to stand living under his non-Christian father, Khama went into exile in 1873. He moved to the Boteti River with some 2,000 followers and most of the white traders. Khama's exodus proved unsuccessful, though, as heavy rains that year

Fighting between pro-Khama and pro-Sekgoma Bangwato.

led to a disastrous outbreak of malaria. After a year, about half of his people had died. He returned to Shoshong in 1874 to live under his father but in 1875 led a revolt that made him kgosi again.

Khama's second reign
Khama, who reigned for fifty years, became the most powerful Tswana leader and a figure of international fame. Yet by the time he took power, there were few elephants left in his territory. He inherited a morafe that had already established its power over a huge area south of the Makgadikgadi. Khama himself had become rich through ivory hunting and trading, while his numerous malata herded his cattle and gave him tribute.

After 1875 hunting became less important in the Bangwato territory. But Shoshong remained a prosperous place. Many traders used it as a base for their operations elsewhere, such as in Zimbabwe or Zambia. Meanwhile, peoples living in the Bangwato territory began to specialize and produce goods for sale. For instance, Bakgalagadi specialized in making karosses from skins, and the Bakhurutshe and Batalaote made money in transport riding. Farmers such as the Batalaote bought ploughs and produced increased yields of crops, which they sold in Shoshong.

Khama himself traded a great deal, exporting cattle and breeding horses. Later in life he even bought a big chain of stores. Although he taxed hunters and banned alcohol sales, he did not try to regulate trade as much as his father Sekgoma and his uncle Matsheng had done. For this reason Khama was seen by whites as a good example of an enlightened African.

Khama's reforms

As a leader, Khama began to alter the laws that had regulated the Bangwato under previous leaders. He was most famous for stopping the brewing of beer and the sale of alcohol in his territory. He went to great lengths to do so and even at on point expelled almost all of the white traders in his territory for disobeying him on this point. Of course, Khama was never successful in stopping beer drinking, but it was typical of his nature to try and turn his subjects into moral people. He wanted to change his people's behaviour in the way a father corrects his children:

Khama with son Sekgoma II in 1881

> I have been amongst my people for a long time and they do not know what to do unless I advise them.

He did not care if the majority opposed his ideas . Though he generally did not interfere with trade, he forbade traders to give goods on credit or to charge high prices during times of famine. Sometimes he stopped grain sales so that there would be enough food in dry years. He prevented people from hunting big animals or cutting trees down without permission. Khama also ended the system of kgamelo and allowed such cattle to become the private property of the holders.

He also introduced a number of Christian reforms, such as forbidding people to work on Sundays. He abolished the bogwera and bojale ceremonies, as well as other non-Christian practices such as bogadi, rainmaking and some forms of magic. He tried to discourage men from taking a second wife and encouraged marriages that were legally recognized by the

British government. Another western practice he brought was to allow women to inherit property from their fathers.

Khama was also anxious to improve his people's moral behaviour. In addition to stopping alcohol sales he forbade all dancing at night and even stopped women walking around at night in order to reduce the potential for love affairs. Men who took concubines were censored One traveller wrote:

> Everything in Khama's town is conducted with the rigour, one might almost say bigotry, of religious enthusiasm, The kgosi conducts in person native (church) services, twice every Sunday, in his large round kgotla, at which he expects a large attendance . . . He has a system of espionage by which he learns the names of those who do not keep Sunday properly and he punishes them accordingly.

Not all of Khama's laws had the effect he desired. Many of them were ignored by the Bangwato. Later, after his death, many were forgotten. But it should be recognized that Khama brought Christianity to the Bangwato for good and that he made a determined effort to change the way his people lived.

The coming of the British

Traders had come into Bangwato territory since the early 1830s, however, after 1867 a great many Cape based British citizens arrived. In that year gold was discovered at Tati by a German, the first time a gold mine was found by Europeans in southern Africa. Large groups of white miners came up through Shoshong and went to find gold there. Matsheng, who was then kgosi, did not claim the Tati as his own land, but tried to make money by charging the miners £1 to go through his territory.

When gold was found, the Boers in the Transvaal tried to claim Tati and other parts of Botswana. This false claim prompted

Matsheng to write to the British government to say that the Boers were lying. He also asked the British to supervise their citizens who were at Tati. The British, though, were not interested in looking after Tati and so did nothing.

Not much gold was ever found at Tati. After a few years most of the miners went back to the Cape, all disappointed. A group known as the London and Limpopo Mining Company took over the mining of the area and brought in expensive steam engines to crush the gold ore. This company worked at Tati from 1871-75, but made little money and was forced to close down. Later in the century British miners would look for gold there again.

Further Bangwato dealings with the British occurred from 1875-6, when a group of Boer religious fanatics, the Doppers, decided to leave the Transvaal. They wanted to trek north to find the "Promised Land," which they thought they would find somewhere in the north of Ngamiland. They camped for two years on the Limpopo River, near Gammangwato. Their presence frightened the Bangwato because they were well armed, unfriendly and obviously intending to settle somewhere. So in 1876 Khama wrote a letter to the British asking for help to stop the Boers entering his country. Khama eventually allowed by the Boers to cross his country and the Kgalagadi desert. When they failed to follow his advice, hundreds of Boers and their herds of cattle all died of thirst in the desert. The survivors stayed at Ghanzi for a year or so, before eventually getting to Angola.

Of all the Batswana, Khama and the Bangwato had the closest relationship to the British. They were very close to British missionaries, who supported Khama's new laws and also had early contacts with the British government.

Questions

1 Why did the Bangwato expand their territory?

2 Why was Sechele interfering with the Bangwato chiefs?

3 Would you have enjoyed living in Shoshong? Give reasons for your answer.

4 In what ways was Khama different from his father?

5 Once the elephants were gone, how did people make a living?

6 What laws did Khama institute as kgosi?

7 Who were the Doppers? How did Khama deal with them?

Chapter 10
British occupation and colonization

In 1885 Britain occupied Botswana, beginning a period of colonial rule that lasted until 1966. During this time the country was known as the Bechuanaland Protectorate. The British hoped that the word protectorate would reassure Batswana that they would not become a colony. Whereas colonies are countries governed by outsiders, as protected rulers the dikgosi were assured that they could continue to govern their own people.

The Protectorate was imposed by the British. No kgosi asked for it and only three; Khama, Gaseitsiwe and Sechele were consulted afterwards. Khama welcomed it, while Gaseitsiwe and Sechele reluctantly accepted. All three knew from the experience of fellow Batswana south of the Molopo that it was impossible to resist Britain's military power.

The imperialist scramble for Africa

Between 1500 and 1900 leading European countries, such as Britain, France, the Netherlands, Portugal and Germany, established many colonies and protectorates throughout the Americas and Asia, as well as Africa. This phenomenon is called imperialism, and the Europeans who participated in it are called imperialists.

Imperialism came to southern Africa in the 1500s when the Portuguese began to occupy coastal areas of Angola and Mozambique. They were followed by the Dutch who established the Cape Colony, whose white settlers became known as the Boers. After the British took over the Cape, some Boers migrated to re-establish their own overrule in the Transvaal and Orange Free State. Despite such activities most of southern Africa was still free of European rule before 1870. Only thirty years later, in 1900, the region had fallen entirely under white control. The same pattern of imperialist expansion occurred throughout all of Africa. By 1912 Liberia and Ethiopia were the only African countries not ruled by Europeans. Botswana's 1885 occupation was part of a wider European 'scramble for Africa'.

Factors contributing to the scramble

Why would Europeans want to take over Africa? A number of factors contributed to the Scramble. For instance, industrialization in Europe created a growing demand for African minerals and agricultural products. Thus the discovery of diamonds in the Batlhaping lands of the northern Cape caused the British to take over that area, while in southern Nigeria it was palm oil production and in Zimbabwe the hope of finding gold.

As European factories produced more goods, imperialists also hoped to make Africans buy their countries' industrial products. The expansion of manufactured imports into Botswana following the Difaqane encouraged such ideas. The traders, themselves, often looked to their home countries for support. Thus, in 1852-53, British traders had urged Sechele to appeal to their government for support against the Boers.

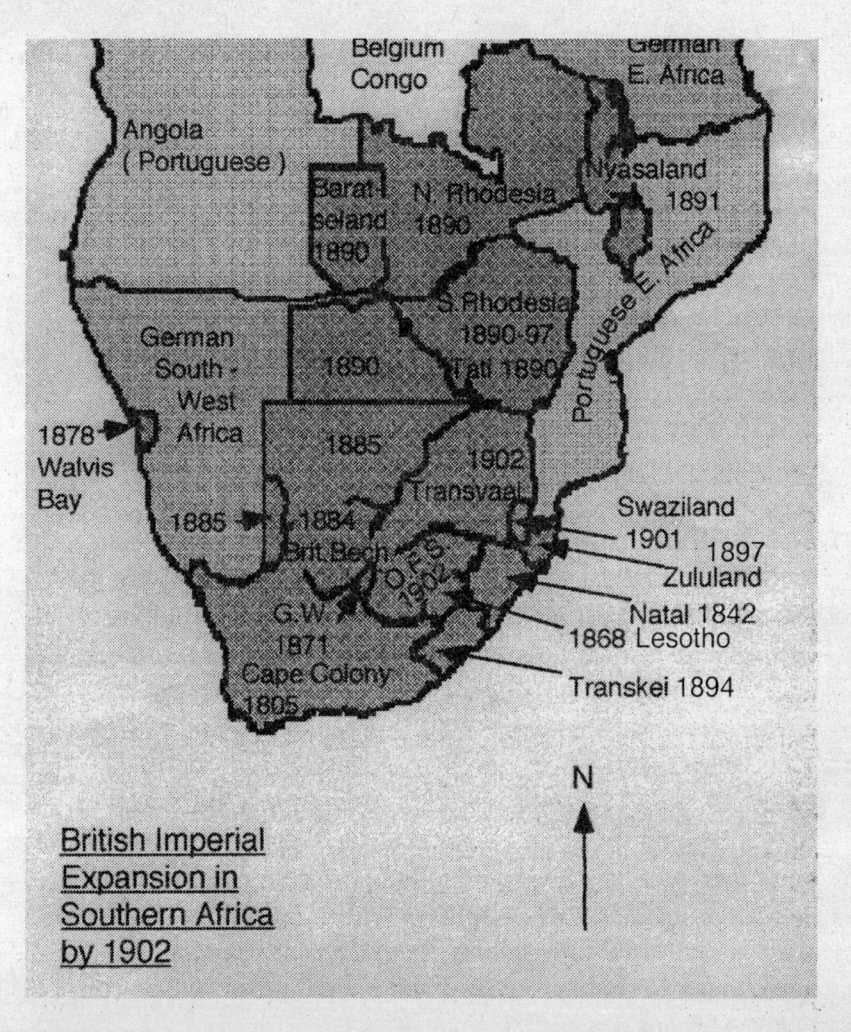

British Imperial Expansion in Southern Africa by 1902

Industrial era technology also encouraged imperialist expansion. The development of new weapons such as carbine rifles, machine guns and better artillery gave European armies an advantage over Africans, including those like the Batswana who had acquired guns. Trains and steamships, along with new medicines like quinine for malaria, made it easier for Europeans to move people and goods through Africa. Cecil

Rhodes, the leading British imperialist in southern Africa, spoke of building a railroad from Cape Town to Cairo through Botswana.

National rivalries also encouraged the scramble. After 1870 Germany emerged to challenge Britain's position as the leading European power. In a desire to maintain their top position, as well as for profits, Britain hoped to exclude Germany from sharing in southern Africa's mineral wealth. Because of Botswana's geographic position at the region's centre, the British were determined not to allow the country to come under German control.

The British imperialists

British imperialists were divided into two groupings. On the one hand were businessmen, civil servants and militarists in Britain who took a global view of their overseas empire. By the beginning of the nineteenth century the British Empire was already vast, with its largest, most profitable, colonies in Asia. Thus, until the discovery of diamonds and gold, the British government in London showed little interest in the southern Africa beyond the strategic ports of the Cape. On the other hand there was a growing population of both English and Afrikaans speaking white settlers in the Cape Colony who were always interested in enriching themselves by expanding northwards to seize more land and coerce more labour from black Africans.

Griqualand West and the Botswana confederation

After 1852-53 Batswana Boer war the merafe living between the Orange and Zambezi rivers had remained free of white domination and were loosely allied. After 1872 communities living south of the Molopo river, mostly Barolong, Batlhaping and Batlharo were conquered by the British. In the process they lost most of their land, which the British government handed over to white settlers.

The British colonization of southern Batswana began with the 1871 annexation of territory containing the newly discovered diamond fields in and around Kimberley. Although over 10,000 Batlhaping lived in the area the British claimed that the entire region belonged to a Griqua group numbering only a few hundred. Conveniently these Griqua had supposedly asked for British protection. The area thus became the Colony of Griqualand West. From 1876 Griqualand West's blacks, including its Griqua, were forced to live in overcrowded 'locations' after most of their land was given to white settlers.

The formation of the confederation

In an attempt to counter further encroachment by either the British or Boers the various Batlhaping dikgosi, along with Montshiwa of the Barolong and Gaseitsiwe of Bangwaketse, joined together to form a confederation of their merafe. The idea was not entirely new. Since the 1852-53 war dikgosi in the region had maintained a defensive alliance. In 1865 Gaseitsiwe, Montshiwa and the Bakwena Kgosi Sechele had threatened to jointly go to war when the Transvaal Boers tried to takeover Lehurutshe. The Boers backed down. The idea of forming a confederation against the common enemy was inspired by Josef Ludorf, a Wesleyan missionary who acted as Montshiwa's secretary. In October 1871 he sent a letter copied to the Bangwaketse, Barolong and Batlhaping dikgosi. He wrote:

> And now chiefs: rulers of the land, I appeal to you. Awake: arise and unite soon before your trophy is torn asunder by wolves; come ye together, make protective laws; stop all breaches and gaps and

close your gaps. Safeguard the heritage of Tau your ancestor. Hear ye all chiefs: Come together and unite.

By November Ludorf had drafted a constitution for "The United Barolong, Batlhaping and Bangwaketse Nation" and had begun appealing for British diplomatic recognition. In the same month Sechele agreed to join the nation building process. After Ludorf's sudden death in January 1872, dikgosi continued to work for his vision of greater unity. But, in the end, they were frustrated by their inability to resist further British aggression.

The British take over the area

In 1878 both the Batlhaping and Griqua in Griqualand West rebelled against white domination. With their guns the Batlhaping put up a strong resistance, defeating one enemy column in the 2 July 1878 Battle of Kho. But, British firepower was far superior. The main body of resisters were surrounded at Dithakong, which fell to the invaders on 24 July 1878, after a three hour artillery bombardment.

Using the supposed need to protect the LMS mission at Kudumane as an excuse a British commander, Charles Warren, then invaded the Batswana lands up to the Molopo river demanding the submission of the local dikgosi. Those who resisted were fined, imprisoned or deposed. A British agent named Alex Bailie was also sent north to the Bakwena, Bangwato and Amandebele to seek their cooperation in supplying labour for the Kimberley mines. When the Bangwato Kgosi Khama asked for British support in keeping Boers out of his territory, Bailie interpreted it as a request for British protection.

Warren's invasion and Bailie's mission were part of a wider policy of British expansionism designed to bring much of southern Africa under their control. Between 1877 and 1881 the British army also fought with the Amaxhosa, Amazulu, Basotho, Bapedi and Transvaal Boers. However, a change in government in London led to a British pullback in 1881. The Transvaal, Kwazulu and Batswana territory north of Griqualand West were temporarily abandoned.

Wars against white mercenaries

Warren's invasion, and the flow of refugees from Griqualand West, had destabilized the Barolong and independent Batlhaping. After the 1881 withdrawal, Montshiwa and his counterpart Mankurwane, the leading Batlhaping kgosi, were attacked by white mercenaries. These mercenaries, who included both Boers and British, claimed to be fighting on behalf of two dikgosi who had already submitted to Boer overrule. Their real interest, though, was in grabbing land for themselves. Mankurwane made his people's situation worse by hiring his own white mercenaries, a group who later turned on him.

In 1882 the mercenaries set up two small states, the Stellaland Republic on Batlhaping land and the Goshen Republic on Barolong land. Imperialists in the Cape Colony, led by the mine owner Cecil Rhodes, now joined local missionaries and traders in calling for British intervention. They maintained that the mercenaries were disrupting the flow of goods and mine labour along the trade route between the Cape Colony and central Africa. Their arguments were strengthened in April 1884 when the Germans occupied the Namibian coast. The British now feared that the two republics would become a land link between the Germans and the Transvaal Boers. They knew that the Transvaal's new President, Paul Kruger, was anti British and pro German.

Soon afterwards the LMS missionary John MacKenzie was told to cooperate with the Stellaland mercenaries in establishing a Bechuanaland Protectorate south of the Molopo. He failed to reach an agreement with the Stellalanders and in August he was replaced by Rhodes. Rhodes quickly won the mercenaries support by recognizing all their land claims against the Batlhaping.

The Goshenites were less successful. Montshiwa's position was strengthened in 1883 when Gaseitsiwe, Sechele and the Bakgatla-Ba-ga-Kgafela Kgosi Linchwe agreed to join him in a new alliance. The Goshenites were then pushed to the Transvaal border farm of Rooigrond. On 12 May 1884 the Barolong raided the farm and burned down the mercenaries camp. When a retaliatory raid resulted in the death of Montshiwa's son Makgetla, the kgosi told his people:

> **Who think you must die for the fatherland if not the princes? Think you an enemies bullet or ball respects a kings son or that a king's son is dearer to his parents any more than a commoners son to his parents? Away with your heaviness of heart: Makgetla has died gloriously because he died as we should be prepared to die; so on with the struggle for our land and freedom.**

Another raid on Bangwaketse and Barolong cattleposts inside Botswana led to the last battle of the war. On 1 August 1884 Goshenite raiders were intercepted by Bangwaketse and Barolong near Mafikeng. In the battle 181 Batswana, including two white sympathizers and some 50 Boers were killed before the raiders retreated back into the Transvaal.

Events came to a head in September 1884 when Kruger claimed that Montshiwa had accepted Transvaal protection! In support of this he produced a false or forged document with an X besides Montshiwa's name. Kruger's attempted bluff convinced the British imperialists that the time had come for stronger action. Even though Kruger soon withdrew his claim, the British sent a 4,000 men commanded by Warren to secure the area.

The 1885 Warren expedition

By the time Warren's forces arrived among the Batlhaping and Barolong in January 1885 the region south of the Molopo had become relatively calm. With MacKenzie serving as his advisor, Warren visited Mankurwane and Montshiwa. The two signed documents, drafted by Mackenzie, in which they agreed to submit to British overrule. Warren also met with Kruger, who promised to prevent further raids on the Protectorate from the Transvaal.

Warren's main task then became the enforcement of land promises made by Rhodes to the Stellalanders. By May 1886 a Land Commission, chaired by Rhodes' close associate Sidney Shippard, had robbed the Batswana living south of the Molopo of 92% of their land. 13% of their land was awarded to the mercenaries, and 79% was taken by the British as Crownlands to be sold to other white settlers. Shippard, who became known to Batswana as Morena Maaka (Lord of Lies), was then appointed as Bechuanaland's Administrator.

The expansion of the Bechuanaland Protectorate

Meanwhile, the British government decided to end any possibility of a link up between German Namibia and the Transvaal by extending the Bechuanaland Protectorate north of the Molopo to include the southern half of Botswana. In March 1885 Warren was instructed to communicate this development to Sechele and Khama. He set out to do this the following month, crossing the Molopo with only seventy men. The timing was appropriate as a small German expedition passed through Botswana only a few months later.

Leading Bakwena had already read about the imposition of the Protectorate when Warren formally notified the Molepolole kgotla on 27 April 1885. There he was immediately challenged by Sechele's son Sebele who asked: "What in us has brought this on that our country should be taken from us?" Warren tried to insist that he had come to establish a Protectorate, not take land, but he was unconvincing. For his part Sechele stated:

> **I do not know the exact object of your coming here. When we see you appear here we do not know if it will be life or death to us, but that we know it will be death to us if you do to us as the Boers do to the Bahurutshe. We shall be dead men if you do to us as the Boers did to the Bakgatla at Rustenburg. If you talk merely in parables we shall not understand you easily. I have seen a newspaper in which it is said I asked for protection, also Gaseitsiwe and Khama. I do not understand this asking. The Bakwena were collected together as they are now when I went to the Cape to get guns and powder to defend myself with. I went with Sanwe, Mr. Sam Edwards, here. There are others who can testify if I ever asked for anything beside to be allowed to buy guns and powder; to be allowed to obtain weapons the same as what the Boers had, to defend myself against them. As to our friendship I do not know why, because of that our country should be taken possession of. Why is known only to you white people and the missionary who lives here.**

Warren at Molepolole kgotla.

After two days of discussions Warren left Molepolole having failed to win Sechele's submission. But, the Mokwena had no illusions about resisting the British. As early as 1868 when asked if he would fight them he stated: "How could I? The great English would eat me up in one day."

Warren proceeded to Shoshong where his announcement of the Protectorate was enthusiastically welcomed by Khama, though most of the Bangwato were opposed to the British presence. On 13 May 1885 he signed a document, drafted by Mackenzie, in which it was stated: "Further I give to the Queen to make laws and change them in the country of the Bamangwato, with reference to both black and white."

Mackenzie also convinced Khama to hand over about one quarter of Botswana's land, much of it not under his actual control, for the English settler. Warren then returned to Molepolole where Sechele was pressured to reach a similar agreement. But, the Mokwena was only willing to give up his own claims to Bakgatla occupied lands east of the Ngotwane and parts of the western Kgalagadi bordering on Namibia "as long as my people should be able to hunt there". He further conceded: "Concerning the laws which shall be established in the country, I wish to rule among my people according to custom, but I give to the Queen to rule among white people wherever they are." Later, when also pressed for an agreement, Gaseitsiwe made a similar gesture, giving up his residual claims to Gamalete and Hukuntsi.

British plans for the area

Though they knew that Gaseitsiwe and Sechele's land concessions were worthless, Warren and Mackenzie hoped to use Khama's "magnificent offer" as the basis for creating a white settler colony. They submitted a plan to carve out 7,000 farms of about 6,000 acres each. Fortunately, this idea was overruled from above. The British government accepted its South African High Commissioner's conclusion that:

> **As to the country north of the Molopo River....it appears to me that we have no interest in it, except as a road to the interior. I would suggest, therefore, that we should confine ourselves to preventing that part of the Protectorate being occupied by either Filibusters (mercenaries) or Foreign powers, doing, for present, as little as possible in the way of administration or settlement. The Chiefs, Gatziziba (Gaseitsiwe), Sechele and Khama, might be left to govern their own tribes in their own fashion and their offer of lands to Her Majesty's Government ...should be refused.**

It was therefore decided that the British presence north of the Molopo would be limited to occasional police patrols to 'protect Sechele's country and the country neighbouring to Shoshong'. This circumstance suited the Batswana who were reported to have an 'utter distaste for the rule or control of the white man'.

On 30 September 1885 the Batswana were administratively divided by the Molopo river. The merafe south of the river, who now lived in the shadow of white settlers, became part of the colony of British Bechuanaland, which was later incorporated into South Africa as the northern Cape. The Bechuanaland Protectorate survived north of the Molopo to become Botswana.

Summary

In 1885 much of Botswana was occupied by the British to keep it from falling under the control of the Germans. This action was part of a wider late nineteenth century scramble for Africa that brought most of the continent under European control. In accepting the imposition of the Protectorate local dikgosi were aware of how the British had militarily crushed the Batlhaping to their south. At first both the British and the dikgosi were able to agree that the later should be left to govern their own people.

Questions

1 a. What is Imperialism?
   b. What were the two types of nineteenth century British imperialists?

2 a. Give four factors that contributed to the scramble for Africa.
   b. When did the scramble occur?

3 a. How did the British acquire Griqualand West?
   b. What other groups claimed the area?

4 a. Why did Batswana try to form a confederation during the 1870s?
   b. How did Josef Ludorf contribute to Batswana unity?

5 a. Why did the Batlhaping fight the British in 1878?
   b. What was Charles Warren's role in the war?

6 a. What is meant by the word mercenary?
   b. Who were the Stellalanders?

7 a. What is the significance of the Warren Expedition?
   b. Why was it sent to Botswana?

8 Compare and contrast the responses of Khama and Sechele to the Protectorate.

Chapter 11
The consolidation of colonial rule

Although the British declared their Protectorate in 1885, they did not begin to exercise full colonial control over Botswana until 1890. As we saw in the last chapter the colonial office initially believed that their interests north of the Molopo were limited. They therefore did not want to spend money establishing a colonial administration.

Before 1890 the British interfered little in the rule of the dikgosi. Thereafter they gradually began to introduce a system of indirect rule. Under Indirect Rule colonial officials ruled through dikgosi, who were no longer free to run their own peoples' affairs without interference. Instead they were expected to obey instructions from above. Indirect rule was based on the imperialists' belief that they alone had the ability to hold ultimate authority.

You may wonder why it was that the British suddenly decided to impose indirect rule? The reason was that their view of Botswana began to change. In 1885 their primary concern had been limited to preventing the Germans in Namibia from linking up with the Transvaal Boers. But by 1890 Botswana had become a base from which British imperialism could expand northward into central Africa.

Rhodes and the British South Africa Company

The leading British imperialist pushing for the expansion of colonial rule into Botswana and central Africa was Cecil Rhodes. He had become one of the richest men in the world through his ownership of South African diamond and gold mines. Rhodes also hoped to control the wealth of central Africa. In this he was supported by his friend 'Morena Maaka' Shippard, the official immediately responsible for the Bechuanaland Protectorate.

In 1888 Rhodes, through an agent named Rudd, obtained a concession from the Amandebele King Lobengula. It granted him exclusive mining rights in western Zimbabwe. This occurred after Shippard had visited Lobengula. He and his assistant J.S. Moffat (son of Robert Moffat), misled the king. If he signed the Rudd Concession, they told him, he would gain British support in his efforts to limit the activities of white fortune seekers in his country. When he saw that he had been tricked Lobengula tried to break the agreement. Rhodes, however, was prepared to enforce his claims by force and Lobengula was unable to gain the support of the British against him.

Rhodes used the Rudd Concession as a basis for asking the British government to give his British South Africa Company (BSACo) permission to take control of central Africa. They agreed. In

Officers of Bechuanaland Border Police.

October 1889 Queen Victoria issued a royal charter. This document gave the BSACo the right to rule Botswana, Zambia and Zimbabwe on Britain's behalf. Because of this document the BSACo became known as the Chartered Company. Rhodes wanted to take over Zimbabwe first, which he believed was rich in gold, before he assumed the cost of running Botswana. He therefore convinced the Colonial Office to temporarily maintain its responsibility over Botswana. In so doing he knew he could count on Shippard's administration to assist him in his conquest of Zimbabwe. Shippard became a Director of the BSACo after he left Botswana. Many of his subordinates, particularly officers in the Protectorate police, were given BSACo shares by Rhodes. Through such corruption Rhodes knew that Protectorate officials would serve his interests.

The Kopong Conference

On his way to see Lobengula, Shippard had disturbed the dikgosi of southern Botswana with loose talk of establishing colonial rule. In the hope of calming them, Shippard accepted Sebele I's proposal that he convene a meeting of the dikgosi. As a result, the southern dikgosi and thousands of their followers gathered to meet Shippard at Kopong in February 1889.

Shippard believed that he could trick the dikgosi at the Kopong Conference by making them show they accepted colonial rule. Instead Bathoen I, Linchwe I and Sebele (acting for his ailing father Sechele) joined together to oppose the continued British presence in their territories. They told Shippard that they would rather be independent than ruled by imperialists. Linchwe said:

> **I do not wish either the Boers or the English to come and take our chieftainship away from us. All Bechuanas (Batswana) should fight together. God will protect us if the Protectorate is withdrawn and God is the greatest Protector.**

Khama, however, broke ranks and promised "to help the English government in every way." Disappointed by Bathoen, Linchwe and Sebele's defiant attitude, Shippard broke up the conference. In his report he noted:

> **Khama who is thoroughly loyal and sincerely attached to the English appears to be completely isolated. He is left out of all the private meetings of the Protectorate Chiefs and seems to be regarded by them with suspicion and dislike as the white man's friend.**

A month later Khama claimed he had blocked Sebele's proposal at Kopong to attack the British. The police report added: "Khama says Chiefs below (i.e. those in the south, Bathoen, Linchwe and Sebele) blame Khama for inviting the white man in and backing them (the British) to the point of fighting them (the southern dikgosi)." Because of Khama's support for Shippard, the dikgosi could not speak with a united voice against the establishment of colonial rule.

The Orders-in-Council of 1890-1

The new kind of colonial rule was imposed through the Orders-in-Council of 1890 and 1891 (an Order-in-Council is an order or decree given in the name of the British monarch). The first in June 1890 made an official called the High Commissioner the Queen's representative in southern Africa. This official was to:

> **provide for giving effect to any power or jurisdiction which Her Majesty (Queen Victoria), her heirs or successors, may at any time before or after the date of this order have within the limits of this order.**

This meant that the High Commissioner had absolute power and was acting for the Queen. He could even cancel laws that had been made in the past. These new powers were necessary because Shippard had to find a way to cancel concessions held by companies other than the BSACo. Bathoen, Linchwe, Moremi and Sebele had each sold concessions in their territories and this contradicted the rights given to the BSACo by the royal charter. Most of these rival concessions recognized the dikgosi, not Queen Victoria, as the sovereigns of the soil (that is, owners and rulers of the land).

Shippard had tried to declare all non BSACo concessions invalid earlier in 1889. He backed down when it was recognized that he had no authority to issue such an order. Then the British gave themselves absolute power in the Protectorate by issuing the Orders-in-Council. These orders extended the Protectorate's border to include all of northern Botswana. The peoples of Ngamiland and Chobe were thus brought into the Protectorate for the first time.

But the dikgosi still claimed to be sovereigns of the soil. In the same month that the 1890 Order was issued their position was upheld by the High Commissioner's own legal advisor, W.P. Schreiner. He thought that the proposals made by Gaseitsiwe, Khama and Sechele, when accepting the Protectorate in 1885:

> "do not per se convey to the Crown (Queen Victoria) any legal jurisdiction within the territories of those Chiefs" so that "the delegation to the British South Africa Company of a legal jurisdiction founded upon the due acceptance of the proposals referred to, would be an act requiring for its validity the approval or assent of the Chiefs concerned."

In other words, he was saying that nothing in the agreements made by the dikgosi handed over sovereignty to Queen Victoria. After the Kopong Conference, Shippard realized that the dikgosi would never voluntarily submit to colonial overrule. Nor would they be willing to submit to the BSACo. Indeed, in 1890 Bathoen, Linchwe and Sebele worked together to block such British acts as the construction of a telegraph, the sinking of wells and the stationing of police in their territories. When their protests failed they turned to lawyers. Their claim to be sovereigns of the soil thus posed a serious legal challenge to making the BSACo the rulers of the Protectorate.

The Bramestone memorandum

To overcome the dikgosi's objections, in February 1891 a senior colonial office official in Britain named John Bramstone drafted a document. It was called "Memorandum as to the Jurisdiction and Administrative Powers of a European State Holding Protectorates in Africa." This document provided the basis not only for colonial rule in Botswana. Other African protectorates such as Uganda and Malawi were also affected. In his memo Bramestone defined Botswana as:

An uncivilized territory to which Europeans resort in greater or less numbers and where, in as much as the native rulers of the territory are incapable of maintaining peace, order and good government among Europeans, the protecting power maintains courts, police and other institutions for the control, safety and benefit of its own subjects and of the natives.

He then argued that sovereignty in an "uncivilized" African territory could be exercised by the same methods as if the ruler had ceded his whole country to her Majesty. He based this conclusion on the Foreign Jurisdictions Act under which Botswana had originally been occupied. The act had been changed to allow the British government to control its own subjects in the "uncivilized" foreign territories. Bramestone then concluded. If Britain was allowed to protect its citizens in

Protectorates then it had the right as a civilized power to place its own courts and government officers in an uncivilized territory.

The Bramstone memorandum is an example of the racist nature of imperialism in Africa. Batswana were labelled uncivilized and thus 'incapable of maintaining peace, order and good government' simply because they were black Africans. Britain's right to rule Botswana was thus justified. It was not meant to protect Batswana from the Boers or any other whites, it was to protect all whites from Batswana.

On the basis of the Bramstone memorandum a second, Order-in-Council was issued in May 1981. It authorized the High Commissioner to enact laws, to establish a court system, to raise taxes and to take additional steps to maintain peace, order and good government of all persons within Botswana. To assure that Batswana accepted the new colonial order Shippard expanded his police force. One large force was stationed at Gaborone to watch over the southern dikgosi.

Gaborone Camp in 1890's

Khama and the founding of Rhodesia

Only one kgosi had been formally notified of the BSACo's royal charter. On 16 December 1889 Shippard wrote to Khama:

> The British South Africa Company has received from Her Majesty most extensive powers not only over the whole Bechuanaland Protectorate, but up to the Chobe and Zambesi Rivers and far beyond..... The powers of the Company include all mercantile operations, digging for precious stones and minerals, the raising, equipping and maintenance of armed forces for preserving order and protecting the territories included in the company's charter and many other rights and privileges. The Company will not interfere in anyway with your rights and powers in the Government of your country and people and Mr. Rhodes hopes to have your support and assistance in his great work of carrying the blessings of civilization not only into Matebeleland and Mashonaland (Zimbabwe), but, in due time and with God's blessing, throughout the interior of Africa.

In his reply to Shippard Khama stated that:

> I trust I may always be found ready to give all the help in my power to open the interior to the blessings of God's Book and all the blessings which the English people have brought to me and my people and to help the English Government in every way in which I gave my promise to you at Kopong to be ready to do.

Khama's letter to the BSACo went further by specifically offering Rhodes soldiers if he started a war against the Amandebele.

Khama had already assisted Rhodes by detaining a number of Bulawayo bound individuals who opposed BSACo interests. This led to an international incident in July 1888 when his men attacked a party of Boers. Piet Grobler, Transvaal's ambassador to the Amandebele, was killed in the ensuing gun fight. Khama had also urged the Balozi and Batonga in Zambia to follow his example by signing agreements with Rhodes' agents. These agreements led to the creation of BSACo ruled Northern Rhodesia.

From 1890 Khama's capital at Palapye served as the BSACo's forward base for conquering central Africa. The Bangwato assisted in the 1890 invasion of Zimbabwe by the company's pioneer column. In the years that followed Khama prospered by providing support for BSACo operations.

Khama was helpful to Rhodes in 1893. He supplied 1,760 troops, (more than the 1,000 requested of him) to join 815 Protectorate police and 1,230 BSACo soldiers in a war against the Amandebele. The conflict had been provoked by BSACo in order to seize more Amandebele territory. In an effort to avoid a fight he knew he would lose, Lobengula sent two groups of messengers to beg for peace from the High Commissioner. This appeal never reached its destination as members of both groups were killed by the Protectorate police. After months of heavy fighting the Amandebele kingdom was destroyed. A new settler colony was established, known as Southern Rhodesia.

Sebele resists colonial rule

By March 1892, southern Botswana was on the brink of war. The Protectorate police were being reinforced at Gaborone in preparation for a possible assault on Molepolole. The region had been drifting towards crisis since the 1891 Order-in-Council. In October 1891 the British used their new authority to impose license fee's on the Protectorate's traders. When the southern dikgosi questioned this decree, they were told that they had no say in the matter. Despite this, Sebele forbade Asian and Boer merchants operating in Kweneng to pay the fees.

In February 1892 Shippard's new Assistant Commissioner for the Southern Protectorate, William Surmon, tried to force the Kweneng traders to pay their fees. Surmon's post had also been created in October 1891 'with the view of keeping in check the somewhat turbulent Chiefs Linchwe and Sebele'. When his police tried to close an Asian shop for non payment, Sebele had it reopened. Then two policemen tried to collect payment from a Boer trader but were stopped by a Bakwena mob. Sebele informed the two that "he refused to allow anyone trading on his ground to pay any license whatever; he was the man to whom licenses had to be paid, not the English government." Shippard then called for tough action:

> **I am of the opinion that the matter is too serious to be safely treated as a mere case of obstructing the police in the performance of their duties...It appears to me beyond doubt that this case is regarded by the other Chiefs and the natives generally in the Southern Protectorate, as a test and that any further attempt to collect licenses or exact payment of fine, will be resisted. I should deprecate any threats or demands which we might not be prepared immediately to enforce.....Towards this end I think the first step should be to come to an understanding with Khama and obtain from him his promise of assistance in the event of trouble arising in the Southern Protectorate. In any case and whether annexation be decided on or not, it appears to me to be necessary to make immediate preparations for coercive measures.**

Soon the High Commissioner authorized preparations for a joint assault on Molepolole by the police and Bangwato. He was afraid, though, that the Bakgatla, Bangwaketse and Batlokwa would join the Bakwena if fighting broke out. The Bakwena, themselves, decided only to fight if first fired on.

Sebele therefore decided to back down by donating ten cattle to Surmon as a sign of his friendship. He added:

> My ancestors kept their villages in good order without acting under the compulsion of others. Friendship does not mean giving laws to another. Friendship is to advise each other.

To Shippard's frustration his superiors in London welcomed this development. They told the High Commissioner that he could impose fees only 'with the consent of the Chiefs'.

The Concessions Commission and Bakaa crisis

The peaceful resolution of the crisis over the imposition of trading licenses did not resolve the larger issue of BSACo rights within Botswana. In August 1892 a British MP with interests in Sebele's Secheleland concession wrote to the Colonial Office protesting continued efforts to have non BSACo concessions cancelled. In reply he was informed that the government had decided to form a commission of enquiry to look into the whole question of concessions.

The 1893 Concessions Commission was not an impartial body. Its task was to disallow those concessions which clashed with BSACo interests. Sebele still insisted that he, not Queen Victoria, had the authority to decide such matters and refused to deal with the commission. Lawyers for the rival concessions also maintained that the BSACo had acquired no rights in Botswana.

By the time the commission issued its report its legitimacy (and/or findings) were challenged. Recognising this, the British then delayed. They wanted to give the BSACo time to make private agreements with the dikgosi and rival concessionaries.

In February 1894 Shippard tried once more to provoke a war against the southern dikgosi. Earlier the Bakaa, who had been living with the Bakwena since 1849, had broken up into two factions following the death of their kgosi, Mosinyi. This split led to disputes over cattle. With the assistance of Bathoen and other neighbouring dikgosi, Sebele awarded the royal cattle to one of the claimants, Segotso. But this was rejected by Shippard, who backed the rival claims of Khama's son in law Tshwene. Shippard recommended that Khama be allowed to impose a settlement. Surmon was then appointed to hold an enquiry with the assistance of Khama's secretary Ratshosa.

Surmon's proceedings shocked the Bakgatla, Bangwaketse and Bakwena who came to witness the proceedings. Surmon ignored the Batswana and simply gave all the cattle to Tshwene, without specifying how many he was owed. When 196 were delivered, Surmon called for another 200. Sebele then decided to oppose the judgment.

Shippard tried to use Sebele's supposed refusal to obey Surmon as a basis for his deposition. New plans were made to burn down Molepolole. In addition to Bangwato soldiers, Shippard tried to get Balete support by promising them Bangwaketse territory. He planned to finance the operation by the seizure and sale of Bakwena cattle. Even though Sebele agreed to send the 200 extra cattle to Surmon, Shippard continued with his evil scheme and made plans to burn down Molepolole. Fortunately the High Commissioner intervened and ordered the police to stand down.

Khama becomes suspicious of Rhodes

It is unclear whether or not Khama was really eager to join Shippard in warring on his fellow Batswana by 1894. At the time he was beginning to understand that Rhodes was a threat to his own position. With Zimbabwe now secure, the final transfer of Botswana to the BSACo seemed imminent. The loss by the Amandebele of most of their land to white Rhodesian settlers after the 1893 war might have been a warning to him. Rhodes himself showed no gratitude to Khama for the Bangwato support he had received. Meanwhile Khama's position as kgosi was being challenged by his junior brothers, Raditladi and Mphoeng, who were rumoured to have Chartered Company support. So Khama became suspicious of Rhodes.

By 1895 Rhodes was at the height of his power, being the Prime Minister of the Cape Colony as well as master of the Rhodesias. Direct control of Botswana now became a necessary stepping stone in the realization of his greater ambition, control of all of southern Africa by seizing the goldfields of the Boer ruled Transvaal.

Bathoen, Khama and Sebele go to Britain

In July 1895 the Bakgatla, Bakwena, Barolong, Bangwaketse and Bangwato all sent petitions to London against BSACo rule. Bathoen, Khama and Sebele then decided to take their merafe's cases directly to the British government and people. Between September and November 1895 the three travelled throughout Britain, speaking out against the BSACo in forty different towns and cities.

Their whirlwind tour of Britain was a public relations triumph. They worked closely with the London Missionary Society, which was celebrating its 100th birthday. The dikgosi presented themselves to the British public as good Christians. This was important because missionaries influenced many voters in Britain. Many citizens then pressured the politicians not to allow the Batswana to be handed to Rhodes.

The three dikgosi won support by accusing Rhodes of sinful commerce: "We fear that they will fill our country with liquor shops, as they have Bulawayo and some parts of Mashonaland and Matebeleland." This appeal worked. To Rhodes' frustration Bathoen and Sebele joined Khama in giving up drinking alcohol themselves.

The dikgosi's campaign also attracted support from many imperialists. Some believed that the Colonial Office could run Botswana, not the BSACo. Others who hated imperialism saw Rhodes as an evil man who needed to be stopped. So these people sympathized with the dikgosi's fears:

> You can really see now that what they (the BSACo) really want is not to govern nicely, but to take our land and sell it that they might see gain... the Company have conquered the Matebele and taken the land of the people they conquered. We know the custom: but we have not yet heard that it is the custom of any people to take the best lands of their friends...Where will our cattle stay if the waters are taken from us? They will die. The Company wants to impoverish us so that hunger may drive us to become the white man's servants who dig in his mines and gather his wealth.

By November 6, 1895 the three dikgosi emerged as a threat to Rhodes' timetable for attacking the Transvaal from Botswana. So the Colonial Office told Rhodes that Gangwaketse, Gammangwato and Kweneng would remain under government control. The rest of the Botswana, though, was given to the BSACo.

The dikgosi thus left Britain with the belief that their own territories were secure from Rhodes. But, even this assumption about their ability to keep a half a loaf was incorrect.

The dikgosi are betrayed

Rhodes was soon reassured that the BSACo could get Botswana once the dikgosi went home and the British people forgot about them. The Colonial Office quickly transferred the Balete, Bakgatla and Barolong to Rhodes 'as instalments of a general settlement with the British South Africa Company with regard to the Bechuanaland Protectorate'. By then the Colonial Office was already planning the destruction of Bathoen and Sebele's domains with Hamilton Goold Adams.

Goold Adams had been bribed by Rhodes and had fought for him against the Amandebele. He was appointed to demarcate the Bakwena and Bangwaketse boundaries in order to ensure that they were left with nothing more than tiny, uneconomic locations. It was agreed that the two merafe would only be allocated villages and farm plots permanently occupied by 'proper' Bakwena and Bangwaketse. Most of their cattleposts, pasture and hunting grounds were to become crown lands. This theft was to be justified by concerns about 'the lawfulness of the relations of the Bechuana tribes proper towards the Bakalahari.' Goold Adams' plan was stopped, though, by the Jameson Raid.

Rhodes plans to invade the Transvaal

Dikgosi exchange gifts with Queen Victoria, whom they called Mmamusadinyana.

By 1895 the Colonial Secretary had given Rhodes the go ahead to invade the Transvaal, though the British government was not officially involved. This was because the British government felt the Transvaal was becoming too independent because of the money it got from gold mining. Germany was very active in the Transvaal and so threatened Britain's control of gold throughout the world. Also, the Transvaal government was not listening to British gold mine owners' demands for cheaper transport, black labour and goods. So the Colonial Office decided to let Rhodes try to take over the Transvaal.

As with the occupation of Zimbabwe, Botswana was to be the forward base for the invasion of the Transvaal by BSACo mercenaries. The eastern border was the staging ground. Thus the area between Ramatlabama and Gaborone was given to the BSACo in 1895.

On 23 December, 1895, a month after they had left Britain, Bathoen, Khama and Sebele returned home. At the border a crowd of several thousand gave them a hero's welcome. The dikgosi's mission to Queen Victoria, was praised as a diplomatic triumph which would stop Rhodes taking over the country. But, with a growing number of British troops stationed between Mafikeng and Gaborone it was not clear that they had really succeeded.

On their way to Molepolole, Khama and Sebele saw the armed force being assembled by Rhodes' top mercenary, Dr. L.S. Jameson. According to newspaper reports its target was Mochudi, where Linchwe was supposed to be resisting the loss of some of his land. These reports were deliberate lies designed to trick the Boers. When Jameson's Bechuanaland Police set off from Pitsane Potlhoko on 29 December, 1895, their true destination was Johannesburg.

The Jameson Raid

Jameson's raid was part of a broader plot to overthrow Kruger's Transvaal Republic. Jameson was to invade from Botswana, while British expatriates in Johannesburg were supposed to lead an uprising there.

Despite much secrecy the plan became widely known by Transvaal President Kruger's secret police. The expatriate rebellion failed after most of its leaders were arrested. Meanwhile Jameson's men were surrounded near Krugersdorp, where they surrendered on 2 January, 1896.

The failure of the Jameson Raid resulted in a huge international scandal. Rhodes' political influence in Britain and in Botswana ended because he was disgraced. Rule by the Colonial Office was restored and Goold Adams's boundaries were forgotten.

Due to good luck, Bathoen, Khama and Sebele were able to defeat Rhodes after all. After the fall of Rhodes the dikgosi's mission to the Britain was now seen by Batswana as a heroic success. Over the years a story grew that Queen Victoria had listened to the dikgosi and stopped Rhodes from taking the Protectorate. Of course, if Rhodes had taken the Transvaal the Batswana would have lived under his government.

Rhodes still kept his economic interests in Botswana after 1896. His company owned the railway and the Gaborone, Ghanzi, Lobatse and Tuli Block. It also continued to own mineral rights over most of Botswana.

Questions

1 What is meant by indirect rule?

2 What is the significance to Botswana and Zimbabwe of the 1889 royal charter to the British South Africa company?

3 Why did the British government want to give Botswana to Rhodes after 1890?

4 a. Why was the 1889 Kopong conference held?
   b. What was its outcome?

5 a. How did the Orders-in-Council of 1890 and 1891 effect Botswana?
   b. Why were they issued?

6. a. What was the concessions commission?
   b. Which kgosi refused to recognize its jurisdiction?

7. a. Why did Bathoen, Khama and Sebele go to London?
   b. Did they succeed in getting what they wanted?

8. Describe two ways in which the dikgosi opposed British officials between 1892 and 1894.

Chapter 12
The new Tswana culture

Throughout this book we have seen how life in Botswana changed after the Difaqane. Europeans, whether Boers, missionaries, traders or government officials have appeared regularly. All these people had some influence on the way in which Batswana lived. Perhaps of all these newcomers, the missionaries had the greatest influence on the lives of Batswana.

Mission expansion, 1816-1885

Missionaries came to work among the Batswana very early in the nineteenth century. Various churches started among the Batswana who lived in areas to the south. During the course of the nineteenth century the missions moved north and eventually were found in most parts of Botswana.

The first mission group to work among the Batswana was the London Missionary Society (LMS), a Protestant group from England. In 1816 they established a headquarters among the Batlhaping at Kudumane and they used this place as a base from which to expand their operations.

It was not long before other missionary groups arrived. In the 1820s another Protestant organization called the Wesleyan Missionary Society began to send people to work among the Barolong and Bahurutshe. During the 1830s, a French Protestant group known as the Paris Evangelical Missionary

Society set up a number of stations in the Transvaal among the Bahurutshe. There were also some failed attempts by American Baptists and English Anglicans to move into the same areas.

Before long the LMS became the main missionary organization in the Cape among the Barolong and Batlhaping. Despite being unsuccessful in converting Batswana to Christianity early on, the LMS was able to gain many converts after the Difaqane.

Missionary Wookey and wife.

In most of Africa missionaries did not have much success in converting ordinary citizens to Christianity. Usually they started off by converting the outcasts of society, such as cripples, albinos, orphans, widows, refugees and people from a slave background. This was because Chiefs, elders and free citizens had their own cultures which they liked and did not want to give up. So when the LMS first arrived among the Batlhaping and Barolong, it is not surprising that they converted only a few widows.

The success of the LMS

All this changed around 1830. After the devastation caused by the Difaqane, there were large numbers of Batswana who became refugees. Many of these people ended up moving to Kudumane, where the missionaries offered them land and the chance to lead a peaceful life. Kudumane was then being run by the Rev Robert Moffat, who was a missionary of great charisma. Moffat, like the other early LMS missionaries, had arrived and failed to make any impression on the Batswana. But after six hard years he finally learned Setswana and eventually became a master of the language. He began to relate the Bible to the Batswana in a manner that they appreciated and also translated many English hymns into Setswana. Because of Moffat's abilities, the LMS gained many converts in the northern Cape area during the 1830s.

Due to the LMS's success, the other missionary societies left the area. The Wesleyans ended up concentrating on the Xhosa and the Batswana of the Orange Free State, while the French focused their efforts in Lesotho.

During the 1840s the LMS began to expand to the north. A young minister called David Livingstone was sent to preach in Botswana and he settled among the Bakwena in 1845. Meanwhile, other LMS people worked among the Batswana in the Transvaal.

The LMS and the Boers
Just as the LMS was expanding, it ran into trouble with the Boers of the Transvaal. This is because Livingstone and other missionaries were helping to defend the Batswana from Boer attacks, by supplying them with guns and promoting ties with traders. After the Battle of Dimawe, the Boers expelled the LMS from the Transvaal. They also put pressure on Livingstone to leave the Bakwena, which he did. Livingstone's support for Batswana armies gave the LMS great popularity thereafter.

When the LMS left the Kweneng and the Transvaal, the Boers wanted to replace it with a church that would support Boer rule. For this reason, the Transvaal government approached a German Lutheran group, based in Natal, called the Hermannsburg Missionary Society. In 1857 the Hermannsburg moved into the Kweneng and then also started a church among the Bangwato.
It was only in the mid 1860s when the LMS moved back into Botswana, that Hermannsburg missionaries agreed to concentrate on the Transvaal. Over the next two decades, LMS missionaries were sent among the Bakwena, Bangwato, Bangwaketse and Batawana. By the year 1900 the LMS called Lontone by the Batswana, became the main church in Botswana and had the support of the Batswana dikgosi.

Conversion of the Batswana elite

Who were the people that the missionaries first interacted with and converted to their way of thinking? In the 1830s Robert Moffat and the LMS at Kudumane gained many converts from the Difaqane refugees. In Botswana the situation was different.

Among the Batswana, in contrast to much of Africa, it was the dikgosi, the royal family members and the traditional doctors, who were the first converts. Why was this the case?

It was partly because the LMS and other missionaries concentrated much of their efforts on converting important people as a means of influencing other Batswana. David Livingstone, for instance, converted only a few people. His first and most important convert was Kgosi Sechele. Following this conversion, many of the other leading Bakwena became Christians.

Among the Bangwato, Kgosi Sekgoma opposed Christianity, but once the missionaries converted his eldest son, Khama, it only became a matter of time before Christianity became important. Khama made Christianity the national religion of

An early Motswana evangelist

the Bangwato after 1875 and imposed various laws in accordance with the dictates of the Bible.

All the Batswana dikgosi had adopted Christianity by 1910 and most of them long before that. Chiefs knew that missionaries brought many benefits with them if they were allowed to operate inside Batswana territory. Missionaries knew a lot about the whites so they could explain and give advice to the Chiefs about how to deal with foreigners. Missionaries also encouraged trading and so brought economic benefits to the Batswana. They often brought valuable practical skills with them, whether in irrigation, construction, carpentry, blacksmithing or gun repair. Missionaries also knew how to read and write and were usually willing to teach Batswana how to do the same. So for these reasons, many dikgosi sent messages to the churches asking for a missionary if they did not have one.

Another important group of converts for the missionaries were the dingaka, who opposed Christianity in other parts of Africa. Perhaps the reason why Batswana dingaka liked Christianity was because many of the missionaries who came to Botswana also had medical training and were able to cure diseases. Men like David Livingstone and the Wesleyan, Joseph Ludorf, cured hundreds of people in their journeys. It seems that many dingaka felt that if they adopted Christianity they would gain increased spiritual power. Thus they would have more power to fight witchcraft and disease.

Missionary teaching

Another factor in the spread of Christianity was the fact that many of the Batswana who had been converted at Kudumane were then sent north to work. Because these missionaries spoke Setswana and knew Tswana culture very well, they were able to convert far more people than the European missionaries. For instance, the LMS sent very few European missionaries to the Bangwaketse, yet that morafe had the most Christians in Botswana by the 1890s. This was because African missionaries sent from Kudumane were very active there.

Christian missionaries were also successful in Botswana after Robert Moffat succeeded in translating the Bible into Setswana in 1857. Moffat's translation, which is still used today, brought the Bible to the Batswana in an appealing and poetic style. This was important because the Bible often did not make sense when translated into another language. And as the Jews in the Bible's Old Testament lived in a manner similar to the Batswana, Moffat's translation brought their way of life and the message of Christianity very directly to them.

Before 1890s the LMS's priority was to keep one missionary in each town to spread the word of God. But after 1890, once they had many Batswana to help them, they became interested in making their presence felt more strongly. This they tried to do through education.

Missionaries emphasized education for several reasons. Firstly, they knew that if more people learned to read and write, then those people would read the Bible. They also hoped to preach religion to the people they taught and so build up a large group of churchgoers. By 1900 they had established schools in all the main towns and even in a few smaller villages such as Lehututu. Conditions were very poor and classes were small with all pupils being taught in the same room. The emphasis was on learning, reading, writing and 'arithmetic. Along with this basic education the students were taught Bible lessons.

Not many children attended school in the years before 1910. This was mainly because Batswana children, especially the boys, worked at the cattleposts all year round. Most of the pupils were the children of the richer people and the royal families, who could afford to replace their children as potential workers. Of the poorer students, most were girls.

Batswana from the leading families were thus the first to become well educated. Due to their training they were able to obtain jobs working for the kgosi, traders, churches and government. Many of these Batswana wanted to get more advanced education and traveled as far as Cape Town to attend secondary school. The LMS finally, in 1904, built a Secondary School with an advanced curriculum for African children. Located near Vryburg in the Cape and was known as the Tiger Kloof Native Institute. This school educated hundreds of prominent Batswana.

Other missions

By 1910 the LMS had churches all over the Bangwaketse, Bangwato, Bakwena and Batawana reserves, as well as in the Chobe and in the Matsheng area of the Kgalagadi. Two reserves had different churches. The Hermannsburg Lutherans began working among the Balete in 1858 and have continued to do so to the present day. When the Balete went to Ramotswa, the Hermannsburgers followed and established a school and later a hospital. Meanwhile, the Boer dominated Dutch Reformed Church had first sent missionaries to live among the Bakgatla-ba-ga-Kgafela in 1864. These missionaries followed the Bakgatla-ba-ga-Kgafela into Botswana when they left the Transvaal in 1870 and still work among them today.

Missionaries and Tswana culture

What the missionaries wanted to achieve in Botswana was to change the way people thought and behaved. They were only partly successful. Some parts of Tswana culture did change after Christianity spread, but not very many. This was because the Batswana and the dikgosi chose what they liked about Christianity and mixed these features with their own culture. The Batswana did not just do what the missionaries told them to.

The missionaries demanded that the Batswana prohibit certain parts of their culture. They said that certain parts of Tswana culture were pagan and thus outlawed by God. Christians had to renounce these practices or they would not be allowed into the Church.

The main success of the missionaries was getting most Batswana to adopt Christian beliefs. Batswana came to believe that Modimo, their old God, had a son, Jesus, who had lived among men. In addition to God and Jesus, there were also two other supernatural forces that the Batswana adopted. These were the Holy Spirit, which promoted God's plans and also Satan, who opposed them.

The end of Bogwera and Bojale

All missionaries attacked the bogwera and bojale ceremonies. The missionaries often did this thinking that the Batswana were worshipping spirits at these ceremonies, even though that was not true. Partly the missionaries objected to the killing of one of the boys at bogwera and the use of bongaka at these ceremonies. But perhaps most importantly, the missionaries knew that bogwera taught all youths about traditional culture. They thought that Christianity would spread faster among people who had not been taught about traditional culture and adopt a new way of thinking.

So the missionaries preached against bogwera and put pressure on the dikgosi to end the ceremonies. They also forbade Christians to send their children to initiation. This was not easy, because Batswana felt that only an initiated person could get married and act as an adult. Some Christian parents obeyed their missionaries and kept their children from bogwera, while others sent their children secretly.

Eventually the missionaries succeeded in ending bogwera almost everywhere in Botswana. Khama banned it first, followed by Bathoen, Sebele and later Mathiba in Ngamiland. After 1900 many missionaries came to feel that bogwera had a positive role to play in educating youngsters and along with the kgosi tried to reinstate a modified version which did not include circumcision and bongaka. So it continued for a while among the Bakgatla and Batawana. Of all the Batswana, only the Batlokwa and Balete still continued to openly practice traditional style bogwera by 1940.

Christian marriage

Another change which the missionaries insisted on was that each man should only have one wife. They did this even though there was no law in the Bible to outlaw polygamy. When Sechele became a Christian in 1847, he was forced to divorce three of his wives. Many other Batswana made the same choice.

The ban on polygamy was followed by other new ways for Christians to get married. Early missionaries felt that bogadi was sinful. They felt that to pay bogadi was similar to buying a slave. A marriage, they felt, should be a contract between two

Christians of equal status who would then raise a family and live according to the laws of God. So they introduced wedding ceremonies where a minister joined the couple in marriage in church. In doing so they tried to replace the old system of marriage, when bogadi joined two families together in an alliance.

Not all of the Batswana Christians opposed bogadi and so the custom has carried on to the this day. Among the Bangwato and Batawana bogadi was abolished for a very long time and has only recently reappeared.

Batswana adopt Christianity to their own lifestyle
All the missionaries were very opposed to the practice of bongaka and boloi, which they saw as the work of Satan. So they tried to promote western medicine to replace bongaka and worked hard to get their own members to use western medicine. This effort had very little success, though. Before 1910 the missionaries did not have enough funds to build hospitals and so most Batswana had to rely on traditional healing. In addition, most Batswana continued to believe in bongaka no matter what the missionaries said. For instance, Kgosi Sechele, one of Botswana's first Christians, kept using bongaka and boloi for the rest of his life. Even those Batswana who became Christians believed that boloi was being used all around them. Many dingaka continued to practice their trade after being converted. These Christian dingaka used the spiritual power of the new religion to improve their own curing ability.

Christian missionaries also opposed rainmaking, which they believed was a pagan practice. Before the end of the century most of the dikgosi had stopped it and instead held Christian prayer services at the start of the rainy season to appeal to God for rain.

The missionaries often went beyond what was in the Bible when they tried to make the Batswana change their customs. For instance, the missionaries tried very hard to get the dikgosi to ban the drinking of alcohol, even though Jesus was known to drink wine. Because of missionary pressure, many dikgosi starting with Khama banned the brewing of bojalwa and khadi. This law did not, however, prevent many Batswana from making and drinking alcohol.

Bolata was also attacked by missionaries when they preached to Batswana about improving their society. Batswana were told that all men were equal before God and that it was therefore a sin for people to own other people. A few Batswana Christians freed their malata, but most refused to do so. Nor did the dikgosi do anything to end bolata. However, in the southern areas of Botswana many malata fled to work in South Africa. So the importance of bolata was reduced in places like Kweneng, Gangwaketse and Kgatleng. In Ngamiland and the Central District bolata continued for a very long time, with many of the owners being Christians.

Some Christian practices were quickly adopted by the Batswana. One was wedding ceremonies. Another new practice was baptism. It replaced the traditional ceremony where dingaka gave protection to newly born children. Instead babies were now treated with holy water by Christian priests. Another example can be found in burials. Traditionally, the Batswana had buried their dead under their cattle kraals under piles of rocks, or their houses. Under missionary influence, burials began to be done in graveyards, with the deceased only being buried after a service conducted according to Christian rites. Missionaries also brought religious holidays, like Christmas and Easter, on which services were held and people were not supposed to work. Likewise, the churches brought with them the calendar and set their services on Sundays. Prior to this, the Batswana did not have any kind of calendar, though they kept a vague count of years. After Christianity came a new rhythm of life was adopted and the concept of the week was introduced, with all people getting Sunday to rest and worship.

The rise of the independent churches

Before the 1890s, all the churches in southern Africa were run by whites. Sometimes they allowed Africans to be in control of a church in a certain village, but these people were not allowed to decide their own policies and sets of beliefs. Because of this, a number of Africans began to criticise their churches, saying that they should have more say in church affairs.

Eventually African Christians began to break away and establish their own churches. This movement was called Ethiopianism. In 1892 in the Cape Province a man called Mangena Mokoni broke away from the Wesleyans, claiming the Wesleyans were racists. He felt that the Wesleyans ignored blacks in church and educational affairs. He founded the Ethiopian Church and soon other black priests began to create their own churches. Hence Ethiopianism spread very fast.

Ethiopianism quickly reached Botswana, because similar conditions affected black ministers there. In 1893 a trained LMS Mongwaketse minister known as Mothowagae Motlogelwa began to assert his independence. He began a school in Kanye which did not charge school fees and competed for students against the LMS school which was not free. This stance eventually brought him into conflict with Kgosi Bathoen, who was a member of the LMS and who viewed it as the only official church in his territory. As Mothowagae became increasingly popular with LMS members and students, the jealous white missionaries tried to send him to live in Lehututu.

At this point Mothowagae separated from the church with about 100 other LMS members and formed the King Edward Bangwaketse Mission Church. This was the first independent church in Botswana. Mothowagae came into conflict with both Bathoen and his successor, Seepapitso and he was eventually exiled to Lekgolobotlo in 1910. But between 1902 and 1910 Mothowagae was successful in organizing three church branches in the Bangwaketse area. He converted Gobuamang, kgosi of the Bakgatla-ba-ga-Mmanaana at Moshupa and most of the LMS members there.

Mothowagae was not the only man to form an independent church in the period before 1910. There was also the Bakhurutshe Free Church in the Tati. Other Africans also preached the Ethiopian message. A number of these ministers went to work among the Bangwato, but always met with stiff opposition from Khama and his fellow LMS members.
In 1901 five Ethiopians began preaching in Palapye and Khama quickly put them on trial because he and other Bangwato alleged the foreigners had asked the Bangwato to worship them. The men were found guilty and their huts were burned down. Their Bangwato supporters were also fined. In later years, Khama and local government officials put other Ethiopians in prison.

All the early Ethiopians met with opposition from the dikgosi and the government and were unable to build up support early on. In later decades, however, a number of independent churches such as Zion Christian Church (ZCC) would go on to build up a large following across Botswana.

Other Tswana cultures
It was not only the missionaries who brought new ways of life to the Batswana. Other Europeans such as traders and government officials also introduced changes.

Traders brought all sorts of goods with them to sell to Batswana and many of these things met with willing buyers. As soon as these traders came to Botswana, they realized that women were interested in buying materials with which to decorate themselves and improve their appearance. For centuries Batswana women had used a shiny kind of clay, known as sebilo, which they put on their hair or on their skin to keep it moist.

Western clothing
White traders had lots of such things to sell, including beads, which were popular until the 1870s. After the 1870s Batswana women began adopt European clothing. Traditionally, Batswana women wore blankets made of leather or skins, which they stitched together and hung around their necks.

They also wore large leather aprons around their waists. But after the 1870s, more of them began to buy clothes from the traders. They wore these clothes to church or weddings and funerals. They bought dresses, scarves, hats and even white bridal gowns for when they got married. Whereas most people used to go barefoot or in sandals, more women began to buy shoes and boots after the arrival of traders.

Batswana men were also quick to adopt western clothes, which they saw whites wearing. Most men began wearing hats, which were useful in a hot and sunny country like Botswana. They also adopted trousers and shirts, which replaced loincloths and blankets draped over the shoulders. Batswana learned how to sew the new kinds of clothes using leather and animal skins.

The new elite

Traders did most of their business with the wealthy people within the Batswana communities. These included the kgosi, his closest relatives and other individuals who produced goods for sale. Because the kgosi controlled most of the trade with outsiders, he and his close supporters gained a lot of wealth from trade. Only after the 1870s or even later, were other individuals allowed to have open and direct dealings with traders when important goods such as ivory or feathers were traded.

To an extent, the members of the new elite lived extravagantly. Kgosi Sechele, for instance, had in his home crystal chandeliers, fine porcelain and silver and even a machine that made soda water. One of his later wives, an Amadebele princess, enjoyed drinking French champagne. Other examples could be given from across Botswana, because some people spent a lot of money on fancy clothing and food.

A new diet

Traders also made a huge difference in the way that normal people behaved, for instance in the way they ate. Long ago, Batswana ate very little meat. They lived mainly on a diet of sorghum, milk, beans and a few vegetables such as squashes and pumpkins. The Batswana drank water, milk or one of the brewed beverages made from sorghum that had small amounts of alcohol. Occasionally, Batswana would eat the meat of animals they hunted or perhaps that of an animal that had died. Only rarely did Batswana kill one of their livestock for food. When traders arrived in Botswana they brought with them mealie meal, a flour made out of maize. Because this was the cheapest kind of starchy food available for money, it soon became a very popular thing for Batswana to eat. In many families it even replaced sorghum as the principal part of the diet. Maize meal was also the main type of food given to workers at the mines, where many Batswana learned to eat it. Although this kind of food was almost unknown about 100 years ago, today it is the most common part of the Batswana staple diet and is locally known as phaletshe.

The early traders sold tea, coffee and sugar to the Batswana. These were previously unknown and offered a great deal of variety to the Batswana diet. Sugar was popular for two reasons: it replaced honey, which was scarce as a sweetener for food and it enabled Batswana to brew beer with a much higher alcohol content. Before sugar arrived, bojalwa had very little alcohol. With sugar added the mixture became more potent. Drunkenness became a far more serious problem among the Batswana. This is perhaps why several kgosi, including Khama, Bathoen and Sekgoma Letsholathebe, outlawed the brewing of strong alcohol at the turn of the century.

Early traders to the Batswana also sold large amounts of hard liquor, concentrating on sales of a potent brandy known as Cape Smoke. These sales stopped, at least legally, after 1890 because the government outlawed the sale of liquor to Africans. So Batswana had to be content with drinking bojalwa and this only if their kgosi allowed them to do so.

Efficient tools

Other items brought by whites allowed Batswana to do more work with less effort. Guns made hunting easier and allowed the main merafe to become rich through selling ivory and other game products. Many wealthy Batswana bought wagons, which made transport much easier. Wagons replaced oxen, which allowed bigger loads to be carried. They were helpful to the Batswana, who moved constantly between the village, lands and cattle post.

Important for farmers were the ploughs brought by the traders. These allowed people to cultivate large areas with much less effort. Before all ploughing was done by hand with a hoe. But by letting oxen or donkeys pull a ploughshare, Batswana were able to produce more crops. Because wagons were available, it was possible for people with large yields of crops to transport the produce into town where they could sell it. This type of farming was only practiced by the wealthier Batswana, who could afford the high prices for ploughs and wagons. But once they had bought these items, they could make a lot of money by selling their crops to traders.

Negative effects

There were some negative effects of the trade boom, however. Goods sold by the traders were often much cheaper than those produced by Batswana artisans, especially iron goods and clothes. This meant that Batswana blacksmiths were forced out of business and today these skills have vanished. Sewing remained for longer than blacksmithing, but by the 1930s was being done by fewer individuals.

A further negative effect of trade was the destruction of Botswana's wildlife and forests, which were very rich natural resources long ago. Early European traders slaughtered thousands of animals and Batswana were able to do the same once they bought guns. No one knows how many animals were killed, but today game is only found in a small portion of the country. Before the 1850s big game could be found in abundance almost everywhere.

Conclusion

A number of changes, religious, social and technological came to the Batswana after the arrival of Europeans. These changes affected some Batswana, but not all. There were not many Europeans in Botswana and not everyone lived near them. Many Batswana who opposed Christianity stuck to a traditional lifestyle. Many Batswana were too poor to obtain the goods that traders had to offer and only a small percentage of children went to school.

More Europeans arrived in Botswana after 1885 once the Protectorate was declared. But these whites, unlike the missionaries, believed in a policy of segregation because they thought they were superior to blacks. Many of these whites lived apart from the Batswana and rarely mixed with them socially. For this reason they did not have much impact on local culture.

From 1840 to 1910 the main changes that occurred in the Batswana way of life were almost all due to the influence of

Europeans. Batswana tended to pick what they liked about European culture, rather than adopt everything they saw. So the Batswana banned bogwera, but they continued to use age regiments; they adopted Christianity, but they continued to believe in bongaka; and they ended rainmaking, but began holding prayer services for rain.

Some parts of Tswana culture changed a great deal. The new kinds of food and clothing almost completely replaced the older types. Christianity became part of everyday life, replacing the old forms of ancestor worship.

Some aspects of Tswana culture remained the same. Bogosi was unchanged, as was the way in which society was held together by the different wards. Even after culture changed, the same families were running the merafe in much the same way as in traditional times. Some of the laws they used to run public events and judge kgotla cases were new, but probably most of their procedure was based on the ways of past generations.

Questions

1 What made Robert Moffat such an important missionary?

2 Which Batswana were the first to adopt Christianity?

3 Describe three ways in which missionaries tried to change Tswana culture.

4 Why did some people try to form Ethiopian churches?

5 What new foods did the Batswana adopt?

6 Which group do you think had more influence on Batswana, missionaries or traders?

Chapter 13
The Mid 1890's Years of Pestilence

During the 1890s the Bechuanaland Protectorate suffered the worst series of natural disasters in its modern history. Years of drought, combined with terrible locust invasions, made it impossible to grow food. At the same time, a terrible new disease, rinderpest, killed about 90% of the country's cattle and a large number of game animals. During this period about 20% of the human population died.

Droughts

Botswana, of course, is a semi arid country that has good rains on an irregular basis. Many elderly people in Botswana say that in 'the old days' it rained every year, but this is not true. During the 1800s there were many severe drought periods.

Droughts were recorded in every decade during the century, with the worst ones being in 1845-51, 1856-62 and 1876-9. The second of these dry periods was particularly severe, and many people died of starvation after a series of crop failures. In times of famine, disease was spread quickly. In 1862, smallpox killed a large number of people.

Because the Batswana lived in such a dry environment, they had developed ways for coping with such problems. People who owned goats, cattle and sheep would, if their crops failed, exchange some of their animals for sorghum. This they could do with Batswana in their own village, those in other villages or perhaps they could sell their stock to white traders. Another way of getting food in times of drought was to hunt. In the nineteenth century there were large game herds in all areas of Botswana. Alternatively people could forage, that is, gather wild fruits and nuts to eat. All the peoples of Botswana knew how to gather such foods.

Migration

People could also survive tough times by finding a job. During the nineteenth century there were not many paid jobs available inside Botswana. Most people were independent farmers who worked for themselves or with family members. Batswana began to look for jobs beyound the Orange river away from the fighting. During the Difaqane some went to work on farms in the Cape Colony in the 1830s, where they herded cattle and sheep. As commercial farming expanded beyond the Cape into the Transvaal later on, more and more Batswana entered the work force.

People who migrate, that is travel far from their homes, to find a job are known as migrant workers. During the nineteenth century the number of Batswana who engaged in migrant labour was not high, but it was continually increasing. After the 1840s, Batswana stopped migrating to the Cape, but many began to work for Boer farmers in the Transvaal after the Batswana Boer War was over. Usually, such people were paid a cow or two a year, about the same rate as if they had worked for Batswana cattleowners.

After diamonds were discovered in Kimberley in 1867, a huge diamond industry developed and this needed large numbers of workers. Many Batswana, along with other southern Africans walked long distances to Kimberley to get work. Most migrants were young men who wanted money to buy a gun or perhaps to buy cattle to pay bogadi. Presumably, other migrants went to the mines to avoid starvation during drought.

Disasters of the 1890s

Locusts had not been seen in Botswana for many decades when they began appearing around 1890. At first, they were merely a nuisance and provided people with variety in their diet. As the 1890s went on the locust swarms became bigger and spread all over the country.

When the rains failed, in 1895, there was no great problem because grain had been stored. But the 1896 rains also failed and whatever had grown was eaten by locusts. A missionary reported:

> **All of the tribes, except perhaps Linchwe's (the Bakgatla), are at present very short of food and many have not sufficient food for their families. They are, however, making an effort to obtain money for the purpose of buying food by going out to work in Kimberley, Jagersfontein, Johannesburg and other places.**

Rinderpest

That same year the drought was compounded by a cattle disease that was more devastating than any other animal disease before or since. This disease was called rinderpest. In Setswana it was known as bolowane. Rinderpest was unknown to Africa before 1893. The Italian army that invaded Ethiopia brought in infected cattle from outside Africa. Because African animals had never been exposed to the disease before, they had no way of resisting it. When a disease comes to a continent for the first time, the situation is called a virgin soil epidemic. These epidemics always result in very high mortality for the species that are attacked.

Rinderpest started in Ethiopia in 1893 and spread south, through East Africa and down through Malawi and Rhodesia. It killed approximately 90 per cent of the cattle in areas that it passed through. But it not only killed cattle, but also many other hoofed animals such as zebra, wildebeest, antelopes and buffalo. It did not kill small mammals, birds or small stock.

The governments in southern Africa knew that rinderpest was going to arrive. But in the 1890s governments in the area were not very powerful and lacked money and manpower. There were no cordon fences then to stop animals moving from one area to another. Travelers used oxen to pull their wagons and so cattle were moving over large distances and spreading the disease quickly. Most governments tried to stop cattle moving along the main roads if they suspected rinderpest was in the area. But this method did not work as people could travel on other roads.

In 1896 rinderpest reached Botswana from Rhodesia and it devastated the cattle along the main road from Francistown to Lobatse. This road was then the main route between South Africa and Rhodesia. In Botswana, as in other parts of Africa, about 90% of cattle died. One traveler, stranded at Ramotswa in May, wrote:

> **Hundreds of dead oxen lying in every stage of decomposition, behind the bushes, in places a dozen a batch! The whole air was vitiated by the stench of them and amidst them we had to camp! I observed that the natives were busily skinning all the dead beasts and apparently making biltong of the flesh ... I don't see how this country can escape a famine now, their crops have all failed from drought and the remnants are eaten by locusts; their cattle are nearly all dead! I suppose a score of live cattle where there should**

have been a thousand or two! Khama alone is said to have lost 70,000 or 90,000 head.

Rinderpest was a tragedy because it destroyed the means by which the Batswana could have avoided starvation. But now there was no cattle to sell for food and no animals to be hunted. All the common game animals, such as springbok, gemsbok, zebra, wildebeest and others, had died just like the cattle.

People began to starve. And 20% of Batswana had died. Not all people died of starvation, but because lack of food weakened them, they often died of diseases like dysentery, malaria and influenza.

Averting the disaster

During 1897 the Batswana were only lucky in one way. The British South Africa Company was building a railway line from the Cape to Rhodesia along the old road through eastern Botswana. Building this railway required a lot of workers, who were obtained from the Batswana living along the railway, like the Bangwaketse, Bakwena, Bakgatla and Bangwato. Many men made some money working in construction. Others made money by transport riding. This is the taking of goods and people between villages by wagon, and had been the highest paying job for many years.

But by the end of the year, the railway had passed through the country to Bulawayo. When it was finished, many Batswana found themselves with no work. With the railway finished and no jobs available locally, Batswana left for South Africa to find work. Villages like Molepolole, Kanye and Mochudi became empty of men, due to the large numbers of deaths and the loss of men to migrant labour.

At this time of need, some British citizens in London stepped in to help the Batswana avoid starvation. They sent food on the train to Gaborone and offered it free to the Batswana. At first, chiefs like Sebele and Bathoen refused to take it, as they valued their independence. But as starvation continued, they relented and sent wagons regularly to get supplies. Khama also refused to take free food, insisting that Bangwato pay the wholesale cost of the food. However, some of his people traveled south and got it free.

In Ngamiland there was no free food distribution as it was too far from the railway. Kgosi Sekgoma took drastic measures there and managed to stop the spread of rinderpest in certain areas by restricting travel. He kept control over existing food to make sure there was no famine. He also took care of orphaned children, sending them out to places where cattle still existed.

During the period of famine, a new way was found to raise some money. After the construction of the railway, it became possible to send wood to Kimberley very easily on the train. Batswana living close to the railway began to cut down trees and sell the timber.

By 1910 almost all of the area along the railway line had no trees left. By cutting so much wood, the Batswana sacrificed long term agricultural prosperity for short term gain. Areas that have no trees tend to be less fertile and more susceptible to drought than areas with forest. No new forests were planted as replacements.

Taxation and its effect on migrant labour

Government officers were not so unhappy that the Batswana had suffered a disaster. Many of them hoped that the collapse of farming would force Batswana to get wage paying jobs and thus serving the imperialists.

In Botswana and indeed throughout Africa, the government demanded hut tax which forced Africans to work. Colonial governments did this because they needed money to pay for their own activities. But they also wanted to force Africans out of agriculture and into taking up jobs. They wanted them to earn money, so that they would buy European products. Europeans also knew that if lots of Africans went to work, then wages would decrease. This was important at a time in history when there not enough people to work in South Africa's mines and businesses.
So in 1899 the government imposed hut tax on all adult men in the Bechuanaland Protectorate. Under the new law, each man had to pay £1 a year in cash to the government.

Nowadays £1 does not sound like a lot of money, but then it was difficult for most men to come up with the amount. This was because there were very few jobs in the Protectorate, which had no large scale business or industry. In addition, now that many cattle were dead and there were few animals left to hunt, few people had any goods that they could sell for cash. Hut tax was introduced at a time when very few people could afford to pay it.

What happened in Botswana is that large numbers of men were forced to leave the country and engage in migrant labour in order to pay their hut tax. Prior to 1899 migrant labour occurred only at times of distress or when someone needed to earn the money to buy something, like a gun. But after taxation began far more people were forced to become migrants.

The government used the money obtained from the hut tax to pay its own officials. Most of these officials were policemen, whose main duty was to collect taxes. Very little money that the government collected went towards helping Batswana increase their standard of living. Few roads were built and there were no government sponsored schools or hospitals for many decades.

Going to South Africa

There was no law that had more impact on the lives of ordinary Batswana, than the one that introduced hut tax to the country. For the next 70 years, most young men would be forced to leave the country in order to find money.

A significant number of men went to work at either the

Kimberley diamond mine or the Johannesburg gold mines. This was the easiest way to obtain work. The mines had employees, called recruiters, in all the villages. These men signed up Batswana to work at the mines, usually for a year, at a set rate per month (usually £3). This arrangement was known as a contract. Mine recruits also got free transport to the mines, as well as free accommodation and food.

Others did not want to work at the mines. They thought that the wages at the mines were very low and that the work was very hard. Also, they did not like the fact that mine workers could not leave the mines after work was finished and that they were forced to work for one contract without a holiday. These people usually walked to Johannesburg or some other town in South Africa, to look for a job outside of mining.

This group of migrants tried to find jobs in businesses, such as factories and shops, or worked for railroads or in construction. These jobs paid more money than the mines, but did not offer free accommodation or food. Batswana with such jobs had to find a house to rent and cope with living costs.

Almost all of Botswana's migrants went to work in South Africa, because it had the highest wages. There were much smaller groups who went to work in Rhodesia, such as Bakalanga who went to Bulawayo and Basubia who worked on the railways and at the Rhodesian mines. Many residents of the Kgalagadi and from northern parts of Ngamiland went to Namibia, where they herded livestock for white farmers.

Women did not have to pay hut tax, because the government wanted to keep them in the Protectorate to engage in agriculture and look after children while their husbands were working in South Africa. In the southern parts of the

Protectorate, though, many women migrated. Initially this was because of starvation. Later on they went for other reasons.

Along Botswana's border with South Africa, there were many Boer farmers who needed people to work for them for low wages. Some Batswana women liked working there because it was close to their homes and it provided them with a way to make money. Sometimes, a family might send one of its daughters to go and earn cash while the rest farmed at home. Many other women, often unmarried, went to work in South African towns, earning higher wages as maids or factory workers.

Almost all of the Batswana migrants returned to live inside the Protectorate. Younger men would work for a number of contracts and then come back and buy cattle. After that, they would be able to sell a beast every year and thus pay their taxes. Other men bought ploughs and tried to increase their yields from agriculture, in order to sell part of the crop to pay taxes. Batswana women tended to return home in order to marry.

The Langeberg rebellion and its effect on Batswana thinking

Why did the Batswana not protest against the fact that hut tax was imposed upon them at a time when they were suffering so horribly? It was not because they failed to realize how difficult it would be for them to pay. Nor because they were grateful for the food the British gave them. The Batswana had seen what had happened to Batswana in South Africa who had resisted hut tax.

In the Cape Colony the Batlhaping and Barolong had been affected by rinderpest and drought just like the residents of the Bechuanland Protectorate. But they were also very bitter about the way the British had treated them. For instance, in 1886, just after the British arrived to protect them, the Batlhaping and Barolong lost 92% of their land to their protectors.

Later, in 1896, when rinderpest was coming through the Bechuanaland Protectorate, the British authorities in the Cape began shooting Batswana cattle there because they claimed it was African cattle that were spreading rinderpest. When rinderpest arrived, the British continued shooting many Batswana cattle. Of course, a Motswana cannot just stand by if his cattle are killed and people began to get angry.

In 1897, when rinderpest had arrived and droughts had caused famine, the British authorities imposed the hut tax on the Batlhaping and Barolong. The Batlhaping, led by Kgosi Luka Jantjie and Kgosi Galeshwe, decided to rebel against British rule. Luka and his Batlhaping retreated into the Langeberg

Hills, where they were surrounded during a five month siege.

Eventually, after the death of over 1,500 men, the Batlhaping were defeated and many of their leaders were executed. Luka, who had been killed in battle, had his head cut off, which a British officer boiled in his kitchen to obtain the skull as a trophy. Meanwhile, about 4,000 Batlhaping were captured and sent to Cape Town, where they were forced to work for white farmers like slaves for many years. This group consisted largely of women and children.

The Batswana in the Protectorate knew what the British were doing in the Cape. Bathoen I of the Bangwaketse called Luka a hero, saying in kgotla "they have killed him, but they did so after he had fought". At that moment he turned to a British policeman, asking him: "How do the white men fight?" He was told, "When the government fights no one gets the best against it; the government always wins".

Now, when Botswana has one of Africa's richest economies, with mining and business and large towns, it is hard to imagine that none of this existed less than thirty years ago. Today very few Batswana work outside their own country, but prior to independence very few worked inside it.

Before 1910 the Bechuanaland Protectorate had no European type of towns of any size, nor did it offer any jobs in business. Not everybody had cattle that could be sold for money. Africans were also excluded from engaging in trading and business. For this reason, the country was highly vulnerable to the kind of troubles that occurred in the 1890s. Severe droughts and loss of cattle led to mass starvation.

So poor was the country, that when the British government demanded £1 from every man, whole villages lost their adult male populations for most of the year. The way in which life was lived changed drastically. In many areas, especially in the south, more than half the population was absent most of the time. Women, children and the elderly remained and they relied to a large extent on money sent to them by their male relatives.

Batswana and the South African War, 1899-1902

Perhaps the main factor that reduced suffering after the disasters of the mid 1890s was the outbreak of the South African War, better known as the Boer War. This war broke out in 1899, after many years of tension between the Boer republic in the Transvaal and the British. The British government wanted to increase British participation in the Transvaal's huge gold mining industry. The Boers refused to back down in the face of British pressure.

Both the British and the Boers tried to keep Africans out of the fighting. They said they were fighting a white man's war. But Africans, including the Batswana, often took part in the action. All the Batswana merafe sided with the British.

When fighting broke out the Boers decided to try to take Khama's capital, Palapye. They wanted to disrupt the British effort by controlling the railway. Khama's men were mobilized rapidly and British troops came in by train. Due to this quick response, the Boers backed off and no fighting took place in Gammangwato.

In the south, the Boers approached Sebele and they agreed not to fight against each other. Bathoen and his Bangwaketse also agreed to stay out of the fighting. Only the Bakgatla, as we shall see, entered the war.

Batswana benefited from the war, because large numbers of British troops entered the Protectorate. A couple of years of reasonable rains allowed Batswana not only to eat, but to sell their crop to the British at very high prices. Many jobs were available at the British camps so there was no need to migrate. During most of the war, the railway was disrupted so Batswana with wagons could earn money by transport riding.

Another way of earning cash was undertaken by more daring people. The Boers had surrounded the British garrison of Mafikeng, which was then the Protectorate's capital. This siege lasted for many months, during which time the inhabitants of Mafikeng had very little food. This inhabitants relied on Africans who brought food close to town and smuggled it in at night while the Boers were asleep. Bakwena, Bangwaketse and Barolong men made a lot of money from this smuggling, because they were in a position to demand high prices. However, many were caught by the Boers.

The Battle of Derdepoort

The Bakgatla of Kgosi Linchwe were very involved in the war. At the outset of the fighting, the British mistakenly thought he might join the war on the Boer side. But Linchwe did not want to join with the people he had fled from thirty years before. Soon after the war began Boer soldiers began to raid Bakgatla cattle posts. They also set up a military camp just across the border from Linchwe, at Derdepoort.

When the British approached Linchwe to help them fight the Boers at Derdepoort, he agreed. The British wanted to do all the fighting themselves but wanted Linchwe's men to guide and support them.

An attack was planned on 25 November 1899, at dawn. Three Bakgatla regiments joined a small British force that was armed with a rapid firing machine gun, the most deadly weapon of that time. The attack was to begin at dawn when the British were to fire on the Boer camp from some hills above. Linchwe's men were eager to fight and began to fire shots. Then they found that the British had left. They kept fighting, pouring rifle fire into the Boer camp from the hillsides. Without British help, the Bakgatla won a clear victory, killing 20 Boers and taking many prisoners.

Why had the British not taken part in the battle? It was due to cowardice. The British got afraid just before the battle and left without telling the Bakgatla. After Linchwe's victory, the British commander, Col. Holsworth, claimed that Linchwe was not following orders and had attacked the Boers without permission.

After winning this victory with no help from the British who were supposed to be protecting him, Linchwe fought the rest of the war against the Boers without paying attention to what the British said. Fighting continued, because Linchwe had not succeeded in driving the Boers out of the Derdepoort area. In December, the Boers retaliated and burned down Sikwane. Linchwe responded in the following months by sending his men to operate in the Transvaal, where they cut off the Boer supplies going to Derdepoort. Due to this pressure, the Boers were forced to pull out.

After the war

In the months that followed, Bakgatla soldiers were sent on cattle raiding expeditions against Boer farmers in the Transvaal. They captured at least 10,000 animals. As a result, the Bakgatla were able to rebuild their herds that had been reduced by rinderpest. By 1901 the Bakgatla men controlled most of the countryside between Derdepoort and Rustenburg. The Boer farmers had been forced to leave. This was land that the Bakgatla had lived on before the Boers arrived in the 1840s.

Once the war was over, Linchwe asked the British for the rights over this land. However, the British protectors once again betrayed their African allies. All over South Africa many Africans had helped the British against the Boers, because they hoped the British would replace Boer rule with a democratic system.

But British policy insisted that the defeated Boers should be treated well so that they would live in a united South Africa. The British gave them all their land back and changed none of their racist laws. Africans, who had supported the British, were left even worse off than before the war.

Questions

1 How did people usually cope with drought in the nineteenth century?

2 What was rinderpest?

3 In what new ways did the Batswana cope with the disasters of the 1890s?

4   a. What was hut tax?
    b. How did it affect the lives of Batswana?

5   a. Did any of your parents, grandparents or older relatives become migrants?
    b. Describe where they worked and what job they had.

6   Why did Batswana not oppose hut tax?

7   In what ways did the Batswana participate in the South African War?

Chapter 14
The Kgalagadi and Chobe

The Kgalagadi and Chobe are Botswana's least densely populated areas. Due to extreme lack of surface water, very few people can live in the Kgalagadi desert, which runs diagonally from Tsabong north east to Chobe. Most residents of the Kgalagadi are Khoe and Bakgalagadi. The two main centres of population in the Kgalagadi were Matsheng and Ghanzi. Chobe is equally dry, with the exception of the area along the Chobe river. Due to the prevalence of tsetse fly and mosquito in the river valley, it also supports a small population. Most Chobe residents are Basubia or Bekahune.

Matsheng, centre of the Bakgalagadi

In the Matsheng area, there are four large pans in close proximity, Hukuntsi, Lehututu, Lokgwabe and Tshane. Matsheng is the base of the Bangologa section of the Bakgalagadi.

Over time the Bangologa of the Matsheng area became heavily involved in the trade of skins to the Barolong and Batlhaping to the south. Every year large groups of Bakgalagadi would leave home with many animal skins, such as jackal skins and sell them for goods such as iron, sebilo, grain and tobacco. The Barolong would then sew the skins into clothes and blankets.

The Bangologa of Matsheng remained independent of Bangwaketse control for most of the nineteenth century. In the

1830s Sebego ruled the area in a violent fashion for several years and occasionally would also visit the area to demand tribute. But for the most part chiefs such as Serame and Lenyadi ruled their own people. Bangologa traded up into the Ghanzi area and in Ngamiland and as a result they settled far and wide. In the 1850s the Bangwaketse made some attempts to take over the Matsheng area. They never really succeeded in this as their time was often taken up by internal feuds and wars with other groups, such as the Barolong.

Throughout the nineteenth century regions of the Kgalagadi, including the Matsheng area, was that of the Batswana tried to dominate trade and politics. They did not always succeed in political domination, but often became involved in trade.

For instance, Kgosi Sebego took many of his people from Gangwaketse into the Kgalagadi after he fought with the Amandebele in 1832. First he set himself up in Matsheng, where he worked hard to establish his political domination over the Bakgalagadi. He demanded tribute from the Bangologa and Bashaga and when a group of them refused he even burned a whole village of them alive. Once he had control of Matsheng, he moved most of his people north to Ghanzi. After 1835 he attempted to subdue the area's Basarwa and Bakgalagadi and to take over the trade going south from Ghanzi to Matsheng to the northern Cape.

Sebego was at first successful, as his mephato were the strongest around. However, his subjects kept harassing him and Sebego had to use force to maintain his authority. Around 1838, Sebego's followers were destroyed by outbreaks of malaria and his cattle found Ghanzi too dry for their liking. He was forced to retreat to Matsheng, which remained his base until 1844. Despite his best efforts, Sebego and his followers (who made up about half of the Bangwaketse) were unable to prosper in the desert. Eventually they left for the Cape, where Sebego was murdered by his enemies.

Bakgalagadi traditions make it clear that they resisted the control of Sebego. One famous Mongologa named Mosuswe is said to have led this resistance in both Matsheng and Ghanzi. He is also said to have fought against other Batswana such as the Batawana.

Ghanzi

The area of Botswana with the largest proportion of Khoesian is Ghanzi. A Khoe speaking group known as the Naro live here. Ghanzi is a region in the western Kgalagadi with an abundance of limestone wells and pans. It has sweet grasses and is fairly well wooded. Well into the late nineteenth century it had a large game population, including big elephant and rhino herds.

The Naro-Khoe had a varied lifestyle. The men hunted animals with bows and arrows and the women gathered wild fruits. But they also were heavily involved in trading as goods from the Okavango were being sent south to be exchanged on the border of what is now South Africa. Acting as go betweens for other groups, they traded ivory egg shell beads, skins and feathers in exchange for tobacco, beads and millet. Moreover, the Naro-Khoe had artisans of their own who made excellent karosses and bone arrow points. They also had smiths to work the metal that they got from the north. This trade must have had its origins in the eighteenth century.

Dukuri's rise to power

When Sebego left the Ghanzi area in the 1830s, a new leader emerged among the Naro-Khoe. This was Dukuri, who organized cattle raids and military expeditions against his neighbours. When white traders began entering his territory in the early 1850s, he sold ivory to them. Dukuri ranked among the more powerful Basarwa leaders, most of whom lived in Namibia. According to Naro-Khoe tradition, Dukuri ruled in this way:

> He stayed over the entire region between Rietfontein in the west, the Grootlaagte in the north, Okwa in the south and deeply in the sandveld along the Epikuro. In the dry season he stayed at Ghanse and Kautsa and in the rainy season he hunted along the Grootlaagte. He was very mighty and surrounded himself with Bushmen at all times . . . His houses were filled with spears and other weapons. He was the supreme warlord. At his summons the Bushmen had to assemble versus neighbouring tribes. He collected annual tribute from the (Naro-Khoe) families, consisting of skins, ivory, ostrich eggshell necklaces and other items. He was, moreover, the supreme judge who adjudicated over family disputes . . . The honor of a kgosi was hereditary in those days and the Bushmen were totally independent. The Batuana (Batawana) did not dare to set foot into their region and the Hottentots only entered it on raids.

Dukuri's downfall

Dukuri's most daring action, which eventually led to his downfall, took place while the Batawana were fighting the Bakololo in 1854 (see chapter 8). During the confusion, Dukuri's men captured large numbers of Batawana cattle. Over the next few years Letsholathebe sent out men to try to get his cattle back. He was unable to defeat the Naro-Khoe, however. Finally, in 1858 Letsholathebe invited Dukuri and other Naro-Khoe leaders to his capital to conclude a peace settlement. Instead of extending friendship Letsholathebe killed them in cold blood. For the next forty years the Naro-Khoe were subject to the Batawana.

Letsholathebe subsequently made the Naro-Khoe malata. As such, the Naro-Khoe had to pay tribute, provide herding and hunting labour when asked and send children to work as domestic servants in the homes of Batawana royals.
Batawana established large cattle posts in the area and headmen gathered tribute. Meanwhile, the Naro-Khoe were given guns to hunt with, with the profits going to the Batawana.

Van Zyl settlers in Ghanzi
This situation changed slightly in 1874 when a Boer from the Transvaal named Hendrik Van Zyl asked to settle in Ghanzi with some of his friends. Letsholathebe agreed, because some Nama Khoe from Namibia had been raiding Ghanzi and presenting problems. He let the well armed Boers run the area on condition that he receive one half of all ivory they shot. Van Zyl, who the Batawana called Raubase, was to be the headman of Ghanzi and was not to interfere in the affairs of other Batawana districts.

Van Zyl did very well as a Motawana headman, using Naro-Khoe labourers to cultivate his fields and tend his thousands of cattle. He also gave his subjects firearms and horses to go hunt for him. The wealth he generated through ivory and trading enabled him to erect a lavish two storey house with stained glass windows and carpets. When Letsholathebe died there was no strong Tawana leader until 1876. Van Zyl began to assert his independence. Moreover, since parties of Boer Dorsland Trekkers (on their way to Angola) stayed in western Ghanzi between 1875 and 1878 Van Zyl had enough guns to do as he pleased.

After 1877, Van Zyl and his Naro-Khoe hunters began to kill large numbers of elephants north of Ghanzi in an area outside his jurisdiction. In two exceptional days apparently he aquired the tusks of about 100 elephants, around 8,000 lbs of ivory. Van Zyl did not pay the required tribute to Moremi, the young kgosi of the Batawana after these expeditions. Van Zyl also enraged Moremi by not going to live at the capital when asked to. But the Boer's heyday was nearly over.

After the second of his famed elephant hunts, Van Zyl heard that Moremi had sent out a regiment to acquire the Sehuba. Sensing trouble Van Zyl invited a number of Nama-Khoe from Namibia to share a large consignment of peach brandy he said he had. When a mounted Nama-Khoe party arrived it found itself confronted by Moremi's regiment. A gun fight ensued, with a large number of deaths. Following this, Moremi burned down Van Zyl's house and drove him west. In 1880 Van Zyl was murdered, apparently by some Naro-Khoe whom the Boer had wronged in the past.

After Van Zyl's death, the Batawana used Ghanzi for cattle herding and also made periodic raids to get taxes and children. But the threat of violence from the Nama-Khoe meant they did not exploit the area fully.

The BSACo takes over Ghanzi

In the 1890s the British government set its eye on taking the Ghanzi reserve as Crown land. The reasons for this are laid out in chapter 11, which described how the government and the BSACo were working together. Cecil Rhodes, of the BSACo, wanted to put Ghanzi under his company's control and government officials he had bribed did their best to meet his wishes.

From 1894 the government sent policemen and officials to get kgosi Sekgoma of the Batawana to give up Ghanzi. He always refused. Meanwhile, Rhodes had organized some 200 Boers in

Shua Khoe at Chobe in 1906

South Africa who were waiting to go and settle in Ghanzi. These Boers were all poor whites who just wanted to receive a free farm, sell it off for profit and then return to South Africa much richer.

Despite Sekgoma's opposition to giving up Ghanzi, the British government prevailed in the end. A number of bribed witnesses were induced to declare that Ghanzi had always been vacant land, inhabited only by a few roving Bushmen. In 1897 Sekgoma eventually agreed to give up Ghanzi if no more of his land was to be taken. The British agreed and in 1898 the party of Boers moved into Ghanzi, taking up their farms. Very few stayed more than five years, but they had obtained ownership of much land. In later years, more Boers would arrive to occupy the area fully.

The saddest aspect of Ghanzi's history is that the Naro-Khoe inhabitants of Ghanzi lost all their land to the Boer farmers. No other group in Botswana lost more due to the arrival of white settlers. They became a landless group, dependent on low paying jobs from the local Boers.

"God has given us this land and then has taken it away from us. We are working for nothing because we no longer own the land," The Naro-Khoe say today.

The Chobe region

The Chobe area has never been part of the territory of any of the large Batswana merafe. In the Chobe region the Basubia are the main ethnic group and they refer to themselves as the Bekuhane. It appears that the Bekuhane are closely linked to the peoples of Zambia and they migrated across the Chobe River into Botswana many hundreds of years ago. According to legends, the Bekuhane once lived with the Hambukushu and Bayei at some hills in the eastern Chobe. In recent centuries the Bekuhane have settled in small villages along the Chobe flood plain. In these places they lived by fishing, farming and owning cattle.

For a long time the Bekuhane were united and maintained their independence despite occasional attacks from Balozi and other Zambian groups. Their land was known as the Kingdom of Itenge, named after one of their rulers. Only around 1876 did they split up. Liswani II fled the area fearing he would be killed by the Balozi. He and his followers settled near the Boteti river.

The other long term inhabitants of the Chobe area are the Shua Khoe, who ruled themselves until the arrival of the British. Though the Bangwato tried to subdue the Shua Khoe and turn them into malata the Shua Khoe resisted. A man named Maruza and his supporters stopped these attempts by killing a number of Bangwato.

Also attracted to the area were refugees from more violent places. Various Bakalanga fled there from Amandebele rule in Zimbabwe and Basarwa and Bayei fleeing bolata also liked Chobe. In terms of religious activity, Chobe was the only place in Botswana where Catholic missionaries settled at in the nineteenth century. They maintained a mission at Pandamatenga. During the twentieth century the Chobe area did not attract many new inhabitants. The Tsetse fly and Malaria-causing mosquito made living there too difficult.

Hunting in the Chobe region

Because Chobe was mostly open territory it became a favoured hunting ground for the Batawana, Bakwena and Bangwato, who sent hunters there as early as the 1850s. Places like the Mababe Flats had huge game herds, which were utilized by hunters for over a century. An English trader named George Westbeech also established a big ivory trading operation at Pandamatenga and operated independently of the various dikgosi. During the 1870s and 1880s he bought ivory from various Zambians and Zimbabweans and then exported it south to Shoshong. Westbeech and David Hume (see chapter 6) were the two biggest ivory traders in Botswana in the nineteenth century.

Chobe became part of the Bechuanaland Protectorate in 1890, and the area was designated Crown land. The British were unable to maintain much presence in the area until 1908, when they stationed an officer at Kazungula. It was only after this that the collection of taxes and the introduction of British law arrived. From that time on, it became illegal to hunt big game in the area.

Events after 1885

After the British government took over the Bechuanaland Protectorate in 1885, it placed the Kgalagadi and Chobe under its direct control. It did this because the land had never been under the permanent control of one of the large Tswana merafe. Except in the case of Ghanzi this was true. Batswana had never ruled the peoples of the Kgalagadi desert, though they had often hunted or moved there in times of danger. Such land was called Crown land and is now called state land.

On Crown land the British recognized local headmen, who had the right to judge cases among their subjects. Thus the Basubia and Bakgalagadi chiefs retained their authority at the local level. In Ghanzi, though, no local headmen were recognized and all people were subject to the laws of Great Britain.

But the fact that such areas were under direct British control made little difference before 1910. No schools were built and few developments took place. Some half hearted attempts were made to restrict hunting. Later on, though, much of the Kgalagadi would be turned into Game Reserves. The local population lost its right to use the areas they had long lived on. Contact with the government was limited to occasional visits by policemen collecting taxes on their camels.

The British government did not oppose Africans settling on Crown land. For instance, when Sekgoma Khama split with his father, Khama III, in the 1890s, he went into exile in the Nata area, in the south of Chobe district. Many Barolong fleeing white rule in South Africa also settled in the Kgalagadi desert. Perhaps the most spectacular new immigrants to the Kgalagadi were the Nama-Khoe of Simon Kooper. Kooper was in fact from Namibia. Between 1904 and 1908 he had engaged in armed struggle against the German colonists. He fought a guerrilla war, fighting a major battle at Sitachwe Pan, inside the Protectorate where the Gemsbok National Park lies today. Despite these successes, Kooper did not command enough strength to overcome the Germans and eventually settled in the Matsheng area in 1908.

During the period after 1885 the Bakgalagadi living in the Matsheng and the Kweneng began to engage in a new kind of trading system. The Bakgalagadi had been long distance traders for some time, but this mainly involved trading south into the Cape province. After the arrival of the Protectorate, they began to move goods north from the Kweneng and Matsheng, selling them in the Ghanzi area and Ngamiland.

Many of these Bakgalagadi traders made clothes and blankets out of skins and they were thought to be the best in Botswana. They would make a large number of items and then perhaps go north with other things like horses or iron goods. Then they would trade their skins and horses for cattle, which they would then trek down to Matsheng.

Not only did such trade bring in a lot of wealth to the Bakgalagadi, but it also led to large scale migrations north into the areas they were trading in. Between 1880 and 1910 many Bakgalagadi left the Matsheng area, settling in Ghanzi and the south west part of Ngamiland. In these new areas they kept trading and seem to have been the most successful of all the merafe at business.

Questions

1 Discuss the similarities and differences between the economic activities of the Bangologa and the Naro-Khoe.

2 a. Who was Dukuri?
   b. What led to his downfall?

3 How did the Batawana control Ghanzi?

4 How did Ghanzi end up in the hands of the white settlers?

5 What was Crown land?

6 The Chobe area was not conquered by any large morafe. What was the result of this fact?

Chapter 15
Changes in the north

A number of the main developments that occurred in the north between 1885 and 1910 have already been covered. For instance the BSACo attempting to take over territory by corrupting the government. Also, the north suffered badly from rinderpest, locust infestations and drought in the late 1890s. Famine was widespread. Still, many other things were going on, both politically and socially.

White settlement in the north

Besides Ghanzi, whites also settled in the Tati and the Tuli Block after 1885. Tati came to be under the control of the Tati Company, though the British government controlled policing and justice in the area. As mentioned earlier, gold had been discovered in the 1860s in Tati in a section of land that served as a neutral area between the Amandebele and Bangwato. Almost all of the residents there were Bakalanga, who paid tribute to the Amandebele. In the 1890s this land was awarded to the Bechuanaland Protectorate and not to Rhodesia.

Lobengula, King of the Amadebele, had awarded the area to some Englishmen who then formed the Tati Company. Before the 1890s the company had a great many problems trying to mine in the area. Wars and political uncertainties regarding the ownership of the area stopped them. The Tati area had mines which were hundreds of years old. But after big efforts were made to mine them in the late 1890s it was clear that there was not much gold left.

White settler farmers at Gaborone; 1900

Since the mines did not produce much gold, the Tati Company found other ways to make money. It had a lot of land, some of which it sold or rented to white farmers. The rest was eventually used to house Africans looking for land to settle on. Some of these groups were refugees from South Africa, such as some Barolong under Kgosi Moroka. The Company also tried to tax the Bakalanga.

In 1894 the Tati Company persuaded Rauwe, the kgosi of the Bakhurutshe, to settle in the Tati area. His father, Sekoko, had lived in the Tati up until the 1860s, but then left for Shoshong as the Amandebele were taking too many of his young people from him. Rauwe signed an agreement with the Company to supply them with mine labourers and to collect land rentals from all the Africans living in Tati. These included the Bakalanga living under Habangana, Mosojane and Masunga.

Rauwe did not live up to his side of the agreement and in 1904 the Company tried to evict him and the Bakhurutshe. The government then stepped in to control the situation. It was suspicious of the Tati Company, which was trying to act independently and to impose its own laws and taxes in Tati. Eventually, in 1911 the government agreed to pay £1,000 a year rent for the Africans in the Tati area, while maintaining the right to rule them and collect hut tax.

Despite government intervention, the Bakhurutshe felt they lacked sufficient land and in 1913 moved into Bangwato territory, settling at Tonota. Tati continued to be overpopulated, though, as a new influx of Africans arrived under Moroka. Meanwhile other Batswana had moved to Francistown looking for jobs.

The Tuli Block was another area of white settlement. It is a small strip running along the Limpopo River. This land had been given away by Khama in 1895 to the British to build a railway. The government gave it to the BSACo.

After the Jameson Raid failed in 1896, the BSACo continued to claim the Tuli Block. Soon a railway through the area had been built, it reached Francistown in 1897. Once the South African war was over, the BSACo marked off a number of farms and sold them to white farmers. Africans in the area, such as the Babirwa, then became subject to BSACo taxation. Like the Bakhurutshe in Francistown, most of the Babirwa left white territory and settled among the Bangwato rather than pay extra taxes.

Most of the farms were operated by white traders operating in Gammangwato, Ngamiland and Francistown. These men would buy cattle from the African populations and then move them to Tuli. They sold off big animals, either putting them on the railroad or smuggling them across the river into South Africa. Younger cattle were fattened and then sold off later. Growing crops, though, never proved successful due to poor soils and drought.

European settlement was small scale and rarely involved great loss of land to the Africans. There were just not enough money in Botswana to attract settlers. Business was light and it was difficult to make money in agriculture.

Events among the Bangwato

Khama III was the favourite kgosi of the government. As long as he was content to support their plans, they were happy to leave him alone in his control of his district. The British allowed Khama, as they did all other Batswana dikgosi, to rule all the groups underneath him as he saw fit. Thus the Bakalanga, Batswapong, Khoe and Bakgalagadi and others continued to be under Bangwato domination.

Many of these groups were not happy about this arrangement. They disliked paying tribute to the Bangwato, providing men for regiments and following the orders of Khama's headmen. Meanwhile, their own traditional leaders were often ignored.

Khama and the Baseleka
Khama did not tolerate any attempt made by subjects to assert their own authority. An example of this policy can be seen with the Baseleka, a small group living near the Limpopo River. In 1885 the Baseleka under Kgosi Kobe engaged in bogwera, allowed a Boer family to hunt in their territory and refused to take orders from Palapye. Khama sent a mophato to

punish the Baseleka. This group of men burned down the Baseleka fields. But the Baseleka refused to back down and killed three Batswapong to make Khama angry.

The British government sent one soldier to try to persuade the Baseleka to give up. After this half hearted attempt was made, the British told Khama to do what he wanted with regard to the Baseleka: "The sole responsibility in the last resort rests not with us but with you," they wrote to him.

Khama responded by massing some 4,000 men. He attacked the Baseleka who were hiding out on Ngwapa Hill. In the ensuing battle, eventually won by the Bangwato, eight attackers and thirteen defenders were killed. Following the bloodshed, most of the Baseleka fled to the Transvaal.

Khama and the Shua-Khoe

Another instance of Bangwato domination can be seen in Nata, where a large number of Shua-Khoe lived. Prior to the 1880s such people had largely been involved in the hunting trade, which was coming to an end as the big game was shot out. But by this time the Bangwato were rich in cattle and needed large numbers of herders to look after these animals.

Khama hoped Nata could be the site of his new cattleposts, as it was fairly well watered and had a sizable population. He sent a number of regiments, under his son Sekgoma, to go and put cattle under the control of Shua-Khoe herders. The people of Nata had no say in the matter. They were rounded up and apportioned to the new cattleposts. Those who resisted faced possible execution.

Thus a new form of life came to Nata. Bangwato headmen controlled the area and cattleowners occasionally came to the area to oversee their cattleposts. Shua-Khoe herders were rarely paid, but were allowed to drink milk. They could not leave the area and were tracked down and punished if they did.

Bolata was against the law in the Bechuanaland Protectorate, as elsewhere in the British Empire. But the government made no attempt to stop it. In the first place the government did not have many officers and lacked the money necessary to hire more. Secondly, the government relied on the slave owners to run large areas of the Protectorate for them. It was the headmen and royal family members of these groups who owned most malata and they ran the courts and collected taxes for the government. The slave owners ran the northern part of Botswana for the British and were not paid for it. So it made no sense for the government to take their malata away.

Bangwato internal conflicts

Though Khama was an extremely strong and capable ruler, he never really succeeded in uniting his people. Various royal family members quarrelled with him and this led to some splits within the Bangwato. For instance Khama fell out with his brother Raditladi, who showed independence of spirit in the kgotla. Raditladi and some of his supporters quarreled with Khama over religious matters and denounced Khama's ban on the drinking of alcohol.

Eventually in 1895 the government decided to let Raditladi and his supporters leave the Bangwato Reserve. This group moved into a large area inside the borders of Rhodesia. Khama, however, ended his ban on alcohol before the Raditladi party left and so it lost support. Raditladi's faction remained in exile for some 20 years.

Not long after this split, Khama fell out with his first born son and heir, Sekgoma. The reasons for the split center around the fact that Sekgoma wanted a significant role in advising his father about tribal affairs, but his father did not let him do much.

Another reason for the Khama Sekgoma split was that Khama sent people to live all over the Bangwato district after 1896. Prior to this the Bangwato had generally lived together in the capital, where the kgosi could oversee the affairs of his people closely. But by the 1890s Khama had acquired all sorts of new land: the Motloutse area from the Amandebele, the Boteti from the Batawana and the area around Lophephe from the Bakgatla and Bakwena. All this land was lying idle and so Khama began splitting up his morafe to occupy it.

Khama's plan of decentralisation
Khama sent the Bakaa and other Bakgalagadi to live at Shoshong, while the Babirwa went to Bobonong. Other settlers went up to the Boteti River. Meanwhile, most of the Bangwato remained behind in the capital, which in 1902 was moved to Serowe. In fact, Khama had abandoned Shoshong in 1889 when the water there ran out. By the late 1890s Palapye was also running dry and so Khama moved to Serowe. Due to the fact that the Bangwato were by this time more spread out than before, the population was small enough for Serowe to support.

To supervise these new settlements, some Bangwato headmen were sent out to new villages like Mmadinare, Bobonong and Sefhope. Rauwe of the Bakhurutshe was headman at Tonota. Nswazwi, a minor Mokalanga chief, was sent from Shoshong to Sebina to rule the Bakalanga even though he had no traditional authority over those people. In these new areas large numbers of schools and LMS churches were opened and white traders and policemen also operated there. Khama was successful in moving his people over a wide area and as a result the Central District today has a widely distributed population.

Khama's plan of decentralization angered Sekgoma, because he was the heir and felt his future position was being weakened. Sekgoma, after some years of bitter relations, was eventually asked by his father to leave. He went with some 2,000 followers to Lophephe in 1899. Then in 1907 he moved to Nekati, on Crown land north of Nata. Only many years later did he return to Serowe.

Sekgoma Letsholathebe's rule in Ngamiland

Though Ngamiland became part of the Protectorate in 1890, not one British government official settled there until 1894. In those four years there was practically no contact between the government and the Batawana.

This changed when Kgosi Sekgoma led a spectacular military expedition into German territory in 1893. Sekgoma, as was seen in chapter 8, had assumed power as regent in 1891. He was extremely ambitious and was looking for ways to increase his political support. He decided to go on a military campaign to gain cattle and slaves to distribute among potential followers.

In 1893 he took a large expedition up the Okavango River up into the Caprivi Strip and Angola. There he captured thousands of cattle and took many slaves in battle. On his way back he stopped off to greet an old Batawana ally, Nyangana, kgosi of the Bagcereku.

Sekgoma and the Bagcereku

Showing Nyangana his large number of cattle, Sekgoma explained that his success was due the medicine that he put on his guns. Nyangana was eager to learn the secret of Sekgoma's medicine and so agreed to meet Sekgoma the next day. Sekgoma said he would apply medicine to all the Bagcereku guns. On the following day Nyangana and his warriors went to a place in the bush, where Sekgoma and his dingaka put all the Bagcereku guns in a big pile.

An elaborate ceremony was begun and after some time Nyangana was asked to crawl through a large noose as part of the treatment. As soon as the Bagcereku kgosi was inside the noose, Sekgoma had it tighten around him. A large force of Batawana soldiers then emerged and killed the defenseless Bagcereku warriors.

This episode, known as the Battle of Lishora, succeeded beyond Sekgoma's wildest dreams. He wiped out almost all adult Bagcereku men with very few losses on his own side, and took large numbers of cattle and guns. Sekgoma's men then went to Nyangana's capital and took hundreds of young women and children as slaves. It was perhaps the biggest slave raid that has ever taken place in southern Africa. On his return to Ngamiland Sekgoma divided up the cattle and slaves amongst his warriors. In this way, he built up a large following of men who were indebted to him.

When the British government heard about Sekgoma's actions, it was outraged. It did not want any friction to develop with the German and Portuguese governments, on whose territory the raids had occurred. So the British sent policemen to Ngamiland to ensure that Sekgoma made no more military expeditions.

The natural disasters of the mid 1890's
Ngamiland like the rest of Botswana suffered badly from the natural disasters that occurred in the mid- 1890's. Severe droughts hit the area from 1895 to 1897 and huge locust swarms covered the area throughout the 1890s. After the droughts began, these locust invasions ate up much of the crops and the grazing for cattle.

Rinderpest arrived in Ngamiland in late 1896 and destroyed cattle and game in huge numbers. But in Ngamiland rinderpest did not kill nearly as many cattle as in southern Botswana. Many areas of the region, especially in the drier parts of the west, were not affected. Most cattleowners were left with several animals after the epidemic passed through.

These natural calamities forced the population of Ngamiland to relocate. Prior to the 1890s, most people lived in the south east around Lake Ngami. However, in 1896 the lake dried up and the water levels in the area sank further underground. As a result, many people moved north up to the edges of the Okavango Delta. This was an area where previously few people lived due to the prevalence of tsetse fly. When rinderpest killed off huge numbers of cattle and wild game, the tsetse fly (which spreads sleeping sickness to cattle and people) also vanished from the Okavango Delta as it had nothing to feed on. Sekgoma moved his capital to Tsau, on the edge of the swamps.

The British West Charterland Company
In the 1890s Ngamiland was the site of one of the largest business ventures ever to have taken place in the Bechuanaland Protectorate. British businessmen raised £400,000 and acquired the concession signed by Nicholls and Hicks in 1888 (see chapter 8). These men were confident that they would find

large quantities of gold and diamonds in Ngamiland and Ghanzi and were prepared to establish a British colony in the area if they succeeded.

This company, known as British West Charterland, (BWC) had exactly the same aims as the BSACo. Because it was not influential with the government, it had to rely on Sekgoma Letsholathebe for support. Sekgoma and BWC ended up collaborating against the government in order to prevent the loss of Batawana land in Ghanzi and Boteti. Despite the huge amount of money it spent, BWC did not to find any minerals in Ngamiland. The company thought that the only place where diamonds could be found was the Boteti River area but, as the British government had awarded the region to Khama they could not prospect there. As a result, diamonds were not discovered commercially in Botswana until after independence.

The arrival of the Ovaherero

In 1904 a new group of people made their appearance in Botswana, the Ovaherero. In fact the Ovaherero are made up of two sections, one called the Mbanderu and the Herero. They speak the same language and live in a similar fashion, but have separate leaders and tend not to intermarry.

When the Germans took over Namibia in the 1890s they came into conflict with both the Herero and Mbanderu because they were unwilling to take orders from the Germans. Many Mbanderu moved to Ngamiland in 1897 to escape Germans domination. Initially, the Herero collaborated with the Germans and helped them militarily. But in 1903 the Herero fell out with the Germans because Samuel Maherero, their leader, refused to let his people live in small native reserves. Then the Herero and the Mbanderu launched a surprise revolt. At this point the Germans told all Ovaherero to leave Namibia or be exterminated.

Despite brave Ovaherero fighting, the German military eventually proved too strong and ruthless. Ovaherero died in extremely large numbers. By 1905 thousands had fled the fighting and sought safety with Sekgoma in Ngamiland. Some Mbanderu went to the Chobe area in subsequent years, but eventually they returned to Ngamiland, settling around Lake Ngami. The Herero stayed in Ngamiland and Boteti for some years and in the 1920s many ended up in Mahalapye.

When the Ovaherero arrived in Botswana they were very poor and had no cattle. To survive they grew crops even though they preferred just to raise cattle. Many of them also acquired mafisa from the richer Batswana often borrowing these cattle often for decades at a time. In this way, they managed to restore their prosperity after the disasters in Namibia.

Features of northern Botswana's society

Sekgoma Letsholathebe was removed from the Batawana bogosi in 1905 by the British. He was replaced by Mathiba II, who ruled for the next twenty eight years. Meanwhile, Khama III continued as Bangwato kgosi until 1923.

By 1910 the similarity between Ngamiland and Gammangwato was great. In both areas, small Batswana minorities controlled large areas of land populated by non Tswana majorities. The same mechanisms of control were used. Large areas of land were divided and put under the control of basimane ba kgosi, who were almost always Batswana.

When hunting no longer produced wealth, both the Bangwato and Batawana relied on cattle. By 1910 cattle herds had been restored from the devastation caused by rinderpest. These animals were kept in areas distant from the capitals. They were often herded by malata or by poorer people who borrowed them as mafisa. In general the Batswana controlled the majority of cattle owned. Their subject populations, the Bayei, Bakalanga and others, relied more on agriculture as a means of livelihood.

Along with the rise in Batswana political power came Batswana culture. Setswana began to replace other languages and was used in public forums such as the kgotla, school and church. The use of Tswana law and custom, forced the subject peoples to drop many of their own customs and act more like Batswana.

But the culture brought by the Batswana was not really the same culture that the Batswana had practiced in the 18th century. Khama himself changed many of laws as he was a Christian. When Mathiba took power in Ngamiland, Khama also impressed upon him the need to adopt new laws in order to get rid of the influence of non-christians like Sekgoma Letsholathebe.

One of the biggest changes made in the north was the abolition of bogadi, in which the family of a man was expected to pay cattle to his wife's family. This change did not occur in southern Botswana. The end of bogadi meant that younger men did not have to struggle to earn cattle to get married. In southern Botswana and all over southern Africa the cost of bogadi tended to increase after 1900. This made it hard for men to get married. They were often forced to go to work at the mines for several years in order to earn enough cattle. The abolition of bogadi in the north meant that fewer men in northern Botswana engaged in migrant labour, at least in comparison with southern Botswana. There were other reasons why there were fewer migrants from the north of Botswana. Malata were not allowed by their masters to move freely. The slave owners relied on their malata and to produce money and products for them with which they could pay their taxes. Very few women migrated from northern Botswana, which again is different from southern areas. This is partly because the north is further away from South Africa. But also, in the north there was much more land than in the south so there was no pressure to force women into work. Those who wanted money or livestock could often obtain it by growing tobacco, which always had a ready market. Finally, the government allowed many residents of the north to pay taxes with goods such as sorghum, maize or skins, rather than with money only. In southern Botswana the government demanded money from all men, and so many were forced to get a job in South Africa to pay their taxes. In the north many men could simply plough an extra field or hunt a few animals to pay their taxes.

Questions

1. a. Where did whites settle in Botswana?
   b. Why did they go to those places?

2. Did the British interfere in the affairs of Khama and Sekgoma Letsholathebe? Explain your answer.

3. Why did Khama and his son, Sekgoma, quarrel?

4   a. For what reason did Sekgoma Letsholathebe attack the Bagcereku?
    b. How was this attack different from Khama's attack on the Baseleka?

5   What was BWC?

6   Why did the Ovaherero move to Ngamiland?

7   How did Tswana culture spread in the north of Botswana?

Chapter 16
Realities of protection in the Bechuanaland Protectorate

Between 1906 and 1910, two developments occurred that showed how politics in the Bechuanaland Protectorate would be run in the future. First, a crucial court case was fought against the government by Kgosi Sekgoma Letsholathebe of the Batawana. The British government won this case. Its officials in the Protectorate gained the right to take any action they wanted. They were under no obligation to respect the wishes of Batswana or to respect the laws of Great Britain.

Second, in 1908 the British government began to press to transfer the Bechuanaland Protectorate to the control of the South African government. It wanted to save money and also to put blacks under the control of whites (which it believed was the best set up). Batswana leaders joined together to oppose this transfer to South Africa. For the first time the idea arose that the peoples of Bechuanaland were a nation and that they could not be located within another country.

Strangely enough, the Batswana leaders who opposed the transfer of the Protectorate to South Africa used an idea taken from the British themselves. Before this period the British claimed to be protecting Batswana, rather than state the selfish reasons for which they had taken the country. By 1910,

Batswana began to say that the British wanted to hand them over to the very same people that they had originally been protected from. The Batswana leaders appealed to the British public not to betray them and then hoped the British public would place pressure on its politicians not to give up the protected Batswana to the South African government.

The legal basis for British power in the Bechuanaland Protectorate

Great Britain took over the area it called the Bechuanaland Protectorate in 1885 under a British law called the Foreign Jurisdiction Act. This act allowed Britain to interfere in the government of other countries to protect the interests of its citizens. At first this act was interpreted to mean that Britain had a right to control the affairs of the British and other white people living in the Protectorate. Batswana would remain under the authority of their dikgosi. As a result Batswana were not entitled to the legal protections of British courts.

In 1891 the British decided to increase their powers over Batswana by declaring that their dikgosi were too uncivilized to rule without the guidence of colonial officials. The British officials wanted to reduce the power of dikgosi who opposed the vast ambitions of Cecil Rhodes. Officials found that they did not have a legal right to hand Botswana over to Rhodes.

In 1891, the High Commissioner issued an Order-in-Council that gave the Protectorate administration unlimited powers over Batswana. At the same time Batswana could still be denied access to British law. Thereafter a Motswana simply had no way to protect himself legally from the abuses of the government.

In Britain, citizens had many legal protections to fall back upon in case they were mistreated by the government. One of these protections was known as *habeus corpus*, which said that no individual could be put into prison without being charged for breaking a law. In this way, a British citizen was not allowed to be put in prison without facing trial. A citizen had to be charged with a crime and given a trial. Batswana were not allowed such forms of protection.

The Sekgoma Letsholathebe Case

Sekgoma Letsholathebe was the kgosi of the Batawana. It was he who actually took the question of British power in Protectorates before the courts. He felt that the way he had been treated was illegal under British law. He was the first kgosi to challenge British laws. He failed to win his case. Unfortunately for he and all other Africans who lived in British Protectorates, government officials in Africa were given unlimited power.

The events leading to Sekgoma's imprisonment

Sekgoma was not the legitimate kgosi of the Batawana. He had taken power in 1891 when his nephew, Mathiba, was three years old. Sekgoma tried to create a large group of supporters who would help him claim the bogosi. He loaned out many cattle and gained many friends. He also took cattle away from some rich men and gave them to poorer people.

Because Sekgoma was not the real leader, he was always opposed by a large group who supported Mathiba. Most of these men were from the royal family, who had wealth and supporters of their own. These dikgosana refused to accept Sekgoma's leadership and called for Mathiba to be kgosi when he became an adult.

By 1905 Mathiba was seventeen. Calls increased for his return from Cape Town, where he was at school. Sekgoma made a crucial mistake at the end of this year, when he divorced his wife (who was the daughter of Khama's brother). He became angry when his wife failed to have children. In late 1905 Sekgoma went to the Francistown court where he succeeded in getting a divorce. During the hearing, Sekgoma's friends told a number of lies in order to win the case. They claimed that his wife had been having an affair with Wetshootsile, the son of the former regent, Dithapo. Sekgoma's move backfired because Dithapo was Sekgoma's most important supporter. Dithapo became angry and began supporting Mathiba. Meanwhile, Sekgoma had gone to South Africa to see a doctor and do some shopping.

Dithapo, Wetshootsile and other dikgosana sent a letter to Cape Town telling Mathiba to come back to become kgosi. Mathiba was soon on the train heading back to Ngamiland. They also sent letters to Khama, asking him to convince the government that Sekgoma was not the real kgosi. Sekgoma heard about the conspiracy. He also got on the train in order to get home quickly. The British government got involved because it did not want fighting to break out between the supporters of the two men.

Sekgoma and Mathiba were both stopped in southern Bechuanaland and placed under close observation. The government sent a delegation to investigate who should be kgosi of the Batawana. In 1906 the Resident Commissioner went to Ngamiland. After consulting the Batawana, he declared

Mathiba chief. Mathiba, he said, was the legitimate kgosi by birth and had the support of the majority. Despite his claims of impartiality, the Resident Commissioner knew that Sekgoma was more popular. Khama and he had decided in advance that Mathiba should be the chief. The Resident Commissioner knew that Mathiba was an educated Christian under the influence of Khama. Mathiba would do what the government wanted. Sekgoma, on the other hand, was strong and independent and was not attracted to western culture.

Sekgoma is imprisoned

Mathiba was installed as kgosi in late 1906. The Resident Commissioner kept Sekgoma in prison. He claimed that if Sekgoma was let free he would return to Ngamiland and start a war. Keeping a person in jail in such a manner was illegal in Britain, because a person could only be arrested after a crime was committed. But Sekgoma was detained because the government felt he might do something wrong.

Sekgoma was left languishing in the Gaborone prison for many years, during which time he kept asking to know what he had done. The government could not move him out of the country, because then Sekgoma would come under British law and be released. Nor did they want to let him go free inside the Protectorate, as they feared a possible war.

The Sekgoma case goes to the courts

But Sekgoma refused to be defeated by the British and he had some faith in British law. He and other Batawana had been to court many times before to collect money owed to them by white traders. Sekgoma had also won his divorce case in a British court. Moreover, his friend, Charles Riley, a Coloured trader, urged Sekgoma to take his case to London and demand *habeus corpus*.

In 1909, after failing to obtain *habeus corpus* in the Cape, Sekgoma sent Riley and two other friends to London. There they hired a British lawyer to fight the case in front of the highest courts. Sekgoma lost. The courts ruled that he was in fact a foreign subject and thus not entitled to the legal protection of *habeus corpus*. Furthermore, the court noted, British law could be extended to the Protectorates. The British judges were uncomfortable denying people under British rule the rights every Englishman enjoyed. But, they noted, their misgivings were:

> **made less difficult if one remembers that the Protectorate is a country in which a few dominant civilized men have to control a great multitude of the semi barbarous.**

And so Sekgoma, who owned a typewriter, shot with modern guns and was married and divorced according to British law, was denied basic human rights due to his semi barbarous nature. Likewise, all the inhabitants of the Bechuanaland Protectorate were classified as uncivilized and were thus seen as unfit to have any legal protection.

Sekgoma was eventually allowed to go to Chobe in 1912, where the majority of Ngamiland's population joined him. He died there in 1914 and his followers quickly drifted back to Ngamiland.

The threat of the Union of South Africa

The Batswana had narrowly avoided becoming part of the BSACo's colony of Rhodesia in the 1890s. After 1907 they again were nearly incorporated into another country. After the South African War of 1899 to 1902, the British betrayed the Africans who had helped them defeat the Boers. The British

wanted to create a new nation called Union of South Africa.
This new country, which they called Union, was to include the
former Boer republics of the Orange Free State and the
Transvaal as well as the British colonies of the Cape and Natal.
Also to be included were the three Protectorates—Basutoland,
Bechuanaland and Swaziland. The Africans of the
Protectorates and the Union were not to be given equal rights.
British politicians felt that the new Union would only be strong
if the defeated Boers of the Transvaal and Free State were
happy. So in 1906 the British rulers gave the citizens of the
Transvaal and Orange Free State (mostly Boers) the right to
elect their own governments and make their own laws.

Dikgosi Bathoen, Sebele speaking against Union of South Africa at 1909 Gaborone meeting

Batswana were quick to challenge their incorporation into the proposed Union of South Africa. The Batswana leaders knew that if they continued to live under the British flag as a protectorate, then at least they would control their own lives in some measure due to the nature of Indirect Rule.

Batswana petition the British government

Peter Sidzumo, Sebele's South African secretary, led the Batswana challenge. In May 1908 he drafted a Bakwena petition opposing incorporation. Then he began building up a united front among the Batswana. He told the Bakgatla that if the Batswana did not join together in protest against the Union they "would be killed by their quietness". To the Bangwato Sidzumo explained the importance of decisive action. "the native question," he noted, "is the only present obstacle towards the closer union of various South African governments". Batswana needed to act fast before "the native question" was solved by the South African whites. Meanwhile, Sidzumo warned BaNgwaketse Kgosi Bathoen I against incorporation, saying:

> **We have found that the white settlers do not like the black people, neither do they appreciate to see them own land, the wealth of which was given to us by God. They only desire to see destruction, hatred, war and poverty for black people.**

Educated spokesmen such as Sidzumo also began to cooperate with the Basotho and Swazi in making their position known to the South African and British public. At the same time they became associated with the rise of black protest politics in South Africa. In that country black controlled newspapers and political associations had arisen to challenge the laws of the new Union.

The Basotho, in particular, became important allies of the Batswana. This worried the British, because they feared that the Basotho were more radical in their hatred of the British than the Batswana. According to High Commissioner Selborne:

> While unrest in Basutoland was not likely to precipitate that 'general native rising' which to some minds is the object of constant apprehension . . .their present form of government constituted a certain barrier between the Basuto and surrounding tribes . . . (and) any change of government which both weakened that barrier and was resented by the Basuto might tempt them to make common cause with other tribes.

Soon after he made that statement, Selborne received petitions against incorporation from Sebele and Bathoen. He had to take their objections seriously. Like the Basotho, the Batswana had not been disarmed. Not long after he received another petition from Queen Regent Labotsibeni of Swaziland. But Selborne still believed in incorporating the three protectorates. He even drafted a set of rules whereby the British colonial office would oversee the territories once they had been transferred.

Selborne's new set of protections angered white South African politicians who wanted a free hand over Africans. Their objections helped the Batswana, Basotho and Swazi, because incorporation was delayed. Everyone had to wait until the British Parliament could vote on the legislation that formed the new Union of South Africa.

During this new period of indecision, the Batswana worked hard to mobilize public opinion for their cause. Bathoen, Linchwe, Sebele and Kgosi Baitlole of the Balete all presented new anti incorporation petitions to Selborne in January 1909. These petitions were sent to England the next month, just as a Basotho delegation arrived in London to make similar protests.

The formation of the People's Delegation
During February Bathoen and Sebele, along with the Basotho King Letsie, became founding members of the Coloured and Native People's Delegation. This group aimed to keep the Protectorates out of the Union and to win the vote for South African blacks. The People's Delegation was the first major multi-ethnic political grouping in Southern Africa. Its members included Rabusana, Dwanya and Mapikela of the South African Native Convention; Jabavu of the Cape Native Convention; Seme and Mangena of the Transvaal Native Congress; Abdurahman, Lenders and Fredericks of the African Peoples Organization; Mohatma Gandhi of the Transvaal Indian Congress; as well as the Zulu leader, John Dube. It also had two white members, the liberal former Cape Colony Prime Minister Schriener and Joseph Gerrans, who was sent by Bathoen and Sebele to represent the dikgosi and people of Botswana.

The delegation left South Africa and arrived in London in July 1909. It tried to counteract the influence of a nineteen member official South African delegation that sought to promote white rule in the new Union as well as incorporation. The British government feared the military strength of the Basotho so it listened to what the Basotho had to say, fearing an expensive war if it ignored African input.

Bathoen and Sebele appeal to the British public
What the Basotho and Batswana needed to do was to get their message before the British public. They hoped ordinary citizens could pressure the government to stop incorporation. Gerrans succeeded in getting Britain's most influential newspaper, *The Times*, to publish a long report in which Bathoen and Sebele gave their views on incorporation. Because Bathoen and Sebele had been in Britain in 1895, they

were fairly well known names. Thus their newspaper article generated a lot of favourable publicity. Bathoen and Sebele presented themselves as kgosi who were loyal to the King and to the British Empire, from which they were being forcibly removed. They also used the old British idea of protection and turned it around to their own advantage. The kgosi claimed that they had welcomed the British for protection from the Boers in 1885. Now they were being betrayed and being given away to the new Union of South Africa. Said Sebele:

> I am under the King—King Edward . . .We are thankful for the protection we enjoy today. To be handed over—no. . . When a man is born under one Government how can he be happy under another? If we go, we go simply as a result of compulsion; but our hearts we leave behind.

Bathoen spoke of the special bond that existed between Britain and Botswana, which had been created when he, Sebele and Khama met the Queen in 1895:

> A ring is the sign of an indissoluble bond. This ring was given to me by the late Queen Victoria . . . as a proof that the promises made would never be broken and that the Bangwaketsi would for ever remain under the protection of Her Majesty.

As a result of this emotional appeal, a number of British MPs took up the Protectorate's cause. They opposed any vote for incorporation. So successful was the newspaper article that the British government soon promised that "the wishes of the natives in the territories will be most carefully considered before any transfer takes place."

The Union of South Africa

In late 1909 the British Parliament approved the Union of South Africa Act, which denied Africans the right to vote. The

Batswana, Basotho and Swazi, though, avoided incorporation. Bathoen and Sebele were partly responsible. The People's Delegation from South Africa had no success, on the other hand, in getting blacks the vote. Many of its members were seen as being against the British Empire, unlike Bathoen and Sebele who praised it.

On May 31st, 1910 the new Union of South Africa came into existence. Though the three Protectorates had not been included in the Union initially, the threat of incorporation remained. In fact, Batswana struggled to remain out of the Union for many more decades, until it gained its own independence in 1966.

The formation of the African National Congress

Two years after the Union was formed, some sixty delegates gathered in Bloemfontein to start a new regional all African organization. Conference organizer, Pixley Seme, stressed that the new party should serve as a united voice not only for black South Africans but for Africans in the Protectorates. He concluded by moving that the delegates and representatives of the great native houses from every part of South Africa here assembled should form and establish the South African Native National Congress. A number of delegates then seconded this motion, including Mokgalagadi Moisakgomo, representing Kgosi Seepapitso II of the Bangwaketse. All the delegates voted to form the new party, which was later renamed the African National Congress (ANC) in 1923.

The move to form the ANC had not just begun in 1912. It was the product of many years of organizing. Many Batswana, including Bathoen, Sebele and Segale Pilane, had been active in supporting the growth of regional African politics. Both

Sebele and Bathoen, unfortunately, died just before the Bloemfontein meeting and never saw their dreams realized. However, the conference recognized the efforts of Batswana by making Khama, Linchwe and Kgosi Lekoko of the Barolong, honorary vice presidents. Khama rejected his appointment. Perhaps he feared that such an alliance would draw the Bangwato closer to the affairs of the Union, which he did not want to join. Linchwe followed Khama's example.

But Linchwe continued to be linked to the ANC for a long time. His brother, Kgari Pilane, served as the ANC treasurer. Meanwhile, Peter Sidzumo's brother, Richard (also Bakwena Tribal Secretary), became the Secretary General of the Bechuanaland and Griqualand West section. For this reason he was later expelled from Botswana by the British. Large numbers of Batswana belonged to Sidzumo's section, while Batswana working elsewhere in the Union joined other branches.

Batswana ties with the ANC remained strong until 1924, when the Congress went into temporary decline. The dikgosi even tried to adopt the ANC constitution when the British allowed them to form their own official body, the Native Advisory Council. Until independence Batswana dikgosi used "Nkosi Sikelela Africa" as their own national anthem on formal occasions.

Conclusion

By 1910, the date that is the cut off for this book, politics in Botswana had moved a long way. No longer were dikgosi just ruling their own people according to traditional law and custom. Batswana instead were involved in national and regional issues of a kind that had never existed in the nineteenth century. Batswana political leaders were looking to form their own alliances and to make their own decisions. Bathoen died in 1910 and Sebele in 1911. Their passing marked the end of a proud era in Batswana history. Before they died, each had educated successors who would continue their policies. Moreover, this new generation was ready to face the challenge posed by the existence of British rule to the dignity of the Batswana nation.

Questions

1 What were the parts of the foreign jurisdiction act that the orders in council sought to replace?

2 What is *habeus corpus*?

3 For what reasons did British courts deny Sekgoma his release from prison?

4 Why did the British want the protectorates to be part of the Union of South Africa?

5 Why did Batswana dikgosi oppose incorporation into the union?

6 What tactics did they use?

7 What was the Batswana role in the formation of the ANC?

18th-19th Century Traditional Rulers.

NB. Most dates before 1840 are approximations based on oral and a few documentary sources. * for Regents (Motswaraledi)

Bakgatla ba-ga-Kgafela:

1. Pheto II (1795-1810)

2. Senwela (1810-15)*

3. Letsebe (1815-21)

4. Motlotle (1821-25)*

5. Pilane (1825-49)

6. Kgamanyane (1848-74)

7. Bogatsu (1874-75)*

8. Linchwe I (1875-1923)

Bakgatla ba-ga-Mmanaana:

1. Kalaota

2. Kontle (1820-35)

3. Pheko (1935-40)

4. Mosielele (1840-71)*

5. Pilane (1871-1889)

6. Gobuamang (1889-97)*

7. Baitirile (1897-1899)

8. Gobuamang (1899-12)*(ruled as Kgosi 1918-40)

Bakwena (ba-ga-Kgabo):

1. Kgabo (broke away from Bakwena ba-ga-Mogopa)

2. Motshudi

3. Motswasele I (1770-85)

4. Seitlhamo (1785-95)

5. Legwale (1795-1803)

6. Maleke (1803-05)*

7. Tshosa (1805-07)*

8. Motswasele II (1807-22)

9. Segokotlo (1822-29)*

10. Molese (1829-33)*

11. Sechele I (1833-92)

12. Sebele I (1892-1911)

Balete:

1. Powe I (1805-30)

2. Mokgosi I (1830-86)

3. Ikaneng (1886-96)

4. Mokgosi II (1896-1906)

5. Baitlotle (1906-17)*

Bangwaketse:

1. Mongala (broke away from Bakwena)

2. Moleta (1770-90)

3. Makaba II (1790-1825)

4a. Sebego (1825-44)* Senthufe (1844-59)*

4b. Segotshane (1830-53)*

5. Gaseitsiwe (1853-1889)

6. Bathoen I (1889-1910)

Bangwato:

1. Mathiba (1780-95)(broke away from Bakwena)

2. Khama I (1795-1817)

3. Kgari (1817-28)

4. Sedimo (1828-32)*

5. Khama II (1832-34)

6. Bobjale (1834-35)*

7. Sekgoma I (1835-58)

8. Matsheng (1858-59)

9. Sekgoma I (1859-66)

10. Matsheng (1866-72)

11. Khama III (1872-73)

12. Sekgoma I (1873-75)

13. Khama III (1875-1923)

Barolong boo-Ratshidi:

1. Leshomo (1790-1815)*

2. Tawana (1815-49)

3. Montshiwa (1849-96)

4. Besele (1896-1903)

5. Badirile (1903-1911)*

Batawana:

1. Tawana (1795-1820)(son of Mathiba of Bangwato)

2. Moremi I (1820-28)

3. Sedumedi (1828-30)*

4. Mogalakwe (1830-40)*

5. Letsholathebe (1840-74)

6. Memo (1875-76)*

7. Moremi II (1876-90)

8. Dithapo (1890-91)*

9. Sekgoma (1891-1906)*

10. Mathiba (1906-1933)

Batlokwa:

1. Bogatsu (1795-1815)

2. Kgosi I (1815-23)

3. Leshage (1823-26)*

4. Bashe (1826-35)*

5. Matlhapeng (1835-80)

6. Gaborone (1880-1931)

Bakalanga:

1. Chibundule Rulers (1450-1680), also known as the Torwa

2. Nichasike Rulers (1680-1840), also known as the Rozwi or Changamire-

    a. Chilisamhulu (1820-1836)

    b. Chigazike (1836-40)

3. Khumalo (Amandebele) Rulers (1840-93)

    a. Mzilakazi (1840-68)

    b. Umnombate (1868-70)*

    c. Lobengula (1870-93)

Bekuhane (Basubiya):

1. Itenge- legendary first Munitenge or Chief

2. Ikuhane- son of above settled along the Chobe

3. Lilundu-Lituu

4. Mwale

5. Shanjo

6. Mafwila

7. Nsundano

8. Liswani I (1830-45)

9. Nkonkwena or Liswani II (1845-76) last ruler of united Bekuhane, fled to Rakops where he died.

Glossary

Amabutho Amadebele term for a regiment of soldiers.

Assegai Short stabbing spear.

Ba- A prefix denoting two or more persons.

Badimo The spirits of dead ancestors which live among the morafe.

Baloi People who use Boloi (see below)

Boloi Sorcery the use of supernatural means to cause harm.

Bo- A prefix denoting an area (eg Botswana) or an institution (eg bogosi).

Bogadi The institution of bridewealth. Cattle are usually given by the family of the groom to the family of the bride. Bogadi was required to legitimize a marriage.

Bogwera Male initiation into adulthood.

Bojale Female initiation into adulthood.

Bojalwa (1) Traditional Tswana sorghum beer, generally having a low percentage of alcohol; (2) Any kind of alcohol.

Bolata Slavery or servitude.

Bongaka Traditional medicine

Dagga A drug which was smoked. It is now illegal and thought to be harmful.

Difaqane The era of wars in southern Africa between 1815 and 1840.

Dikgosi See Kgosi

Dingaka   Traditional doctors. They use bongaka to treat medical and witchcraft cases, both human and veterinary.

Gammangwato   The territory of the Bangwato (Central District)

Gangwaketse   The territory of the Bangwaketse

Hxaro   A Sesarwa institution of reciprocal gift-giving.

Kgalagadi   The large arid bush-covered veld that covers the western parts of Botswana. It is often referred to as a desert.

Kgamelo   These are cattle lent out by the dikgosi of the Bangwato and Batawana to commoners whose support they wish to gain.

Kgosana   A royal family member closely related to the kgosi.

Kgosi   The executive, judicial, and legislative leader the morafe; (2) the eldest son of the ranking wife of a deceased Kgosi.

Kgotla   (1) A meeting place for the ward or merafe. (2) A meeting for the discussion of matters concerning the morafe. (3) A court for settling disputes within the group according to customary law.

Khadi   An distilled from sorghum, which is made stronger through the addition of sugar and other ingredients.

Mafisa   Cattle loaned from one person to another.

Magwane   Boys undergoing bogwera

Makgotla   Wards; a residential section of a morafe, with its own kgotla and headman.

Malata   Slaves; people who are owned by others.

Masimo   Fields; lands.

Merafe   See morafe.

Mo- Refers to a single person (e.g. Motswana).

Modimo God

Mohumagadi A title of respect given to the Kgosi's highest-ranking wife.

Mophato (pl **mephato**) A group of men or women initiated together that is expected to perform public duties. A men's mophato will fight together in war time.

Morafe (pl **merafe**) The people ruled by a Kgosi; a tribe.

Moruti A teacher or a minister of a church.

Motse A morafe's main village

Mwali A being believed by the Bakalanga to be the son of God. Mwali would help ordinary people solve their problems under the right conditions.

Sebilo A shiny clay used by Batswana as a skin moisturizer.

Sehuba Tribute; an annual payment given to a senior group by a junior one.

Serara A marriage between two first cousins.

Xhaihasi A Sesarwa term denoting a leader or the owner of a piece of land.

List of suggested further reading

This book has drawn upon a wide range of archival and otherwise unpublished as well as published sources on the nineteenth century history of Botswana. A guide to most of these sources can be found in Barry Morton's Pre-Colonial Botswana, An Annotated Bibliography and Guide to the Sources (Gaborone, Botswana Society, 1994). Many articles have also been locally published by the Botswana Society in its annual Botswana Notes and Records. The following is a select bibliography of additional books on the period that may be of interest to the general reader.

Agar-Hamilton, J. The Road to the North (London, Longmans & Green, 1937)

Chirenje, J.M. A History of Northern Botswana, 1850-1919 (Cranbury N.J., Associated University Presses, 1977)

Chirenje, J.M. Chief Kgama and His Times, c.1835-1923: The Story of a Southern African Ruler (London, Rex Collings, 1978)

Eldredge, E.A. and Morton, R.F (edits.) Slavery in South Africa, Captive Labour on the Dutch Frontier (Pietermaritzburg, University of Natal Press, 1994)

Janson, T and Tsonope, J. The Birth of a National Language: The History of Setswana (Gaborone, Heineman, 1991)

Kumile, M. and Wentzel, P.J. Nau DzabaKalanga- A History of the Kalanga, 3 volumes (Pretoria, University of South Africa, 1983)

Landau, P.S. The Realm of the Word, Language Gender and Christianity in a Southern African Kingdom (London, Heinemann 1995)

Maylam, P.R. Rhodes, the Tswana, and the British: Colonialism, Collaboration, and Conflict in the Bechuanaland Protectorate, 1885-1899 (Westport CT, Greenwood, 1980)

Mgadla, P.T. Missionaries and Western Education in the Bechuanaland Protectorate 1859-1904: The Case of the Bangwato (Gaborone, University of Botswana, 1989)

Molema, S.M. Montshiwa, Barolong Chief and Patriot (Cape Town, Struik 1966)

Parsons, Q.N. New History of Southern Africa (London, MacMillan, 1982)

Parsons, Q.N. The Word of Khama (Lusaka, Historical Association of Zambia, 1972)

Ramsay, F.J., Morton, B.C. and Morton, R.F. Historical Dictionary of Botswana (Metuchen N.J. & London, Scarecrow Press, 1995)

Schapera, I. (edit.) Diterafalo tsa Merafe ya Batswana (Alice, Lovedale Press 1940- to be republished by Pula Press Gaborone)

Schapera, I. Praise Poems of the Tswana Chiefs (Oxford, Claredon Press, 1965)

Schapera, I. A Short history of the Bakgatla-baga-Kgafela (Reprint Mochudi, Phutadikobo Museum 1980)

Setilaone, G.M. The Image of God among the Sotho-Tswana (Lieden, Balkema, 1975)

Shillington, K. The Colonization of the Southern Tswana 1870-1900 (Braamfontein, Raven Press, 1984)

Sillery, A. The Bechuanaland Protectorate (London, Oxford University Press, 1952)

Sillery, A. Founding a Protectorate: A History of Bechuanaland 1885-1895 (The Hague, Mouton, 1965)

Smith, E.W. Great Lion of Bechuanaland: The Life and Times of Rodger Price, Missionary (London, L.M.S., 1957)

Tlou, T. A History of Ngamiland (Gaborone, MacMillan, 1985)

Tlou, T and Campbell, A. History of Botswana (Gaborone, MacMillan, 1984- revised version forthcoming)

Van Waarden, C. Oral History of the Bakalanga of Botswana (Gaborone, Botswana Society, 1988)

Index

African National Congress (South African Native National Congress): xvi, 254-55.
Amandebele (Matebele): x-xii, xiv-xv, 41, 61-62, 65-67, 70-78, 80-81, 107-108, 118, 124-26, 133-36, 139, 150, 160, 166-67, 171, 173, 193, 224, 228-29, 234.
Amaxhosa (Xhosa): 41, 151, 180.
Amazulu (Zulu): 62, 151.
Angola: 39, 81, 118-19, 143, 146, 220, 235.
Archeology: 4-6, 10.

Babirwa: ix, 8, 15, 27, 37, 69, 132, 135, 230, 234.
Bagcereku: 235-36.
Bahurutshe: xii, 8, 15, 31, 66, 70, 87, 88, 94, 105, 111, 178-79.
Bakaa: xi, 8, 15-16, 31, 75, 89, 109, 132, 169-70, 234.
Bakalanga: ix, xi, 8, 10, 16-17, 28, 31-32, 34, 36-38, 56, 65, 67-68, 75-78, 81, 132-33, 135, 207, 224, 228-29, 231, 234, 240.
    Balilima: 37, 75.
    Banyayi: 37-38, 68, 75, 77, 133.
Bakhurutshe: 8, 15, 31-32, 77, 132, 140, 191, 229-30, 234.
Bakgalagadi: ix, 8, 13-14, 19-24, 31, 38, 40, 77, 103, 106, 114, 117, 119, 127, 132, 135, 140, 216-18, 225-26, 231, 234.
    Babolaongwe: 14, 21-22.
    Bangologo: 14, 21, 40, 216-18.
    Bakwatlheng: 14, 21, 23, 38.
    Baphaleng: 14, 21, 38, 75.

    Bashaga: 14, 21, 217.
Bakgatla: 6, 8, 81.
    Ba-ga-Kgafela: xii-xiii, xv, 6, 66, 72, 101, 108-114, 152, 168, 170-71, 185, 187, 204, 212-14, 230.
    Ba-ga-Mmanaana: x-xi, 67, 72, 87-90, 94, 104-06, 109-11, 168, 191.
Bakololo (Bafokeng ba-ga-Patsa): x, xii, 61-62, 64-70, 80-81, 118-19, 121, 133, 219.
Bakwena: x-xvi, 6, 8, 14-15, 22-29, 37, 42, 65, 67-68, 74, 76, 85-99, 101-14, 120, 135, 149-50, 154-56, 168, 170-71, 173, 180-82, 185, 204, 212, 224, 234, 250.
Balete: xii-xiii, 8, 87, 94, 101, 105, 109-12, 170, 173, 185, 187, 251.
Bailie, Alexander: 150-51
Balozi, Bulozi (Malozi, Barotseland): xiii, 69-70, 126, 167, 223.
Bangwaketse: x, xii-xiii, xv-xvi, 8, 15, 19, 23, 25-26, 29, 37, 42, 65-66, 70, 72, 74, 87, 89-91, 101-114, 149-50, 152, 168, 170-71, 173, 181, 184-85, 190-91, 204, 210-12, 216-18, 250, 253-54.
Bangwato: xi-xiv, 6, 8, 15-16, 19, 25-27, 31, 42, 65-66, 68-71, 74-77, 95, 103, 106-08, 113-14, 119, 132-43, 150, 155-56, 168, 171, 181-83, 185, 188, 191, 204, 223-225, 228, 230-35, 250.
Bantu (language group): ix, 6, 8,

10-11, 17.
Bapedi: ix, 8, 15, 37, 74, 151.
Barolong: x, xiii, xv, 8, 14-15, 21, 24, 31, 65-66, 72-74, 81, 94-95, 102-04,112-13, 149-53, 178-80, 209, 212, 216-17, 225, 229.
Basarwa *(see Khoisan)*
Baseleka: xiv, 8, 231-32.
Basotho: 64, 151, 250-52.
Basubia (or Bekuhane): ix, xiii, xiv, 8, 16-17, 69-70, 116-19, 129, 207, 223, 225.
Basutoland *(see Lesotho)*
Batalaote: 8, 16, 31, 38, 75, 135, 140.
Batawana (Bampuru): xi-xii, xiv-xvi, 8, 15, 32, 63, 69-70, 113, 116-130, 132, 134,181, 185, 187, 219-22, 224, 234-240, 245-48.
Bateti *(see Deti-Khoe)*
Batlhaping: xiii-xv, 8, 64,81, 95, 146, 149-53, 178-80, 209-10, 216.
Batlaro (Batlharo): 8, 103, 149.
Batlokwa: xii-xiii, 8, 66, 87,94, 101, 109-11, 168, 187.
Bathoen I: xv-xvi, 161-64, 170-74, 176, 187, 190-91, 194, 204, 210-11, 249-50.
Batswapong: 8, 15, 28, 31, 38, 55, 69, 75, 132-135, 231.
Bayei (Bayeyi): ix, 8, 16-17, 31, 39, 55, 69, 117, 119, 121-23, 125-28, 240.
Boers (Afrikaners): x-xiii, xv, 2, 6, 62-64, 73-74, 80-99, 101, 104, 108-09, 111-112,123, 142-43, 146-52, 154, 159, 165-66, 175, 178, 181, 185, 200, 208, 211-14, 220-23, 248, 253.
Bongaka (Setswana medicine): 7, 47-49, 188-89.
Bogadi (bride wealth, lobola): 45, 187-88.
Bogwera *(see initiation)*
Bojale *(see initiation)*
Bolata (servitude/slavery): 19, 22, 31-32, 36, 63-66, 105, 119-23, 126, 133,136,189, 220-21, 223, 233, 236, 241.
Boloi (sorcery): 48-49, 188.
Boteti (river/region): 31, 69, 119, 135, 234, 238-39.
Bramestone Memo: 164-65.
British, Britian (United Kingdom): ix, xiii-xv, 2-3, 58, 63, 87-88, 92-93, 97-99, 128-130, 138, 142-43, 145-57, 159-76, 209-14, 231-33, 235, 250, 248-53, 255.
British South Africa Company (Charter Company)(BSACo): xiv-xv, 160-76, 204, 221-23, 228, 230, 238-39, 248.
British West Charterland Company: 237-38.
Bulawayo: xv, 107, 126, 172, 204.
Bushmen *(see Khoisan)*
Butwa, Kingdom of: ix, 11-12, 15, 36-37, 56.

Cape (former Colony/Province): x, xv, 1, 59, 63-65, 81, 84, 87, 97-99, 103, 120, 142-43, 146, 151, 157, 171, 180, 190, 200, 204, 209-10, 217, 226, 249.

Cape Town: 96-97, 123, 136, 147, 185, 210, 246.
Caprivi Strip: xvi, 129, 235.
Changamire *(see Nichasike)*
Chibundule (Tolwa or Torwa Dynasty): 12, 36.
Chobe (river/region): xiv, xvi, 16-17, 36, 69, 118, 121, 126, 160, 163, 185, 216, 222-26, 248.
Christian, Christianity *(see also missionaries)*: 7, 46, 58-60, 138-39, 141-142, 172,178-91, 196-97, 240, 247.
Coloureds: 33, 64, 136, 247.

Dalaunde (Ntalaote): 16, 38.
Deerdeport (battle site): 212-14.
Deti-Khoe: 8,69.
Difaqane (Mfecane): 61-79, 116, 118-19, 138, 146, 178-81, 200.
Dimawe (battle site): xi, 88-93, 95, 181.
Dithubaruba: x, 68, 91, 93, 98, 104.
Dukiri: 121, 219-20.
Dutlwe: x, 72.
Dutch, Netherlands: 1, 145-46.
Dutch Reformed Church: 185.

Education: 49-54, 99, 184-85.
Ethiopianism (religious movement): 190-91.
European(s): 36, 58-60, 64, 82-99, 122, 127, 136, 142, 145-46, 164, 178, 184, 192,195, 197, 210.

Francistown: 4, 230, 246.
Foreign Juridictions Act: xiv, 164, 244.

Gaborone (place): 165, 167, 174-76, 204, 247.
Gaborone (Kgosi): 110.
Gangwaketse: 98, 101-104, 113, 172, 217.
Gammangwato: 98, 113, 128, 132-43, 172, 211, 230, 239.
Gaseitsiwe: xii, 102-04, 106, 112, 145, 149, 152, 154, 156.
Gatawana *(see Ngamiland)*
Germans, Germany: xiv-xvi, 17, 58, 82, 98, 129, 142, 145, 148, 151-52, 154, 157, 159, 174, 181, 226, 235-36, 238-39.
Gerrans, Joseph: xvi, 252.
Ghanzi (Gantsi): xii, xv, 118, 121, 143, 176, 217-223, 238.
Goold-Adams, Hamilton: 173, 175.
Goshenites, Goshen: 151-52.
Great Trek *(see also Boers):* x, 84-85.
Griqua (Gri-Khoe): xi, 64, 72-73, 77-78, 82, 94, 149-50.
Griqualand West: 113, 148-50.
Grobler, Piet: 116.

Hambukushu: ix, 8, 16-17, 31, 39, 56-57, 117, 126, 128.
Hermannsburg Mission (Evangelical Lutheran): xii, 98, 138, 181, 185.
Historical evidence, sources of: 3-7.
Hottentotes *(see Khoe)*
Hukuntsi: 24, 216.
Hume, David: 82, 224.
Hut Tax: xv, 206.

Indirect Rule: 159, 250.
initiation (bogwera & bojale): 27, 51-54, 141, 186-87, 197, 231.

Iron Age: 10-12.
Itenge *(see Basubia)*

Jameson Raid: xv, 173-76, 230.
Johannesburg: 175, 207.

Kanye: 91, 93, 102-03, 190, 204.
Kgalagadi (Kalahari): x, 2, 9, 14, 19-23, 69, 97, 102, 135, 143, 185, 207, 216-22, 225-26.
Kgamanyane: 108-110
Kgari I (of Bangwato): x, 32, 67, 118, 132-33, 135. also Kgari (son of Sechele I): 96. Kgari (son of Matsheng): 108.
Kgaraxumae: 36, 117.
Kgatleng: 20, 27, 108-114.
Kgwebe Hills: 32, 40.
Khama III: 7, 75, 107-08, 138-43, 145, 150, 154-56, 162-63, 166-68, 17074, 176,182, 187, 189, 191, 194, 203-04, 211, 230-35, 239-40, 246-47, 255.
Khoe: 8-10, 20-22, 33-34, 39, 64-65, 69, 82, 105, 117-19, 121-23, 127, 132, 218-23, 225, 231-33.
Khoikhoi (Cape Khoe/"Hottentots"): 33, 41.
Khoisan (language group): 8-10, 20-22, 31-37, 39, 57-58, 64, 135, 217-18.
Khutiyabasadi (battle site): xiv, 124-26.
Kimberley: xiii, 110, 149-50, 200-01, 205, 207.
Kolobeng: xi, 82-83, 88-89, 93.
Kruger, Paul: xii, 108-09, 152-53, 175.
Kobe: 231-32.

Kooper, Simon: xvi, 225-26.
Kopong: xiv, 105, 161-63.
Kudumane (Kuruman): 82, 150, 178, 180-81, 183.
Kweneng: 20, 31, 38, 98, 101-14, 128, 135-36, 168, 172, 181, 189, 226.

Labour migration: 204-09.
Langeburg Rebellion (Second Anglo-Batlhaping War): xv, 209-11.
Lehurutshe: xii, 149.
Lehututu: 21,184, 191, 216.
Lesotho (Basutoland): 64, 249.
Letsholathebe I: xi, 69, 87, 116, 118, 120-23, 134, 219-20.
Limpopo: 12, 31, 36, 135, 143, 230-31.
Linchwe I: 7, 109-12, 152, 161-64, 168, 175, 212-14, 251, 255.
Livingstone, David: xi, 59, 82-87, 91, 120, 180-83.
Lobatse: 98, 176.
Lobengula: 160, 167, 228.
London Missionary Society (LMS): ix, 58, 89, 150, 152, 172, 178-85, 190-91, 234.
Ludorf, Joseph: xiii, 149-50, 183.
Luka Jantjie: 209-10.

MacKenzie, John: 152-53, 155-56.
Mafikeng: xv, 152, 175, 212.
Magane: 22-23.
Mahalapye: 17, 31, 239.
Makaba II: x, 26, 29, 66-68, 102.
Malete: 38, 135.
Mambo (Bakgalanga kings): 36, 38, 76.
Mankurwane: 151-53.

275

Marico (Madikwe, Mariqua) river/
region: 92-95.
marriage: 44-45, 189.
Matebele *(see Amandebele)*
Mathiba (of Bangwato): 26-27, 32.
Mathiba (of Batawana): 187, 239-40, 245-47.
Matsheng (place): 103, 185, 216-18, 226.
Matsheng (Kgosi): xii-xiii, 107-08, 135-36, 139-40, 142-43.
Mbanderu *(see Ovaherero)*
Missionaries: 7, 58-60, 73, 80, 178-91, 196-97.
Mochudi: xiii-xvi, 4, 13, 27, 68, 109-112, 204.
Moffat, Robert: 29, 59, 86, 107, 160, 180, 184.
Mogalakwe: 116, 119-20.
Mokgadi: 26-27
Molepolole: 4, 14, 83, 99, 104-05, 154-55, 167-68, 175, 204.
Molopo: xiii-xv, 145, 149-50, 152-54, 156-57, 159.
Montshiwa: xii, 72, 88, 94-95, 102-03, 110-14, 149, 151-53.
Moremi I: 116, 123-26, 129-30, 163.
Moshaneng: 93, 95.
Mosielele: 88-90.
Mothowagae Motlogelwa: 190-91.
Motebele: 70-71.
Motloutse: 135, 234
Motswasele I: 26-27
Motswasele II: 27, 61-62, 67, 78, 80.
Mozambique: 62-63, 81, 146.
Mzilikazi: 70-78, 107, 135.

Nama (Nama-Khoe, Namaqua): xv-xvi, 220-21, 225-26.

Namibia (South West Africa): xiv-xvi, 17, 56, 69, 81, 129, 151, 154, 156, 159, 207, 220-21, 226, 238-39.
Naro (Nharo-Khoe): xii, 69, 121, 219-23.
Nata: 36, 232.
Natal: 62-63, 181, 249.
Nichasike (Changamire): ix, 12, 36-37.
Ngami, Lake: 32, 40, 237, 239.
Ngamiland (Gatawana): xi, xiv, 15-17, 39-40, 69, 87, 116-130, 163, 204, 207, 226, 230, 235-40, 247-48.
Nswazwi: 77, 234.
Nyangana: 235-36.

Okavango: 9, 39, 117-19, 121, 124, 218, 235, 237.
Orders-in-Council: xiv, 162-65, 167, 244.
Orange River Sovereignty: 93, 97, 146, 180, 249.
Ovaherero (including Mbanderu): xv, 8, 69, 117-18, 238-39.

Palapye: xv, 167, 191, 211, 231, 234.
Peoples' Delegation, Coloured and Native: xvi, 252-54.
Police, Bechuanaland Border: 167, 175, 221, 225, 236.
Portuguese, Portugal: ix, 62-63, 81, 145-46, 230.
Pretorius, Andries: 87-88, 90, 92-96, 98.
Pretorius, Marthinus: xii, 98.
Protectorate: xiv, 145, 152, 155,

157, 159-76, 196, 199, 206, 208-10, 212, 224-25, 228, 233, 243-45, 247-49, 251-53.

Raditladi: 171, 233.
Ramotswa: 185, 202.
Rauwe: 229-30, 234.
Rhodes, Cecil John: 146, 151-53, 160-76, 244.
Rhodesia(s): 166-67, 171, 202, 204, 228, 248.
Riley, Charles: 247-48.
Rinderpest (bolwane): xv, 201-04, 209, 237.
Rock painting: ix, 4, 34-35.
Rozwi *(see Banyayi, Nichasike)*

Samkotse: 17, 117.
San (see Khoisan)
Sand River Convention: 87-88, 97-98.
Scholtz, Commandant-General Piet: 88-93, 95-96.
Schreiner, William: 163, 252.
Sebele I: 7, 99, 161-64, 167-70, 172-75, 187, 204, 211, 249-56.
Sebego: x, 67-68, 72, 74, 78, 102, 217-18.
Sebetwane:x, 66-70, 118.
Sebilo: 28, 192.
Sechele I: x-xiv, 67-69, 74, 77-78, 85-99, 102, 135-36, 138, 145, 149-50, 152, 154-56, 161, 163, 182, 187-88, 193.
Sekgoma I: x-xiii, 7, 68, 74, 77-78, 95, 133-140, 182.
Sekgoma II: 141, 225, 232-35.
Sekgoma Letsholathebe: xiv-xvi, 129-30, 194, 204, 221-22, 235-37, 239-40, 243, 245-48.

Senthufe: xii, 91, 102.
Seretse Khama: 2-3, 5.
Shaka: 63, 70, 76.
Shippard, Sir Sidney (Morena Maaka): 153, 160-63, 165-66, 168-71.
Shoshong: xi, xiv, 15-16, 31, 83, 132, 135-38, 140, 155-56, 224, 229, 234.
Shua (Shua-Khoe): 36, 222-23, 232-33.
Sidzumo, Peter: 250, 255.
Slavery *(see bolata)*
Sotho-Tswana (language sub-group): 8, 10, 12-17.
South Africa: xvi, 1, 13, 38, 136, 204, 206-14, 218, 222, 231, 241, 243-44, 248-54.
South African Republic *(see Transvaal)*
Stellaland: 151-53.
Stone Age: xi, 9-10.
Surmon, William: 168-69.
Swazi (Masawati), Swaziland: 249-51, 254.

Tati (region): xiv, 12, 142-43, 191, 228-30. Tati Concession/ Company: 143, 228-30.
Tonota: 230, 234.
Toteng: 119, 121-22, 126.
Traders: x, 2, 58-60, 68, 80, 192-96.
Transvaal (South African Republic): 12, 59, 66-68, 84-88, 92-93, 95, 99, 104, 106, 108, 111-14, 137, 142-43, 146, 149, 151-54, 159, 166, 172, 174-76, 180-81, 185, 200, 211, 213-14, 232,